Geoff Harper shows that Leviticu[...] Church. At its heart is the joyful p[...] the sacrificial rituals expressing th[...] Desire for God, not legal requirem[...] The aim of Leviticus is to foster the holiness of the people[...] And to be holy is also to be joyful.

Harper draws on all his technical knowledge as a skilled Biblical interpreter, but his concern is to show how the text addresses the reader. He highlights its literary quality, drawing out features such as narrative and structure, and the nuanced use of language. His own writing has flair and imagination. The book is designed both as an encouragement and a resource for preachers. It really does the job of going from informed theology and exegesis to preaching the text, both individual sermons and whole series. In each section, themes for preaching are opened up, sermon outlines, with alternatives, are proposed, and thought-provoking questions supplied. Both the scholar and the pastor-teacher are warmly present here.

J. GORDON MCCONVILLE
Professor Emeritus of Old Testament Theology,
University of Gloucestershire, UK

This is a brilliant book! Most preachers do not have Leviticus at the top of their 'must-preach-before-I-die' list of Bible books. Geoffrey Harper claims that Leviticus, while underappreciated, is 'essential for grasping the full-orbed message of the gospel' (p. 11). Living with God's holy presence is the key issue of the book, he argues, and 'Leviticus instructs Israel about how to approach and survive that divine presence' (p. 17).

Teaching Leviticus is worth getting simply for the masterly introduction with its overview of the Pentateuch and excellent advice on how to preach Christian messages from the Old Testament. But it is far more. It opens up, in engaging language, how to preach a series from Leviticus. Geoffrey Harper is one of that rare breed – an academic abreast of the latest literature and at the same time a practising expositor who is able not merely to write about preaching but to preach most helpfully!

JOHN SAMUEL
Senior Minister, Duke Street Church, Richmond, London, UK

For many of us the book of Leviticus feels unfamiliar, difficult, and, if we're completely honest, it even feels a little bit odd. We know that this section of the Bible is part of the whole, but we're just not sure how it fits or what it means.

In this work, *Teaching Leviticus*, Old Testament scholar Geoff Harper skilfully takes that which is daunting and unfamiliar and provides us with a framework of understanding the book that is both accessible and highly engaging. Harper's work is exegetically nuanced, theologically robust, and at the same time is pastorally informed and audience focused. With wisdom and warmth, *Teaching Leviticus* not only provides a resource for understanding Leviticus, but it also gives impetus as to why we ought to preach and teach it. A much needed work.

MALCOLM J. GILL
Associate Minister, St Andrew's Cathedral, Sydney, Australia

If you're like me, then you probably find Leviticus overwhelming. There are bizarre instructions about mildew, bodily discharges, and feasts. What can they possibly have to do with me today? This is where I thank God for Geoff Harper's *Teaching Leviticus*. This book is easy-to-read, witty and winsome, and gave me many *ah-ha* moments. I can finally read and understand Leviticus and see how it relates to me today.

SAM CHAN
City Bible Forum
Author of *Evangelism in a Skeptical World* and
Topical Preaching in a Complex World

This guide to Leviticus is exegetically robust, theologically rich, and full of helpful ideas for modern application. It handles the details well while helpfully staying focused on the big picture of the text. Harper has given us a true gift for teaching or preaching through Leviticus!

JAY SKLAR
Professor of Old Testament and Vice President of Academics,
Covenant Theological Seminary, Creve Coeur, Missouri, USA

TEACHING LEVITICUS

From text to message

G. GEOFFREY HARPER

PT RESOURCES

CHRISTIAN
FOCUS

Copyright © Proclamation Trust Media 2022

Paperback ISBN: 978-1-5271-0899-8
Ebook ISBN: 978-1-5271-0926-1

10 9 8 7 6 5 4 3 2 1

Published in 2022
by
Christian Focus Publications Ltd.,
Geanies House, Fearn, Ross-shire,
IV20 1TW, Scotland, Great Britain
with
Proclamation Trust Resources,
116-118 Walworth Road, London, SE17 1JL
England, Great Britain.
www.proctrust.org.uk
www.christianfocus.com

Cover design by Moose77
Printed by Bell & Bain, Glasgow

MIX
Paper from
responsible sources
FSC® C007785

Contents

Author's Preface

This volume is the result of many years of grappling with the ever-intriguing text of Leviticus. In writing, I have been reminded of how essential Leviticus is for the church – and inspired afresh to continue to preach and teach this part of Scripture. I hope that readers, likewise, might be encouraged to venture into these rich pastures.

Teaching Leviticus was substantially written during a period of study leave granted by the board of Sydney Missionary and Bible College, where I have taught for the past eleven years. I deeply appreciate the provision of time to research and write, and the colleagues who shouldered extra responsibilities during my absence. The book was completed amid some serious medical issues. I am profoundly grateful for the friends and family who stood by us during difficult days. Jesus's words in Luke 18:29-30 have consistently proven true in our stint 'down under'.

Jon Gemmell, who accepted this volume for publication, was a welcome (and needed) source of encouragement in the early stages of the process. His successor at the

Proclamation Trust, Stephen Boon, admirably continued that trend. Special thanks are also due to William Chong, who not only set up the original contact with Jon, but read the manuscript in its entirety. Others too have added their corrections, suggestions, insights, and encouragements along the way: Kit Barker, Josh Reeve, Tim Bradford, Luke Padgett, Wendy Fan, Hannah Paduch, and Alastair Crouch. I am also indebted to the second- and third-year students who used a draft of *Teaching Leviticus* to preach through Leviticus in chapel services during Semester 2 in 2020. Their feedback has been invaluable. Thanks, Netani, Andrew, Darren, Joel, Ben, Tom, Jotham, Tim, Steven, Andrew, and Sam.

Any writing project like this would not be possible without the support of one's immediate family. On that front, I am deeply grateful to my wife, Laura, and to our two children. LEGO, bedtime stories, and rugby balls are constant reminders that there is more to life than the ritual texts of the Old Testament. Thus, it is with a father's grateful affection that I dedicate this book to Samuel and Abigail.

G. Geoffrey Harper
Croydon
January 2022

How to Use This Book

This book aims to help the preacher or teacher understand the central aim and purpose of the text, in order to preach or teach it to others. Unlike a commentary, therefore, it does not go into great exegetical detail. Instead, it helps us to engage with the themes of Leviticus, to keep the big picture in mind, and to think about how to present it to our hearers.

'Introducing Leviticus' examines the setting and narrative role of Leviticus within the Pentateuch, as well as Leviticus's own structure and message, and helps us to think through why and how we should teach the book for the benefit of Christians today.

The remainder of the volume contains separate chapters on each preaching unit identified in the introductory chapter. The structure of each chapter is the same. It begins with a brief introduction to the unit. This is followed by 'Listening to the text', which outlines the context and structure of the unit and takes the reader through a section-by-section analysis of the text. Under

the heading 'From text to message', a main theme and aim
for the preaching unit is suggested, as well as ideas for
application. Each chapter concludes with suggestions for
preaching, and some questions that could form the basis
for a group Bible study.

Introducing Leviticus

Getting our Bearings in Leviticus

Each year, I ask my students to tell me what adjective they would use to describe Leviticus. After a brief pause, presumably to work out how honest an answer I am looking for, the inevitable response spills out: 'Boring!' From there, the proverbial floodgates open. When the dust settles, someone will usually put up their hand and ask me about my answer to the question. It is always the same: 'underappreciated'.

With Leviticus we come to what is, for many Christian people, one of the most unfamiliar parts of the Bible. Beyond the famous command to 'love your neighbor as yourself' (19:18), and perhaps the currently infamous 'Do not lie with a man as one lies with a woman' (18:22), the book remains a mystery. Many seem happy to leave that mystery unsolved, which is a great pity, for Leviticus is not just theologically rich, it is essential for grasping the full-orbed message of the gospel.

Literary setting

The importance of Leviticus becomes clearer when we consider its wider literary setting. While the books of the Torah (the Jewish name for the first five books of the Bible) or Pentateuch (i.e. 'five books') come to us as distinct units – Genesis, Exodus, Leviticus, Numbers, and Deuteronomy – they are best approached as connected rather than unconnected works. So, while each book can be fruitfully read on its own, its full force is only appreciated when read as part of the collection.

The Pentateuch as story

The connectedness of these five books should not be surprising. There is a narrative storyline that runs from Genesis through Deuteronomy. Sometimes, that storyline is front and center as, for example, in the ancestral narratives of Genesis 12–50. In other places, the storyline recedes to the background but is still evident in the narrator's voice and the sequence of events. The Torah has been arranged as a single overarching story, albeit containing lots of inserted material: genealogies, poems, lists of instructions, and so on.

Realizing that the Pentateuch is shaped as a story has important implications when it comes to reading it. First, the material cannot simply be rearranged. One cannot simply collect all the narratives together or itemize the regulations in a neatly arranged appendix without doing violence to the text. The instruction contained in this part of Scripture works precisely in its *blend* of story and law (however much some readers might wish things had been done differently).

Second, as with any story, sequential order is important. Think of how a novel works. Of course, one can simply skip to the end to see how everything turns out, but much would be lost by missing the development of characters, the artful weaving of material, the shocking twists in the plot, and so on. Doing so would also ignore any use of flashback and flash-forward, both of which are significant when reading the Pentateuch. You really do miss something if, for instance, you don't realize that the blessing God pronounces to Noah in Genesis 9 reverberates both with what He had said to humans in Genesis 1 and with what Israel hears in Leviticus 26. Following the order of the story is important.

Third, stories have purpose. There is a reason for telling them (with good stories at least!). It might be to make an excuse, or to give an account of how work went, but we tell stories to achieve certain ends. The same holds true for biblical stories. Recognizing this raises important questions that we need to ponder: What is the purpose of the Pentateuch? Why is this story being told, in this way? And what role does Leviticus play in it?

The purpose of the Pentateuch

Even for casual readers, the shift of focus in the Pentateuch's story at Genesis 12 is obvious. Genesis 1–11, with all the tricky questions it raises, merely sets the scene for the main topic: the emergence of Israel. From Abra(ha)m through to the plains of Moab, the author's primary interest lies in charting the relationship between this fledgling nation and its God. Yet even modern histories attempt more than simply listing a sequence of events. This was even more so the case in the ancient world where the primary purpose of history writing was exhortation. Events were described in order to teach readers something, or to confront them, or to commend (and thus implicitly command) a particular virtue. Likewise, the Pentateuch does more than simply recount the past for the past's sake. As it informs readers about former people and events, the Torah critiques, questions, and judges in relation to that past. For example, Abraham's faith regarding what God had told him (e.g. Gen. 15:6) is not just a description of a long-distant past; it also asks readers, *Do you have the same trust in God's promises?*

In this way, the Pentateuch's story aims to persuade as it unfolds. Old Testament scholar, Terence Fretheim, nicely sums up the goal of that persuasion:

> It is now more evident that the Pentateuch as a whole is fashioned to shape the faith and life of its readers .... [T]he most basic effect desired for readers is not that they become better theologians or better informed about their history and traditions. The end desired is more deeply religious, namely, that the relationship with God become what God intended in the creation.[1]

The Pentateuch has been written with purpose. First and foremost, it tells readers about past people and events. Yet, because the account also records God's interactions with people, the story reveals His nature and character. In turn, this emerging picture of God helps readers evaluate the kinds of things He finds pleasing and those He does not. In this way, the story pronounces a verdict on readers' lives. They are invited to conform to God's ways rather than resist them. So, the Torah seeks to shape and transform the community of God's people, or even to call such a community into being where none exists. The Pentateuch, therefore, becomes a means of addressing a

---

1. Terence E. Fretheim, *The Pentateuch* (Nashville: Abingdon, 1996), 62.

broken divine-human relationship and restoring God's creation purposes.

Within these overarching goals, what role does Leviticus play?

The role of Leviticus in the Pentateuch's story

A key issue for understanding any story is to discern the point of tension, the problem that propels the narrative forward. There is usually an issue that the storyteller is trying to resolve (think about the last movie you watched). It is the journey towards resolution that gives direction to the story. That is why there is a feeling of relief and satisfaction when the problem is overcome (or why we complain if this aspect of the story is missing). Accordingly, identifying the point of tension is crucial for understanding any story. What tension is the Pentateuch seeking to resolve?

Eric Zenger has proposed the following overview of the Pentateuch's storyline.[2]

Genesis	Exodus	Leviticus	Numbers	Deuteronomy
Creation, fall, and the promise of a land	From Egypt, through the wilderness, to Sinai	At Sinai	From Sinai, through the wilderness, towards Moab	Instructions for life in the Promised Land

Zenger's scheme is geographical. There is a movement from the promise of a land (Genesis) through the wilderness (Exodus) to Mount Sinai (Leviticus). From there, the story progresses back through the wilderness (Numbers)

---

2. Erich Zenger, ed., *Einleitung in das Alte Testament* (7th, rev. & exp. ed.; Stuttgart: Kohlhammer, 2008), 68.

to the plains of Moab and the giving of instructions for
life in Canaan (Deuteronomy). In this overview, land is
the dominant concern. The narrative tension is the loss of
Eden; the sought-for resolution is gaining the Promised
Land. Yet, if this is the point of tension, the story remains
unresolved, because the Israelites do not enter the land.
Indeed, the account finishes with Moses dying *in Moab*.

   For this reason, I think the following is a better way to
summarize the story of the Pentateuch.

Genesis	Exodus	Leviticus	Numbers	Deuteronomy
Creation, fall, and loss of access to God's presence	God's presence fills the tabernacle	Living in proximity to God's presence	God's presence goes with Israel	Instructions for ongoing life in God's presence

The overall scheme this time is theological. In the beginning,
God formed a (sacred) place in which He and humans could
dwell together. Accordingly, the real loss in Genesis 3 is
access to God's presence. This is the tension that propels the
rest of the story: How can a holy God live with people again?
Regaining access to God's presence becomes the dominant
theme. Of course, land is still important – Canaan will be
the place where God will establish a permanent dwelling
place – but it is not the central concern. Thus, the highpoint
in Exodus is not rescue from Egypt, but construction of a
tabernacle to house God's glory (cf. 40:34-35). In Numbers,
God's presence travels with the people through the
wilderness. Even though Moses dies outside the Promised
Land in Deuteronomy, God remains with His people.

   Now, the importance of Leviticus becomes clearer. A holy
and terrifying God (cf. Exod. 20:18-19) has come to reside

in the tabernacle, right at the heart of the Israelite camp. Accordingly, Leviticus instructs Israel about how to approach and survive that divine presence. All the book's instructions and regulations now become necessary, vital even.

And it works! Leviticus opens with Yahweh speaking to Moses '*from* the tent of meeting' (Lev. 1:1).[3] This simply continues the scene from the end of Exodus where everyone, including Moses, is excluded from the tabernacle when God's glory descends (Exod. 40:34-35). This is the fate of humanity since the Garden: exclusion and separation from the presence of God. But Numbers 1:1 testifies to a profound reversal. Here, echoing the opening words of Leviticus, we read that Yahweh spoke to Moses '*in* the tent of meeting'. Moses entered and survived! How did that happen? Well, that is what the book of Leviticus will explain. It is therefore not all that surprising to find Leviticus placed at the structural, and, arguably, theological, heart of the Pentateuch. This book is crucial.

Structure

When it comes to working out the structure of Leviticus, things are not straightforward. Even a brief skim through the commentaries reveals a bewildering array of options. This serves as a reminder that few biblical books are written so tightly that only one structure is possible.

---

3. Throughout, I use 'Yahweh' and 'Lord' interchangeably. 'Yahweh' reflects the underlying Hebrew. Following the LXX (i.e. the Greek translation of the Old Testament), 'Lord' is the preferred term in English translations. Each teacher will need to make up his or her own mind. My own practice is to use 'Yahweh' when preaching and teaching at college or in a setting where the name will be understood, but to use 'Lord' when preaching elsewhere.

Nevertheless, there are some divisions within Leviticus that are commonly recognized. These can at least provide a starting point for considering how the book's various sections might fit together.

Chapters 1–7 are tied together by a focus on sacrificial procedures and are concluded by a formal summary statement (7:37-38). Also belonging together are chapters 8–10. The uniting factor this time is genre, which – unusually for Leviticus – is narrative. Chapters 11–15 focus on matters related to ritual purity. Chapter 16, outlining the Day of Atonement, is probably best regarded as an independent unit.

Subdividing chapters 17–27 is more complicated. Chapter 17 deals with sacrifice and the importance of blood. Chapters 18–22 are set apart by the contrast they establish between 'holy' and 'common' – in relation to the moral purity of the people (18:1–20:27) and the ritual status of priests, sanctuary, and offerings (21:1–22:33). Leviticus 23:1–24:9 is concerned with sacred times (Sabbath and feast days). The short episode in 24:10-23, like chapters 8–10, is narrative and discusses a case of blasphemy. Chapter 25 expands the concept of Sabbath, outlining in turn a 'Sabbath year' and a 'Year of Jubilee'. The highpoint of the book comes in chapter 26 which announces the blessing or cursing that will accompany obedience or disobedience, calling the reader to make a choice. Chapter 27 returns to the topic of voluntary offerings made to Yahweh.

Putting all this together is a matter of some difficulty! Different arrangements are possible depending on which features are given more prominence. I have previously suggested the following outline for the book, arranged as a palistrophe (chiasm) centered on the Day of Atonement:[4]

A Instructions for Entering the Tabernacle as Sacred Space (1–7)

  B Narrative about Profanation of Sacred Space (8–10)

    C Separating Clean and Unclean (11–15)

      D The Day of Atonement (16)

    C' Separating Holy and Profane (17:1–24:9)

  B' Narrative about Profanation of Sacred Name (24:10-23)

A' Instructions for Entering the Land as Sacred Space (25–27)

Jay Sklar arranges the material somewhat differently. He proposes an eight-part structure with a more linear, logical progression:[5]

1. Laws on offerings (1:1–7:38)
2. Public worship at the tabernacle begins (8:1–10:20)
3. Laws on the causes and treatment of ritual purity (11:1–15:33)
4. The Day of Atonement (16:1-34)
5. Laws on the proper slaughtering and eating of animals and the proper use of their blood (17:1-16)

---

4. G. Geoffrey Harper, *'I Will Walk Among You': The Rhetorical Function of Allusion to Genesis 1–3 in the Book of Leviticus* (BBRSup 21; University Park: Eisenbrauns, 2018), 78.

5. Jay Sklar, *Leviticus* (TOTC 3; Downers Grove: IVP, 2013), 78-84.

6. Laws on living as God's holy people (18:1–20:27)
7. Laws on showing due reverence for the Lord's holy things and holy times (21:1–24:23)
8. Laws anticipating life in the Promised Land (25:1–27:34)

Both proposals have merits; each also has drawbacks. This simply demonstrates the difficulty of discerning *the* structure of Leviticus.

Nevertheless, the outlines sketched above provide insight into the overall logic of the book. There is a movement from outlining the cultic procedures and personnel necessary for approaching Yahweh, climaxing with the Day of Atonement, to consideration of the moral and ethical implications for a people invited to live in proximity to God. This does not mean a neat divide between 'ritual' (Lev. 1–16) and 'moral' (Lev. 17–27) concerns, however. As we will see in Part II, these concepts are often intertwined and remain inseparable.

Message

Irrespective of how one decides to divide up Leviticus, the book's central concern is clear: preparing people to live near Yahweh's earthly presence and survive the encounter. Several key words and phrases highlight the theme:

- 'Before Yahweh' and 'tent of meeting' (26 and 34 per cent of Old Testament uses respectively) draw attention to Yahweh's immanent presence which now governs reality for Israel.

- A concentration of the terms 'impure', 'pure', and 'holy' indicates who or what may come, or must be excluded from coming, 'before Yahweh' or into the tent.

- Leviticus contains 48 per cent of the Old Testament's uses of the verb 'to make atonement', emphasizing the means by which persons and objects are made fit to approach God.

- Likewise, the word 'priest' (25 per cent), as well as the specific terms for the various offerings are also clustered here, all of which are necessary for securing atonement.

The Day of Atonement ceremony (Lev. 16) brings these core emphases to a head. The ritual's purpose is to deal with the accumulated impurities and sins of the people (16:30). Atonement is made by the high priest, who enters behind the curtain – *into the very presence of Yahweh* – to sprinkle blood on the ark (16:12-15). The procedure not only allows the high priest, representing the people, to survive his entry to the most holy place but it also enables the people to continue living in the presence of God.

The necessity of dealing with ritual and moral violations is emphasized by the book's two narrative sections. Chapter 10 records a ritual transgression which results in the incineration of the offenders, Nadab and Abihu (10:1-2). The narrative of 24:10-23, on the other hand, concerns a moral transgression. The result, however, is the same: death (24:23). Hence, these episodes drive home the same point: the glorious presence of Yahweh is an ambiguous reality, with potential for life or death. The common denominator is the holiness of God. The variable factor is the stance of the worshipper.

Nevertheless, the message of Leviticus remains one of grace. This is demonstrated by a repeated phrase found thirty-seven times throughout the book: 'The LORD said to Moses,

"Speak to …"'. The result is that 85 per cent of Leviticus is presented as God's direct speech. It is God who desires to live with His people, and it is God who provides means and instructions to make such an arrangement possible.

Author and audience

The related issues of identifying the author and audience of Leviticus are complicated. The matter is, of course, related to determining who is responsible for the Pentateuch as we have it. However, in line with ancient world conventions, the corpus does not record who composed it. Even so, Moses has traditionally been understood as the author or compiler. At the same time, it is widely acknowledged that he cannot have written everything now contained in the Pentateuch (e.g. Deut. 34:5-12). Indeed, the command to 'write down this song' in Deuteronomy 31:19, for instance, is a *plural* command. The resulting complexity regarding authorship should be neither disturbing nor unexpected; it simply fits with what we know of how texts were produced in ancient times.

This is certainly not the place to survey all the proposed solutions or to assess their relative merits. Hence, I will simply employ the term 'author' throughout to designate the person(s) responsible for the text as we have it. Readers can fill this in as they see fit. The crucial factor to remember is that the Pentateuch (like the rest of the Scriptures) is the product of dual authorship. Even if the human side of the equation is messier than we would like it to be, the text is nevertheless God-breathed. It remains His authoritative word for His people.

One feature of the text that we must be sensitive to is the role of the narrator. In Leviticus, the narrator is the first and last voice we hear. His comments make up about 13 per cent of the book. As with all stories, it is the storyteller who shapes the account and who decides which details to elaborate upon and which to leave out. He or she determines our reading perspective. While the narrator throughout the Pentateuch could be Moses, it is also possible that a later writer has woven together material stemming from the time of Moses. Various suggestions have been made for who this might be, including Joshua, Solomon, and Hezekiah.

Again, irrespective of what we conclude about the identity of the narrator, as interpreters of Leviticus we need to think about two audiences. There is the audience within the narrative (i.e. Israel, encamped at Sinai, hearing Yahweh speak through Moses), and there is the audience addressed by the narrator (that is, the people for whom the book was written). We need to be careful not to conflate the two. Although this might initially seem strange, the situation is the same with the Gospels. The Gospels record things Jesus did and said (some of them at least; see John 21:25), but the Gospels were not written by Jesus or for the people Jesus interacted with. Therefore, while we must pay heed to what Jesus said to His hearers about sheep and goats (Matt. 25:31-46), for example, we also need to consider what Matthew's purpose was in narrating the parable. Both audiences need to be kept in view to hear the message of the text correctly.

Aim and purpose

In light of the above, we are now in a better position to consider the aim and purpose of Leviticus as an interdependent book within the Pentateuch. What kind of text is Leviticus and what is it here for?

An instruction manual?

Although many label Leviticus an 'instruction manual', that designation is problematic. Correctly identifying genre (i.e., what type of literature this is) is crucial when reading any text, as it sets expectations for what we will find and how we ought to interpret it. But instruction manuals (by very definition) are boring; no one in their right mind reads them expecting to delight in the literary crafting. Assuming Leviticus to be a manual simply sets readers up to expect a dull and dry text. Moreover, if Leviticus is understood as an instruction manual, whether for the priests or for the Israelites, then readers immediately face the problem of seeming irrelevance. What possible use would these ancient instructions have for modern people? (Surely no more than an instruction manual for a 1960s TV would have.)

But a bigger problem emerges too. If Leviticus is an instruction manual, then it is a very poor one (on a par with flat-pack furniture assembly instructions). It might strike us as being detailed and comprehensive, but that is far from the case. Think about the sacrificial procedure in chapter 1, for instance. Instructions are given, but not enough to actually perform a sacrifice. A host of necessary information is left totally unaddressed: What kind of knife should be used? How sharp does it need to be? Which arteries do you sever? In which order? How long does the animal need to bleed out for? How do you stop the blood from coagulating before it gets splashed on the altar? All of this suggests that to regard Leviticus merely as an 'instruction manual' would be misguided at best. The book, it seems, has other purposes.

What Leviticus is doing

What might those purposes be? One helpful way to approach the question is to consider what Leviticus as a text is *doing*. Framing the question this way recognizes that authors compose texts to accomplish certain ends, that they attempt to *do* things with their words (e.g. to rebuke, encourage, teach, explain, and so on). It is also a recognition that the biblical writers are seldom, if ever, only trying to convey content (which has implications for our preaching). While they write about, or reflect upon, real people and events, their purpose extends far beyond simply providing information.

Leviticus is doing multiple things. As is immediately apparent, the book makes declarations about ritual and ethical matters. There are lots of lists and lots of instructions. With these instructions, Leviticus prohibits readers from certain courses of action while also permitting or even commanding others. Because the instructions come directly from God, Leviticus also imposes this legislation upon readers and demands obedience.

So far so good. But Leviticus does more than simply impose rules. By making demands about ritual and ethical practice, the book also declares who or what may come before Yahweh. In this way, it makes assertions about God's character – for example, that He is a holy God who cannot be approached lightly or carelessly. Yet the portrait of God that emerges and the corresponding boundaries that become necessary are aimed at inviting Israel to come and live safely with Him. In this way, lists of instructions become the means of equipping Israel to experience life and blessing.

Yet even as Leviticus extends an invitation to readers, it also sounds a warning. Yahweh invites His people to draw near, but only on His terms. The book's two narrative

sections (especially 10:1-2; 24:10-23) drive home the
message that failure to carefully heed the divinely given
instructions will end in disaster. Accordingly, Leviticus
urges obedience. Even more than that, and uniquely in the
Old Testament, the book calls its readers to become holy,
just as Yahweh is holy (11:44-45; 19:2; 20:7, 26).

Here, we can see that a central purpose of Leviticus is to
transform individuals and community in conformity with
the likeness of Yahweh. Even more broadly, Leviticus aims
to transform time and space (think of all the holy times and
places prescribed in the book) and thereby begin to reorder
and restore a world fractured by human sin and impurity.
Thus, Leviticus not only testifies to the loss of a 'very good'
world, but also hints at, and perhaps even promises, its
ultimate restoration.

Outlining what the book of Leviticus is doing (even if
only a brief sketch) is essential preparation for looking at
individual sections in Part II. The danger of not doing this
sort of work is that we can read (and teach) a given passage
without due consideration of how it serves the book's
wider aim(s). Interpreters must work at both levels: what a
particular section is doing *and* what role it plays in the whole
composition. This is not a simple step-by-step process, but
rather an organic understanding of the text that emerges
only as one spends time (and prayer!) wrestling with it.

Why Should We Preach
and Teach Leviticus?

Hopefully, seeing as you have made it this far, you are
already mildly serious about teaching Leviticus in some
way! Nevertheless, I think it is worth articulating the

potential benefits of doing so. If nothing else, the vision will help during the long hours of preparation that lie ahead.

Gordon Wenham, in his excellent commentary on the book, notes that Leviticus is the first book of the Bible that Jewish children read in the synagogue.[6] That could hardly be further from the case when it comes to Christian churches, where there is a definite Leviticus-shaped void in the average preaching and Sunday School programs. Indeed, in a threefold series of volumes which recorded the 'best sermons' of the year in the USA (four volumes in 1924–27; ten volumes in 1944–68; and seven volumes in 1988–94), Leviticus does not fare well. Out of the 879 sermons published, only two (0.22 per cent) look at a passage from Leviticus. While the *Best Sermons* series only contain a tiny sample of the (probably) millions of sermons preached across those years, the picture is nonetheless telling.[7] Anecdotal evidence would suggest it is not far off the mark.

This should raise questions about the biblical diet of our churches. If we met someone who only ate apples, or only ate bread, we would have legitimate cause for concern. The same is true with respect to preaching and teaching. Keeping up the diet analogy, God has given us a wonderful variety of sixty-six 'Scripture delicacies', all of which are essential for our wellbeing. But, on reflection, how balanced is our 'eating'? A minister friend of mine took up a position in a well-established church and was shocked to discover

---

6. Gordon J. Wenham, *The Book of Leviticus* (NICOT; Grand Rapids: Eerdmans, 1979), vii.

7. For further analysis, see Brent A. Strawn, *The Old Testament Is Dying: A Diagnosis and Recommended Treatment* (Grand Rapids: Baker, 2017), 28-38.

that the preaching program over the past ten years had consisted of *only* the Gospels – not including John! He promptly started a series on 1 Samuel. Another friend has made it his goal to preach through every book of the Bible before he hangs up his boots. Last I heard, he was tackling Jeremiah for the first time – a wonderful demonstration of a healthy doctrine of Scripture overflowing into ministry practice. So, if people have been overindulging on Pauline pastries at church, then perhaps it is time for a well-seasoned Leviticus steak. There are many side-benefits to such a culinary adventure. Here are four.

Confronting misconceptions

As mentioned earlier, whenever I lecture or preach on Leviticus and I ask people what their impressions of the book are, the two most consistent answers are 'boring' and 'irrelevant'. For many, Leviticus is a book to be endured only when trying to complete a read-the-Bible-in-a-year plan (or it is the place where such a well-intentioned plan goes awry).

If for no other reason, teaching through Leviticus is an opportunity to confront this sort of faulty thinking. The saying springs to mind which reminds us that the Bible is *never* boring (even though sermons on the Bible can be). Leviticus does nothing to counter such sage wisdom. The book is a consummate work of literary artistry – so much more than a mundane list of regulations about infectious skin diseases and bodily fluids. It is forceful, yet subtle; cosmic in scope, yet intimate; straightforward to understand, yet profound. It is filled with wordplays and puns, intricate structural patterns, and allusions. There is beauty here for those with eyes to see.

And, as we will investigate more fully in Part II, Leviticus is strikingly relevant. Like the rest of Scripture, Leviticus contains hard truths about humanity: it confronts us head-on with our once unavoidable fate of being banished from God and His blessing. But it also reveals the graciousness of a God who was not willing for that to remain our fate. In Leviticus, God speaks and acts to make possible an alternative future. I can still remember someone at church telling me about the tears that had run down his face as he listened to a sermon on Leviticus 16 – not because it was Leviticus, but because of the overwhelming picture of God he had encountered. Irrelevant? Not a chance.

Assumed knowledge

Readers unfamiliar with Leviticus can run into problems elsewhere in the Bible. The reason for this is that many biblical authors – in both Old and, especially, New Testaments – simply assume their audiences know Leviticus well. After all, why wouldn't God's people be conversant with the Scriptures? Therefore, not being familiar with Leviticus can, at best, lead to missing the nuance of what a given writer is getting at; at worst, it can result in complete misunderstanding. There are lots of places where Leviticus becomes essential assumed knowledge. Here are two examples to make the point.

1. **Romans 12.** If you ask someone at church to define 'sacrifice', the answer often runs along these sort of lines: a sacrifice is an animal offered as a substitute on behalf of someone who has sinned so that, by its shed blood, atonement can be made and the sinner forgiven. But how then are we to understand Romans

12:1, where Paul commands readers 'to offer your bodies as a living sacrifice, holy and pleasing to God'? Are Christians to offer themselves to achieve atonement? Are they acting as substitute for someone else? Of course, the answer is no, but it is knowledge of Leviticus that clarifies what Paul is getting at. Sacrifice in Leviticus is multifaceted. There are different kinds of sacrifice which served different purposes. Sometimes, atonement for sin was the aim, sometimes not. In Romans 12, Paul is evoking the offering of Leviticus 1, an offering usually made to present a gift to God as an expression of great thankfulness. It is this idea that looms large in the apostle's mind: the call to offer oneself wholly to God is presented as the only reasonable response to His mercy. Understanding the complexity of sacrificial language in Leviticus helps us to hear better how the New Testament authors use the concept.

2. **Hebrews 9.** In Hebrews 9–10, the argument of the book reaches a climax as it proclaims the full assurance believers now have to enter God's presence by the blood of Jesus (10:19, 22). The running metaphor used to explain this accomplishment is adopted from Leviticus 16 – the ritual enacted on the Day of Atonement (or Yom Kippur). In Hebrews, Christ, pictured as high priest, moves through the heavenly tabernacle (9:11, 24). Instead of sprinkling the blood of sacrificed animals, He offers His own blood in the most holy place (9:12). In this way, Christ both purifies the heavenly tabernacle with His better sacrifice (9:23) and brings a full and final end to

sin by virtue of His once-for-all offering (9:26).
Without understanding the Leviticus background,
readers are hard pushed to make sense of what the
author of Hebrews is talking about.

Therefore, those who teach and preach Leviticus well can
help people not only discover hidden riches there, but also
equip them to hear the rest of the Scriptures more clearly.

Theological themes

Many important biblical themes have their most sustained
treatment in Leviticus. The following list is representative:

- The nature and functions of sacrifice
- Atonement for sin and impurity
- The cultic use of blood
- Priests and priesthood
- The parameters of sacred space
- Ritual and moral defilement and cleansing
- Sexual ethics
- Love of neighbor
- Social justice
- The Year of Jubilee

In order to get to grips with any one of these concepts,
engaging with Leviticus is essential. Again, doing so is vital,
not only for reading the remainder of the Old Testament,
but the New Testament also. Take away the concepts of
blood, sacrifice, atonement, purification, and priestly
mediation from a theology of Jesus's life and ministry and
you quickly end up with an anemic portrait. On the other

hand, spending time teasing out these ideas in Leviticus can foster a new understanding of, and appreciation for, what Jesus accomplished. I can remember preaching on a ritual text from Leviticus at a conference. Someone came up to me afterwards to say that, though they had been a Christian for some time, they had never before understood their need for atonement. Now, thanks to Leviticus (and the illumination of the Holy Spirit!), the penny had finally dropped.

Understanding God better

Like the rest of the Scriptures, Leviticus reveals God. Here, readers encounter Yahweh's terrifying holiness that can literally consume (10:2!). They encounter Him as lawgiver, dictating the parameters of sacred space, specifying who and what may approach Him, and when it is safe to do so. They become aware of the tremendous gulf that separates unholy and impure people from the living God and yet also become aware of His gracious provision of cleansing and forgiveness. Thus, a compelling picture emerges of a God who longs to live among His people and to be their God (26:11-12), but who is also fully aware of the danger that such proximity poses to their wellbeing.

Perhaps the best analogy to encapsulate the picture of God presented in Leviticus is of a nuclear reactor. Depending on what country one lives in, attitudes to nuclear energy are different. Nevertheless, even in places where this kind of power production is embraced, one can never fully avoid the shadow cast by events such as Chernobyl or Fukushima. There is an inescapable ambiguity that surrounds nuclear power. With it lies potential for great blessing or unmitigated disaster. The same can be said for the God revealed in Leviticus. His immanent presence among the people holds out promise for untold blessing (see 26:3-12). Yet, events like the Nadab and Abihu episode (10:1-2) cast a shadow over the book. One cannot simply waltz into the most holy place and behold Yahweh's glory. Thus, Leviticus maintains a degree of tension. Is Yahweh's presence with His people a good thing or not? It depends on the stance of the worshipper(s).

Lest we relegate the ambiguous nature of God's presence to a (presumed sub-Christian) Old Testament understanding, it is worth considering some examples of how the theme resurfaces in the New. Jesus warns His disciples that His Father will 'cut off' any branch that does not bear fruit in Him (John 15:2). Ananias and Sapphira are struck dead for lying to the Holy Spirit (Acts 5:1-10); unsurprisingly, '[g]reat fear seized the whole church and all who heard about these events' (Acts 5:11). The book of Hebrews calls Christians to 'worship God acceptably with reverence and awe, for our "God is a consuming fire"' (Heb. 12:28-29). For this reason, Paul advises the Corinthian church to purify themselves from everything that contaminates body and spirit because, quoting Leviticus 26:12, God walks among them (2 Cor. 6:16–7:1). Leviticus has much to add to our understanding of God.

Conclusion

In sum, there is much to be gained by teaching Leviticus. Correspondingly, there is much to be lost if we do not. Old Testament scholar, Walter Brueggemann, urges Christian people to become 'text-saturated'.[8] By 'text' Brueggemann means the Bible; by Bible, he means all of

---

8. Walter Brueggemann, *Theology of the Old Testament: Testimony, Dispute, Advocacy* (Minneapolis: Fortress 1997), 79.

it. As preachers and Bible study leaders, it is our privilege
and responsibility to facilitate that goal.

Ideas for a Preaching or Teaching Series in Leviticus

Although shorter than many Old Testament books (it is
the shortest book in the Pentateuch), Leviticus is probably
too long to tackle chapter by chapter in most contexts.
Hence, the preacher or Bible study leader will need to
decide how best to divide up the material. Several factors
weigh in on that decision. There are portions of the book
which can be tackled as larger units. However, this needs
to be held in balance with having sufficient opportunity to
get into the details of a given passage. The time available
for a series is, therefore, a major factor. So, too, is audience
familiarity. There might well be wisdom in doing a short,
bird's-eye overview of Leviticus in four or five weeks as
preparation to come back later and explore the book at
greater length. Doing so can help give a congregation or
study group an overall understanding of the book into
which to fit the various pieces. (I have used the Bible
Project video summary of the book to achieve the same
ends.)[9] One could, of course, also add a sermon or study
on the entire book to the beginning of a series.[10]

An eighteen-part series

The breakdown I will follow in this book divides
Leviticus into eighteen teaching units. A longer series

---

9. See https://thebibleproject.com/explore/leviticus.

10. Mark Dever provides examples of how this might be done in *The Message of the Old Testament: Promises Made* (Wheaton: Crossway, 2006).

could follow the chapter divisions (a twenty-seven-part series) or the introductory speech formula (a thirty-seven-part series; cf. Lev. 1:1; 4:1; 5:14; etc.). However, I think breaking the book into eighteen units strikes a good balance between pace (moving through the material in good time) and detail (opportunity for in-depth engagement). The eighteen units could also be broken into two nine-part series.

1. Selfless devotion — Leviticus 1:1-17
2. Table fellowship — Leviticus 2:1–3:17
3. Purification for sin — Leviticus 4:1–5:13
4. Making restitution — Leviticus 5:14–6:7
5. The Lord of worship — Leviticus 6:8–7:38
6. Priests who need a priest — Leviticus 8:1–10:20
7. Time for a new diet? — Leviticus 11:1-47
8. Defilement and cleansing — Leviticus 12:1–15:33
9. The Day of Atonement — Leviticus 16:1-34
10. Sacred blood — Leviticus 17:1-16
11. Let's talk about sex — Leviticus 18:1-30 and 20:1-27
12. Holiness everywhere — Leviticus 19:1-37
13. Acknowledging the holy — Leviticus 21:1–22:33
14. Holy time — Leviticus 23:1-44
15. The ever-present Lord — Leviticus 24:1-23
16. God's society — Leviticus 25:1-55
17. Obedience brings blessing — Leviticus 26:1-46
18. Extraordinary thankfulness — Leviticus 27:1-34

A ten-part series

A briefer series that would allow Leviticus to be taught across one term, yet still engage with the text reasonably well, might be achieved in ten weeks. Doing so would probably mean not covering all the material within each section, so the series would be more akin to extended highlights.

1. Honoring God with gifts   Leviticus 1–3
2. Dealing with sin and guilt   Leviticus 4–7
3. Priests who need a priest   Leviticus 8–10
4. Time for a new diet?   Leviticus 11
5. Defilement and cleansing   Leviticus 12–15
6. Bloody Atonement   Leviticus 16–17
7. Holy living   Leviticus 18–20
8. Sacred people and times   Leviticus 21–25
9. Obedience brings blessing   Leviticus 26
10. Extraordinary thankfulness   Leviticus 27

A five-part series

As I mentioned above, there may be occasions when a much shorter series is desirable. A Leviticus 'taster' is possible in five talks. Ideally, this sort of mini-series would serve as an appetizer for a more extended look at the book. It could also be utilized for a church weekend or camp.

1. The LORD's sacrifices   Leviticus 1–7
2. The LORD's priests   Leviticus 8–10
3. The LORD's cleansing   Leviticus 11–17
4. The LORD's standards   Leviticus 18–24
5. The LORD's land   Leviticus 25–27

A thematic or topical series

In addition to the expository approaches outlined above, which move systematically through the book, Leviticus provides a great starting place to explore crucial biblical themes.[11] I listed a number of these above under the title, 'Why should we teach and preach Leviticus?' Any of the listed themes could be explored in this manner. The advantage of this approach is that it allows teachers to grapple with themes systematically – that is, to draw out what Leviticus as a whole has to say on the matter. In turn, this could become a point from which to explore how the theme develops across the canon (i.e., an exercise in biblical theology). A possible series, with key Levitical passages, is outlined below.

1.	A theology of sacrifice	Leviticus 1–6; 16; 27
2.	Understanding atonement	Leviticus 4–6; 9; 16–17
3.	A theology of priesthood	Leviticus 8–10; 16; 21–22
4.	Understanding pure and impure	Leviticus 10–16
5.	Interpersonal wrong-doing and forgiveness	Leviticus 5:1–6:7; 19:17-18
6.	Biblical sexual ethics	Leviticus 15; 18; 20
7.	Old Testament law and the Christian	Leviticus 18–20

---

11. For an excellent treatment of topical preaching, see Sam Chan and Malcolm J. Gill, *Topical Preaching in a Complex World: How to Proclaim Truth and Relevance at the Same Time* (Grand Rapids: Zondervan, 2021).

8. Disability in the Bible   Leviticus 19:14; 21:16-24;
                              22:17-25

9. Sabbath   Leviticus 23:1-3;
                              25:1–26:2

10. Social justice and care   Leviticus 19; 25
    of the vulnerable

11. Obedience and blessing   Leviticus 26

Teaching aids

One final point in relation to teaching Leviticus
concerns the use of visual aids. Helping people see or
imagine what Leviticus is speaking about pays dividends
in relation to understanding the text. This is not only
because many people are visual learners but is also a
recognition that the world of the Old Testament can be
an alien place to the uninitiated. The potential is endless: charts, maps, diagrams, pictures, videos – even a
virtual tour of the tabernacle. All can help illuminate
what is happening in a passage. Although not suitable
for every context, there really is nothing quite as effective
when teaching Leviticus 1 as playing a video of an animal
being sacrificed.

Preaching and Teaching
Old Testament Law

One of the immediate issues arising for anyone who wants
to teach Leviticus is what to do with Old Testament law.
Does Old Testament law apply to Christians or can it be
safely set aside? If it does apply, then how much does? Only
the Ten Commandments? All the so-called moral law? The
law in its entirety? These are perennial questions that have

occupied Christian thinkers since the earliest days of the church (see Acts 15). Each of the above positions has been defended and opposed, sometimes trenchantly.

This is not the place to survey (let alone resolve) every difficulty or proposed solution.[12] All I can reasonably accomplish is to make my own thinking on the topic clear in order to make sense of decisions made in Part II. In short, my answer to whether Old Testament law applies to Christians is always yes. This part of the Bible continues to function as Christian Scripture. Even a quick skim through the New Testament reveals that its writers reuse Old Testament commands frequently, including those found in Leviticus (e.g. Mark 12:29-31; 2 Cor. 13:1; 1 Pet. 1:15-16). So the more important question to ask is, *How* does Old Testament law apply to Christians? It is obvious to most interpreters that something significant has shifted with the coming of Jesus and the globalization of the gospel. But what exactly has changed and how should that shape our teaching and application of Old Testament law?

In order to think about these issues, I want firstly to consider the nature and purpose of Old Testament law before thinking about how one might helpfully teach and preach this part of Scripture.

The nature and purpose of Old Testament law

Our understanding of Old Testament law has dramatically increased in the last fifty years. There are several reasons for this. In recent decades, the Pentateuch has become the focus of increased research interest – especially the oft-neglected books of Leviticus and Numbers. Unsurprisingly,

---

12. For further discussion, see the 'Resources for further reading' at the end of this section.

more interpretative effort has led to better understanding
of how these books work. Also, renewed thinking about
how texts work to persuade readers has opened a window
into the purpose of both the narrative and legal sections
of the Torah. Additionally, archaeologists have continued
to discover and translate other ancient legal codes and
court texts. These finds have substantially increased our
understanding of how this type of literature functioned in
the ancient world. These factors have a direct bearing on
our interpretation and application of Old Testament law.
There are several things worth teasing out.

Torah as instruction

The first issue relates to translation. What does the
Hebrew word *torah* mean? Most English versions render
torah as 'law'. For instance, in Deuteronomy 1:5 we read,
'Moses began to expound this law [Heb. *torah*]' (likewise, ESV, KJV, NASB). However, when Moses begins to
speak, he tells the *story* of Yahweh's prior dealings with
the people (Deut. 1:6) and, in fact, continues doing so
for several chapters. Certainly, lots of commands also
follow (see Deut. 4:1-2; 5:6-21, etc.), but it is clear that
torah encapsulates both commands *and* story. Therefore,
the designation 'law', at least as the term is understood
in Western thinking, does not quite fit (if you went to
a lawyer for advice and he or she started telling you
stories, you might well ask for a refund). For this reason,
many have suggested that the translation 'instruction'
or 'teaching' may work better. This is not to suggest that
what we have in the Pentateuch is mere take-it-or-leave-it
advice; there are imperatives here (lots of them!). What
it does draw our attention to is the purpose behind this

combination of story and command (and poems and genealogies). *Together*, this blend of material delivers Yahweh's instruction to His people. Quite appropriately, therefore, the New Testament authors draw on both core elements to instruct Christians: story (e.g. 1 Cor. 10:1-11) and command (e.g. 1 Cor. 9:7-10).

Torah as story and command

Noting the relationship between command and story in the Pentateuch has important implications. First, commands cannot be neatly separated from their narrative context. There is an interplay that must be recognized. The developing storyline reveals the shifting contexts that explain why commands sometimes change (e.g., the regulations for how meat can be obtained in Lev. 17:3-5 and Deut. 12:20-25). On the other hand, the rules and regulations often address issues that the narratives have raised. The aim is sometimes prohibitive. For example, the danger posed by unresolved anger in Genesis 4 is addressed in Leviticus 19:17-18 with a command to rebuke wrongdoers, instead of taking vengeance. The story-law relationship can also be restorative. The sexual ethic outlined in Leviticus 18, for instance, promulgates the creation description of one man, one woman, one flesh of Genesis 2. In these sorts of ways, command and story work together. Interpreters must be sensitive to this dynamic.

Second, the story of Yahweh's deliverance of Israel sets the context for the giving of commands (see especially Deut. 6:20-25). God rescues His people *before* He instructs them regarding how they are to live. The exodus precedes Sinai. Or, in other terms, salvation comes before obedience. Obedience is expected, but always as a response to having already experienced God's grace. Hence, Old Testament faith runs along the same lines as New Testament faith.

Third, commands are given so that the people might experience life (see Lev. 18:5). When, at the end of Exodus, Yahweh takes up residence in the tabernacle (Exod. 40:34-35), Israel's reality is immediately changed. Transformation is required. Accordingly, righteous behaviors are commanded and extolled; warnings are sounded regarding things that result in death and banishment. The goal of these commands is to enable Israel to enjoy the blessing of living with God. Thus, Old Testament law is not opposed to grace; it is, in fact, an expression of grace. God graciously instructs His people so they may successfully live with Him.

Torah as common law

As any readers with a legal background know, there is more than one way to conceive of law.[13] A body of regulations may be considered statutory law – that is, a system of legal instruction laid down by a lawgiver which is final and complete. In this understanding, legal texts function as a definitive source. Only what is written in the code is regarded as binding. However, a legal system can also be based on common, or case, law.[14] Here, legal decisions are governed by cultural and collective concerns and are based on past precedent; laws are forever evolving and adapting as new situations arise. Legal texts in this conception are a

---

13. Here I summarize the very helpful treatment in Joshua Berman, *Inconsistency in the Torah: Ancient Literary Convention and the Limits of Source Criticism* (New York: Oxford University Press, 2017), 107-17.

14. In Commonwealth jurisdictions, the distinction might better be phrased as being between statutory law and *judicial law* (which includes both common law and equity). Either way, the analogy still stands. (My thanks to Ben Mackay for the point of clarification.)

resource, a record of past decisions which provides wisdom for future deliberation.

The crucial matter arising from this distinction between statutory and common law determines which conception of law best applies to the legal sections of the Pentateuch. Of course, there is a danger of imposing modern terminology and concepts on an ancient text. Nevertheless, I think the exercise is useful. Are the commands found in the Torah a full and final statement of everything that must be done or not done (akin to statutory law)? Or do they form a repository of past decisions aimed to instruct subsequent judicial thinking (akin to common law)?

It is worth noting that, while a statutory approach to law reflects many modern legal systems, as well as Greek and Roman law, it does not fit with what we know about law codes from Mesopotamia (the primary context for ancient Israel). Instead, Mesopotamian codes display a common-law approach to decision making. Texts are treated as resources, not definitive sources. So, while legal codes, like the Laws of Hammurabi, were widely available (based on archaeological evidence), no Ancient Near Eastern court text yet discovered cites any one of these codes.

Old Testament law functions similarly.[15] Nowhere are judges instructed to consult written sources. Accounts of

---

15. James Watts notes in this respect, 'There is no ancient evidence that written laws directed legal practice until the third or second century BCE' (*Understanding the Pentateuch as a Scripture* [Hoboken: Wiley Blackwell, 2017]). Increasingly, the Pentateuch came to be understood as prescriptive law, normative for Jews and Samaritans. For further exploration of this development, see Gary N. Knoppers and Bernard M. Levinson, 'How, When, Where, and Why Did the Pentateuch Become the Torah' in Gary N. Knoppers and Bernard M. Levinson (eds.), *The Pentateuch as Torah: New Models for Understanding Its*

trials (e.g., 1 Kings 3) do not include reference to law codes. Provision is made for a judicial decision-making process that would replace Moses (Deut. 17:8-12) in which the verdict reached by the priest and judge (v. 10) becomes a *torah* ('law' or 'instruction') that must be obeyed (v. 11). A paradigm of common law better accommodates the data than viewing Old Testament law as statutory. At the same time, Yahweh's role must be remembered. Laws and rules are not simply social constructs; they have a divine origin and, hence, constitute authoritative instruction.

Torah as moral formation

One immediate implication of the distinction between statutory and common law is that Old Testament ethics cannot simply be equated with Old Testament law. In other words, Old Testament commands were not the ethical benchmark for Israel. Rather, these commands, especially the prohibitions, defined the outer limits of acceptable behavior beyond which punishment was prescribed. Take, for example, the command, 'You shall not murder' (Exod. 20:13 and Deut. 5:17). Those who did commit murder were to be punished (with the death penalty). However, that does not mean that the moral ideal in Israel was simply to avoid 'going too far' – that anything short of taking someone's life was permissible. Far from it. Israel's ethical goal was to become like Yahweh, to do as He would do. This is why the legal material in the Pentateuch is sprinkled with so many recollections of Yahweh's past action. Israel was to remember and act accordingly. The

---

Promulgation and Acceptance (Winona Lake: Eisenbrauns, 2007). (My thanks to Joshua D. Reeve for pointing out the Knoppers and Levinson reference.)

people were to embody the same kindness, mercy, fidelity, and generosity they had experienced from the hand of God.

It is precisely this understanding of Torah that Jesus illustrates in Matthew 5. Speaking to His disciples He says, 'You have heard that it was said to the people long ago, "You shall not murder, and anyone who murders will be subject to judgment." But I tell you that anyone who is angry with a brother or sister will be subject to judgment' (Matt. 5:21-22). In saying this, Jesus was not adding something new, but was clarifying for His audience what Old Testament law was meant to produce in people: transformation of the heart towards loving God and loving others.

Here, we begin to see that a fundamental purpose of the Torah was to form people ethically. It is much more than a list of 613 rules to be obeyed. Remember, the Torah is a mix of story and command. While we are generally better at discerning how narrative works to shape ethical thinking, it is important to recognize how the legal material seeks to achieve the same goal.

Again, this is where comparison with other ancient law codes can aid our understanding. While these codes display many similarities with biblical law, they also serve to illustrate the differences. Perhaps one of the most striking differences is the Bible's use of purpose clauses. Old Testament commands are saturated with phrases beginning with 'so that', 'because', or similar (e.g. Lev. 17:10-14; 20:14; Deut. 12:12; 15:7-11). Even the recurring statement, 'I am Yahweh' functions towards the same end (e.g. Lev. 19). Noting this helps illustrate what I suggested above. While there are commands to be obeyed (with resulting consequences), biblical law is concerned with more than mere command delivery. The presence of so many purpose clauses reveals that transformation of moral reasoning is the goal. Commands are worded in such a way that the hearer's understanding is shaped. Israel was meant to grasp the *why* behind the commands – presumably so that the same ethical principles could help people negotiate new situations as they arose.

Torah as demonstration

In light of the above, it becomes evident that the primary purpose of Old Testament law is to make a statement about Yahweh. In the ancient world, law codes presented a compendium of legislation as a model system of justice. The aim was to picture the ideal in order to highlight the just and wise character of the lawgiver – most often the king. Biblical law functions similarly. Of course, from a biblical perspective, Yahweh is the lawgiver (Moses, in the main, acts as God's spokesperson). Thus, the system of just and wise instruction conveyed by Torah proclaims the justice and wisdom of Yahweh. This was intended to have a secondary impact with respect to how Israel was perceived. The nation's obedience was meant to portray the magnificence of their God and so be attractive to outsiders. This logic is explicitly at work in Deuteronomy 4:6-8 where Moses says regarding God's commands,

> Observe them carefully, for this will show your wisdom and understanding to the nations, who will hear about all these decrees and say, 'Surely this great nation is a wise and understanding people.' What other nation is so great as to have their gods near them the way the LORD our God is near us whenever we pray to him? And what other nation is so great as to have such righteous

decrees and laws as this body of laws I am setting before you today?

Torah as delightful

It is not hard to see why the Torah was viewed as being delightful and beneficial or, in Paul's terms, as holy, righteous, and good (Rom. 7:12). It is here, perhaps, that we need to let the testimony of Scripture speak on its own terms and let it challenge our (Western, Protestant) disinclination towards Old Testament law. For Israel, the law was premised on grace and was itself an expression of grace. It provided needed instruction for people to continue to live in proximity to Yahweh's glorious presence. Its purpose went beyond simply informing thinking to shaping character – to bring about transformation – and so form a worshipping community gathered around God. For these reasons, the psalmist exclaimed:

> The *torah* of Yahweh is perfect,
>> Bringing back life.
> The testimony of Yahweh is established,
>> Making wise the simple.
> The precepts of Yahweh are right,
>> Gladdening the heart.
> The commandment of Yahweh is pure,
>> Giving light to the eyes.
> The fear of Yahweh is pure,
>> Standing forever.
> The judgments of Yahweh are true,
>> All together righteous.
> More desirable than gold,
>> Even much pure gold;

Sweeter than honey,
>   Even oozing honeycomb.

>>   (Ps. 9:7-10; my translation)

Preaching Old Testament law

Hopefully at this point you are thinking, 'Let me at it! I want to teach Old Testament law!' But how do we preach and teach Old Testament law well? The good news is that many of the (perhaps intuitive) interpretative skills we employ elsewhere serve us here too. Things a preacher or Bible study leader will need to think about include the meaning of words, historical setting, literary context, purpose, and so on.

Truth is, the same work must be done to teach *New* Testament commands well. For example, in 2 Corinthians 13:12, Paul says, 'Greet one another with a holy kiss.' The sentence is a command delivered by the apostle to a Christian church. So why do we not regularly greet one another with a 'holy kiss' at church? Are our churches failing to heed the clear teaching of Scripture? Of course, we need to remember that Paul's letter was written to a church in first-century Corinth, not directly to us. So, what would Paul's command have meant to its original readers? What cultural factors influence the instruction? How does this command fit with the rest of the letter? These are the kinds of questions that must be addressed *before* considering what the command for holy kissing might mean today. Interpreting Old Testament law works similarly.

Israel as paradigm

Before we get to the nitty-gritty of dealing with Old Testament commands, it is worthwhile taking a step back to get a sense of the bigger biblical picture.

There is a movement across the Scriptures from a focus on Israel in Canaan to consideration of the nations (including Israel) upon the earth. There is a broadening of scope, or a widening of the lens. Of course, God has always been concerned about the nations and the earth, but there is a progression in emphasis. You see this movement at play in Ephesians 6, where Paul restates the command to honor one's parents, but expands the location where one will enjoy long life from 'land' to 'earth' (vv. 2-3; cf. Deut. 5:16). He does a similar thing with respect to Abraham's inheritance in Romans 4:13 ('Canaan' to 'world').

This observation has a direct impact on how we teach Old Testament law. The law given to Israel represents the embodiment of divine values *in a particular time and place*. The broadening of scope from Israel to the nations and from the land of Canaan to the world, however, means we need to understand Israel as a paradigm rather than look for, or assume, one-to-one correspondence. The values or principles underlying a given command will remain, but the outworking or application may be different. The following diagram (adapted from Chris Wright) illustrates this dynamic (see *Figure 0.1*, page 50).[16]

Wright helpfully teases out the implications for teaching and preaching:

> So we can preach OT law, not seeking to enforce it litera-
> listically, but looking for what it taught and required
> within that inner triangle (OT Israel) that still addresses
> and challenges the context in which we live in the outer
> triangle – whatever that may be. It still has the capacity,

---

16. Christopher J. H. Wright, *Old Testament Ethics for the People of God* (Rev. ed.; Leicester: IVP, 2004), 183.

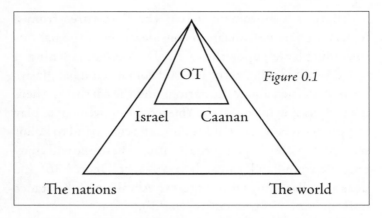

Figure 0.1

OT

Israel   Caanan

The nations   The world

rightly handled, to challenge church and society on issues of social ethics and justice. We stand, as it were, among the observing nations of Deuteronomy 4:6-8, asking questions not only about the kind of God Israel worshipped and the kind of society they were meant to be, but also about how the answers to those questions can help us in engaging our own contexts in our preaching within the community of faith.[17]

Questioning the text

With that broader framework in mind, we can now think about questioning the biblical text (in a good way!). The following is a series of interpretative questions that we need to think through as we approach the task of teaching Old Testament law. These are not steps to follow mechanically; there is no neat progression from one to the next. Nor will each always have equal relevance. Rather, these eight questions are designed to shed light on various dimensions

---

17. Christopher J. H. Wright, 'Preaching from the Law,' in 'He Began With Moses …': Preaching the Old Testament Today (ed. Grenville J. R. Kent, Paul J. Kissling, and Laurence A. Turner; Nottingham: IVP, 2010), 53.

of the passage in question. With some focused pondering, a clearer picture will emerge.

1. **What cultural factors do I need to consider?** It almost goes without saying, but sometimes still needs to be said: the Bible was written by ancient people to other ancient people. So how did *ancient* people think – about themselves, about the world, about God? What were their cultural conventions? What was expected, or frowned upon? Of course, good commentaries will help in addressing these sorts of questions, but we also need to become students of the ancient world; to develop, as best as we are able, an understanding of the times and places (and languages) referred to in the Scriptures. It is amazing how doing so can reveal things in the text that remained hidden before. Original readers would have sensed the implications immediately; we have a bit more work to do, but it is effort that pays dividends.

2. **How is this instruction connected to the wider storyline of the Pentateuch (or vice versa if working on a narrative text)?** Sometimes, connections are made explicit in the immediate context. For example, Leviticus 24:16 reads, 'Anyone who blasphemes the name of the LORD is to be put to death'. The reason for the command is found in verses 10-12, which narrate the actions of an Egyptian-Israelite man and the resulting quandary about what to do. At other times, the story-command connection is less explicit. Leviticus 18:18 states, 'Do not take your wife's sister as a rival wife'. While more can be said

about the injunction, a careful reader will recall the
consequences of sisterly strife between Rachel and
Leah (Gen. 29-30) and ponder the wisdom of the
Levitical prohibition in that light.

3. **How does the rest of the canon bear on this
   instruction?** This question explores context in
   its widest possible sense as it considers how the
   rest of the Scriptures – Old Testament and New
   Testament – influence our reading of the passage
   in front of us. Has the command been 'updated'
   or changed in any way (e.g. Exod. 20:17; cf. Deut.
   5:21)? Do later instructions impinge on, stand in
   tension with, or even nullify the original (e.g. Lev.
   17:3-4; cf. Deut. 12:15)? Does the New Testament
   reiterate the command (e.g. 1 Cor. 9:9-10) or raise
   questions about it (e.g. Mark 7:19)? What does an
   instruction given to Israel mean when applied to
   Gentiles (e.g. Lev. 19:2; cf. 1 Pet. 1:15-16)?

4. **What does this instruction reveal about the
   lawgiver?** As we discussed above, ancient legal
   codes presented an ideal in order to make a
   statement about the person responsible for the
   laws. A vital question to consider, then, is what
   do Old Testament laws reveal about God? What
   does a given instruction say about His nature or
   character? What insights do we gain about the way
   God has ordered and arranged the world? What
   divine virtues are on display? What does God abhor
   and take a stand against? Legal passages, like any
   other part of the Bible, are an expression of divine
   self-revelation.

5. **In what ways does this instruction foster love for God and/or love for one's neighbor?** As Jesus rightly noted, loving God (Deut. 6:5) and loving one's neighbor (Lev: 19:18) encapsulate the heart of the law. Many commands and instructions serve one or other of these ends, or sometimes both. Being attentive to this can help when working out the rationale for regulations that seem odd at first. Why should I build a parapet around the edge of my roof (Deut. 22:8)? Because it is an act of love, at my expense, towards guests staying in my house (and thus sleeping on the roof in the context of ancient Israel). Why do I need to write God's commandments on the doors of my (presumably parapeted) house (Deut. 6:9)? That is so I might express love to God by not forgetting Him or all His goodness to me (Deut. 6:10-12).

6. **How is this text trying to shape the moral imagination of readers?** As mentioned earlier, one of the distinctive features of Old Testament law is the presence of purpose clauses and explanations. Often, what we have is more than bare imperative. Readers are meant to grow in their understanding of *why* these things have been prohibited or commanded. For example, Exodus 22:21 commands, 'Do not mistreat or oppress a foreigner'. The prohibition makes sense by itself; yet a reason is also given: 'for you were foreigners in Egypt.' Israelite readers were meant to reflect on their national experience of being immigrants – mistreated and exploited immigrants at that. Evoking that memory was designed to

transform Israel's view of foreign workers in the land, and how such people were to be treated. The instruction subtly asks, 'You don't want to be like your (hated) Egyptian slave masters, do you?'

7. **What is this text doing?** Too often, interpreters stop at hearing only an assertion or command. Certainly, Old Testament law is doing those things. But there are often other actions that the text is performing by way of making commands. For example, Leviticus 11 could be summarized as: 'Things Israelites were not to eat or touch'. The chapter obviously contains imperatives to that effect. Yet, as we will see in Part II, there is much more going on in Leviticus 11. The way the commands are worded recalls the use of similar language in Genesis 2–3 (which also talks about things not to be eaten or touched). Thus, by hearing the commands in Leviticus 11, readers are also *reminded* of the Garden story; they are *warned* about the consequences of disobeying God's commands regarding food; and they are *invited* to choose differently and remain in God's blessing rather than experiencing banishment. Interpreters need to be sensitive to the range of things biblical law may be doing.

8. **How is this instruction useful?** The baseline is set by Paul in 2 Timothy 3:16 when he says, 'All Scripture is God-breathed and is useful for teaching, rebuking, correcting and training in righteousness'. When Paul wrote this, there was no New Testament. In view, then, were the Old

Testament Scriptures. Based on his frequent use of citation and allusion, Paul had in mind *all* the Old Testament Scriptures. Here is the starting point for interpreters: Old Testament law is *useful* – for Christians. It is Christian Scripture, through which God continues to teach and rebuke, to correct and train. We must set our expectations accordingly.

Resources for further reading

The following list contains some helpful resources for thinking further about the nature, purpose, and application of Old Testament law. None is the final word on the matter, but each provides good material to provoke reflection.

Roy E. Gane, *Old Testament Law for Christians: Original Context and Enduring Application.* Grand Rapids: Baker, 2017.

Hetty Lalleman, *Celebrating the Law? Rethinking Old Testament Ethics.* 2nd ed. Milton Keynes: Paternoster, 2016.

William S. Morrow, *An Introduction to Biblical Law.* Grand Rapids: Eerdmans, 2017.

Brian S. Rosner, *Paul and the Law: Keeping the Commandments of God.* New Studies in Biblical Theology 31. Downers Grove: IVP, 2013.

Joe M. Sprinkle, *Biblical Law and Its Relevance: A Christian Understanding and Ethical Application for Today of the Mosaic Regulations.* Lanham: University Press of America, 2006.

Christopher J. H. Wright, *Old Testament Ethics for the People of God.* Rev. ed. Leicester: IVP, 2004.

I.
Selfless Devotion
(Leviticus I)

Introduction

The keynote in Leviticus 1 is joy. This makes for an astonishing beginning to a book that many regard as being legalistic, onerous, or even oppressive. The picture presented is exactly the opposite: voluntary gifts, of great value, spontaneously offered to God by anyone who chooses to do so, without tangible benefit for the one offering. Could there be any better portrait of the uninhibited worship that ought to characterize the blessedness of people dwelling with their God? This passage is meant to inspire.

Leviticus opens with an extended focus on five major types of sacrifice and Leviticus 1 addresses the first of these, the ascension offering. While it can feel like we have stumbled across an ancient how-to document for Israel's priests, filled with procedural details, it is important to recognize that the chapter revolves around themes of relationship, worship, and adoration. As such, Leviticus 1 continues the extended focus on the tabernacle from Exodus 25–40. Exodus, therefore, provides essential background that the preacher and Bible study leader will need to bear in mind (and, somehow, communicate to their audience).

In context, Leviticus 1 relays the very first words that Yahweh speaks from His new abode at the heart of the Israelite camp. This is a vital development in the storyline of the Pentateuch. The word of God, which had been so powerfully present at Mount Sinai, would continue to be heard by His people as they travelled to Canaan. And the first item on the agenda concerns ascension offerings. Even though this type of sacrifice had an atoning function (see below), that facet is somewhat muted here. Instead, the dominant focus is on the gathered people of God approaching His immanent presence to present costly gifts in joyful recognition of what He had done for them (deliverance from long bondage to a cruel and repressive regime) and of who He is (their new master, deserving of total allegiance).

Listening to the text

Context and structure

In Hebrew, the first word in Leviticus is 'and'. This connects all that follows to the wider storyline of the Pentateuch and indicates the book ought to be read as a sequel to Exodus. Readers should therefore have Israel's deliverance from Egypt and the building of the tabernacle in mind as they approach Leviticus. It ought not to be surprising, then, to find the book's opening chapters dominated by themes of corporate worship and the institutions central to the proper functioning of the tabernacle – namely, sacrifice (Lev. 1–7) and priests (Lev. 8–10).

The structure of Leviticus 1 is straightforward. The opening two verses set the narrative context and indicate the theme that will dominate the first seven chapters of the book:

offerings presented to Yahweh. The remainder of chapter 1 consists of three blocks of material which outline variants of the first type of sacrifice: the ascension, or burnt, offering.

> Mediated instruction regarding offerings (1:1-2)
> Ascension offerings (1:3-17)
>> From the herd (1:3-9)
>> From the flock (1:10-13)
>> From the birds (1:14-17)

Working through the text

Mediated instruction regarding offerings (1:1-2)

The section opens with Yahweh calling to Moses from the tent of meeting. This picks up the narrative from the end of Exodus where, in 40:34-35, the glory of the LORD fills the newly erected tabernacle, thereby preventing everyone from entering, including Moses. This is the scenario envisioned by Leviticus 1:1. Moses, standing outside the tent, is addressed by the God who had just taken up residence. The tabernacle thus becomes the location from where Yahweh will exercise lordship over His people through His word. In this way, the tent effectively becomes a portable Mount Sinai. The voice that had spoken from the cloud-concealed glory atop the mountain (Exod. 24:16) would continue to address the Israelites from the cloud-concealed glory dwelling within the tabernacle (Exod. 40:34) as the people journeyed towards Canaan.

Moses's role as mediator would also continue (cf. Exod. 19:3; 20:18-19). In 1:2 God tells Moses, 'Speak to the Israelites and say to them'. Variations of this formula occur a further thirty-six times throughout Leviticus (4:1; 5:14; 6:1; etc.). The repeated phrase is important. It is a constant reminder that the instructions found in Leviticus are not arbitrary, let alone silly or unnecessary; rather, they originate from Yahweh and are communicated through Moses to the people, presumably for their benefit and blessing. Presented as direct speech from God, instructions conveyed by Leviticus are vested with supreme authority. Israel must not only hear these words but be very careful to obey them.

The first thing Yahweh speaks to His people about is making offerings. There is a nice wordplay in Hebrew that connects the act of bringing with the offering made: perhaps, 'when anyone *offers* an *offering*', or 'when anyone *presents* a *present*' to Yahweh. The term translated 'any of you' (1:2) is as wide-ranging as it sounds. This is remarkable in its ancient world setting. Presenting a present to Yahweh was open to anyone. It was not simply the prerogative of the priests; ordinary people could bring their gifts too. Nor were offerings restricted to the rich; poor people could bring less costly gifts that still achieved the same results. Elsewhere, women (e.g. Hannah in 1 Sam. 1:24) and even Gentiles (like the resident foreigner in 17:8 or Jethro in Exod. 18:12) are recorded as making ascension offerings to Yahweh. So, even while Leviticus is primarily concerned with ancient Israel, there are nevertheless hints of God's global intent (cf. Gen. 12:3). In Leviticus 1:2, an invitation is extended to anyone made in the image of God to draw near and offer his or her gift. Yet, at the same time, it is not a free-for-all. Yahweh gives strict instructions about *what* and *how* gifts are to be given.

Ascension offerings (1:3-17)

The first type of gift considered is frequently labeled the 'burnt offering' (so NIV, ESV, NLT). The term 'burnt' captures the idea that this kind of sacrifice in its entirety was to be burned on the altar (except for the skin; see 1:6; cf. 7:8). For this reason, some prefer the designation 'whole offering'. The Hebrew word itself (*'olah*) is derived from a root meaning 'to go up, to ascend' which suggests something like 'rising offering' or 'ascension offering'. If you think about it, this is exactly what happens: the animal is literally turned to smoke and goes up into the air. In the end, each of these possibilities captures something important. This type of offering, unlike those that follow in subsequent chapters, is wholly consumed by fire on the altar and rises as smoke before God. That the animal is turned to smoke is not just stating the obvious. The altar fire does not merely *destroy* the animal; it is a means of *transferring* the offering to the divine realm. For this reason, and in keeping with the sense of the Hebrew, I use the term 'ascension offering'.

The chapter discusses three grades of ascension offering of decreasing cost. There is the deluxe gift (a bull, 1:3-9), the standard gift (a sheep or goat, 1:10-13), and the budget gift (a dove or young pigeon, 1:14-17). In line with what we observed about the universality of the invitation to present an ascension offering to Yahweh, there is an option for everyone. No one is too poor to give a gift to God.

The procedure outlined in 1:3-9 is representative of how one should present this kind of gift. Here, the offering is from the herd. The animal must be a 'male without defect' (1:3), that is, a prime specimen. The animal is to be brought to the entrance of the tent of meeting, where the offerer is to lay his or her hand on its head. This action is a means of identification, a way of saying, 'This animal is mine and represents me'. It also brings to the fore the personal connection between worshipper and God: you cannot have someone else present a gift on your behalf.

The personal involvement rachets up in 1:5-9. There, we find that it is the *offerer* who must slaughter the animal (1:5), skin and dismember it (1:6), and wash the intestines and legs, presumably to remove fecal matter (1:9). This is worship that requires an apron! The procedure for sheep and goats is virtually identical; birds, being smaller and more fiddly, require slightly different handling. Nevertheless, in each case, the animal is entirely burnt on the altar and is made to rise up as smoke before Yahweh.

At the same time, it is vital to note what the worshipper *cannot* do. Many of the required actions must be carried out by 'Aaron's sons the priests' (1:5). It is they who must collect the blood and splash it against the altar (1:5). It is the priests who must arrange wood on the altar and lay the pieces of the animal upon it (1:7-8). So, while the worshipper may be more involved than he or she would like to be, there are things that remain strictly off limits. Hence, already in the opening verses of Leviticus we are brought face to face with a reality that will be elaborated time and again: it is not easy or safe to approach Yahweh. Caution is required. Instructions are given – for the people's sake, to keep them from harm as they draw near to the tabernacle. There is a genuine invitation from God for anyone to come to the tabernacle, but that person must heed the house rules. And, graciously, God makes those rules clear. It is as if God is saying, 'Come and offer your gift, but here's what I like to receive and how I like it to be given'. And, when worshipper and priest fulfill their respective roles in line with God's instructions, the result is an ascension offering which rises as 'an aroma pleasing to the LORD' (1:9, 13, 17).

The fronting of the ascension offering in Leviticus is suggestive of its importance, a fact amply borne out in the rest of the Old Testament. This is the preeminent offering. But what was it for? Elsewhere, this type of offering accompanies prayers of praise and thanksgiving (Ps. 66:13-15); it emphasizes the seriousness of petitions (1 Sam. 7:9; 2 Sam. 24:24-25); it is used to ratify covenants (Exod. 24:3-8). Strikingly, after the flood, it is ascension offerings which placate Yahweh's wrath (Gen. 8:20-21). Ascension offerings thus have a rich array of uses.[1] Leviticus 1:4 indicates that making atonement is a core function. Yet, at this point, we may have work to do to rightly understand what 'atonement' signifies. It is an important concept in Leviticus; the effort is worth it.

Atonement is often assumed to mean something along the lines of 'the removal of sin to make a person right with God'. However, such a definition quickly runs into trouble in Leviticus where 'atonement' is made for places (e.g., 16:16) and things (e.g., 8:15) as much as for people. Moreover, Leviticus requires that 'atonement' be made in situations where sin is not a factor (e.g., 12:6-7). Whatever

---

1. It should also be noted that in the Pentateuch ascension offerings *precede* the narrative setting of Leviticus 1 (e.g., Gen. 8:20; 22:3; Exod. 10:25). This is another indicator that Leviticus 1 is not simply a how-to manual, as sacrificial processes were already known. The purpose of the text lies elsewhere. The same holds true for tribute offerings (e.g., Gen. 4:3-4) and fellowship offerings (e.g., Exod. 18:12; 24:5). The purification and reparation offerings in Leviticus 4:1–6:7, however, seem to be novel (depending on how one translates Gen. 4:7).

definition we decide on needs to be broad enough to accommodate all the data.

The Hebrew verb (*kpr*) translated 'to make atonement' has two related meanings.[2] The first connotes the idea of 'purging'. This fits contexts where a person needs to have sin removed. It also works for cases where impurity rather than sin is the issue (as in the example from Lev. 12 above). Places and objects, likewise, can require purging to render them fit for use. In all these cases, the blood of the animal acts like a cleansing agent to remove sin and/or impurity. The second concept conveyed by *kpr* is that of 'ransom'. Making atonement thus also addresses the danger posed by sin and impurity, especially when in proximity to God (see 15:31; 20:2-3). A ransom payment, while costly, is significantly less than the alternative consequence (usually death or banishment). In this sense, the animal functions as a substitute; its life is offered as a ransom payment instead of the worshipper (see further at 17:10-12). Both senses of *kpr* need to be borne in mind as one reads Leviticus. Often, either purging or ransom is foregrounded, but the connected idea is never far behind. The difficulty is finding an English word that adequately encapsulates such a rich concept. Sklar suggests the term 'ransom-purification'.[3]

A key facet of the ascension offering, then, is maintaining an ongoing relationship with God. For sinful humans, approaching God always requires propitiation and cleansing. At the same time, dealing with specific sins or ritual faults is the role of the purgation and reparation

---

2. This paragraph follows the argument presented in Jay Sklar, *Sin, Impurity, Sacrifice, Atonement: The Priestly Conceptions* (HBM 2; Sheffield: Sheffield Phoenix, 2005).

3. Sklar, *Leviticus*, 53.

offerings (see Lev. 4:1–6:7). Ascension offerings adopt a more generalized function. This is perhaps captured in Exodus 29:38-46, where ascension offerings are required daily, morning and evening. It is as if all of Israel's existence was lived under the auspices of these ongoing offerings which opened the potential for life with Yahweh.

What is really striking in Leviticus 1 is that, while there are commands about *how* to make an ascension offering, there is no imperative *to* make one (even though such commands are found elsewhere, e.g., 23:12). The effect is to portray these offerings as entirely voluntary. Nevertheless, the text assumes that such offerings will be made ('when anyone ... brings an offering'; 1:2). Yet, in an agrarian culture like ancient Israel, an animal from the herd or flock would represent a substantial percentage of a peasant farmer's assets. What might possibly motivate someone to offer such a gift?

This is where the context of this chapter again becomes important. As noted above, the events of the exodus are essential to bear in mind. Why would anyone spontaneously offer a gift of great cost to the God who had rescued them from Egyptian bondage? Why would they not? The offering of a whole animal is symbolic of the consecration of one's whole self to God. Thus, the cost is ultimately not the animal's value but the utter devotion to God that the offering signifies.[4] As Joshua Berman puts it, the ascension offering 'symbolizes our willingness to devote our entire existence to

4. L. Michael Morales, 'Atonement in Ancient Israel: The Whole Burnt Offering as Central to Israel's Cult,' in *So Great a Salvation: A Dialogue on the Atonement in Hebrews* (ed. Jon C. Laansma, George H. Guthrie, and Cynthia L. Westfall; LNTS 516; London: T&T Clark, 2019), 34.

the service of God'.[5] In this way, Leviticus opens by imagining a joyous, openhanded, celebratory response to what Yahweh has done for His people. This is an invitation to true worship.

From text to message

The surprising nature of Leviticus 1 ought not to be missed. One of the challenges facing any would-be teacher of this book is the almost inevitable antipathy people feel towards it. It is, for many, simply a collection of (outdated) commands that have no bearing on Christian life or faith. This chapter represents a wonderful opportunity to expose and correct the misguided thinking which underlies that sort of conclusion. Here is a book designed to evoke (and regulate) true worship of the living God. While the forms of worship may look different in other times and places, there is an expected affinity when it comes to the heart response of God's people towards Him. The author of Leviticus 1 and the psalmist concur: the ideal response remains 'What shall I return to the LORD for all his goodness to me?' (Ps. 116:12).

Getting the message clear: the theme

As Israel's Deliverer and King, Yahweh is worthy of supreme devotion. Accordingly, all are given permission to come voluntarily and present Him with a gift of great cost. This is portrayed as one's reasonable act of worship and symbolizes the wholehearted giving of oneself to God.

Getting the message clear: the aim

While Leviticus 1 regulates how ascension offerings were to be made, the passage does more than merely convey

---

5. Cited in Morales, 'Atonement in Ancient Israel,' 34.

instructions. One of the ways that the Scriptures work to move and change us is to portray an ideal world and then invite us to enter and participate in that world. In other words, the biblical texts seek to reshape and transform our imaginations. Leviticus 1 contributes to that end by presenting a scenario and by assuming its normalcy: a person desiring to give a gift of great expense to God as a tangible expression of his or her internal disposition, not because they have been commanded to do so, but simply as a spontaneous act of adoration. Thus, a picture of the ideal worshipper emerges which either affirms any similar desire in readers or instead chides them for its absence.

A way in

Thankfulness is important. That is why parents spend so long trying to instill good manners in their children, encouraging them time and again to say 'thank you' when they receive something. If that is the response expected when given an ice cream or a new bike, then what about the response to a truly magnificent gift? Think about the salvation we have received, our redemption and new life in Christ. What would an adequate response be in the face of such generosity? Sure, we can say 'thank you' to God and it is right and proper for us to do so. But are there other tangible acts of devotion we might perform as a way of expressing gratitude? What kind of gift would God like anyway?

The incident in Simon's house, recorded in Matthew 26:6-13, is striking. Unbidden, a woman approaches Jesus and empties an alabaster jar of expensive perfume on His head. The response from onlookers is outrage at the waste of resources that could have been used for more sensible ends. But this spontaneous, costly gift is received by Jesus as a pleasing aroma. Thus, with this unnamed woman, we find the same portrait of the ideal worshipper presented by Leviticus 1. There is a biblical model with which we are being invited to compare ourselves. It is worth considering how our acts of devotion compare.

Ideas for application

- God exercises lordship over His people, past and present, through His spoken and written word.

- It is not our prerogative to determine what acceptable worship looks like. God alone dictates when and how and why we ought to worship.

- God is holy and, hence, off limits to unholy people. The only way we may safely approach Him is to heed the means He has provided.

- God is worthy of acts of devotion. He invites us to respond to His kindness by presenting Him with costly gifts, freely given, without thought of benefit for self. Such thankfulness is the hallmark of both Old Testament (e.g., Ps. 116:12) and New Testament (e.g., 1 Thess. 3:9) faith.

- God's generosity towards us ought to provoke a similar attitude of generosity in us. This is Paul's point in 2 Corinthians 8:7-9. Jesus becoming poor in order to make us rich demonstrates what generosity towards others looks like, while at the same time motivating change by reminding us of grace received.

- Paul, in Romans 12:1, speaks of Christians offering their bodies as living sacrifices. They should do this, he says, 'in view of God's mercy'. The type of sacrifice he has in mind is the ascension offering – a gift wholly given to God with nothing left over for the offerer. Paul assumes the underlying symbolism of Leviticus 1: ultimately, it is not sheep or goats that God desires, or even a bull. The only reasonable act of adoration for Christians is to offer their entire selves to Jesus, rather than to the idols of our time.

Suggestions for preaching

Sermon 1

One of the dangers facing any would-be preacher of this text (and those which follow) is to get so caught up in the details that the bigger picture is lost. The opposite pitfall is also ever-present: to miss the richness of the passage at hand by merely summarizing or skimming over the details, or by too quickly trying to 'get to Jesus'. A good sermon will strike a balance between these extremes. Only by doing so is it possible to adequately work out what God was saying to the original audience, which is the necessary basis for determining what God is saying to His people today.

- **Acts of devotion.** The experience of God's saving grace in the lives of His people invites an appropriate response. Yet, gratitude and thankfulness cannot simply be taken as granted. Too often a right response is crowded out by less acceptable alternatives: forgetfulness regarding what God has done; praise best described as lackluster; service motivated by duty and obligation rather than joy. Leviticus 1 can help reorient our attitudes and actions.

- **Presenting an ascension offering.** Bringing an offering to the LORD was a bloody and involved affair. The visceral sights, sounds, smells, and tastes associated with sacrifice are something many Western people have not experienced firsthand. There is a confronting edge to this text. Even more confronting, perhaps, is the realization that priests are essential to the procedure – that many of the places and activities associated with worship are forbidden to ordinary people. Thus, not only are mediators required, but one becomes intensely aware that God is not safe to approach 'just as you are'.

- **Hearing the unexpected.** Interspersed throughout the passage are several surprising details. The instructions are remarkably inclusive. All can present gifts to God; no one is excluded from coming. Additionally, even though these gifts are costly, there is no command to bring them – just the assumption that people will do so. This immediately raises the question of motive: Why would anyone offer gifts like these when they do not have to? The implicit answer which arises is simply that God is worthy of such selfless adoration.

- **Sacrificing today?** It can be tempting to conclude, in light of the coming of Jesus, that sacrifice and offerings are finished for God's people. Yet that is not an option that the New Testament allows us to have. If anything, the New Testament raises the expectation that God's people will present their offerings to Him. This is where correctly understanding the various types of sacrifice becomes important. Not all sacrifices are linked to atonement or the forgiveness of sins. Some, like the ascension offering, could also display deeply-felt thankfulness and selfless devotion. That is exactly what we are called to do. In view of God's mercy to us through Christ, we now offer Him our very lives as living sacrifices, holy and pleasing in His sight.

Sermon 2

Another sermon could focus on 1:1-2 as an introduction to the book, leaving the ascension offering (1:3-17) for a second talk. The benefit for the preacher is more time to situate Leviticus within its wider biblical context, especially its relationship to the book of Exodus. In turn, this would help address the unfamiliarity Christians often experience with this part of the Bible by filling in some of the essential background that Leviticus simply assumes. It really is vital that readers remember the exodus from Egypt and the subsequent gathering of the people around the tabernacled presence of their new Master. The starting point for Leviticus is grace already received. Missing this can quickly lead to distorted understandings of Leviticus. The sermon might also want to give a 'big picture' overview of Leviticus in preparation for the more detailed explorations to follow. It can be incredibly useful for people to have a sense of the whole into which they can fit the parts.

Suggestions for teaching

Questions to help understand the passage

1. In what ways does Leviticus 1 continue from where Exodus left off?

2. Why does Moses need to act as a mediator of God's words to the people? Have a look at Exodus 19:9, 20:18-21, and Deuteronomy 5:22-27.

3. What do you think 'atonement' means?

4. There are different types of sacrifice outlined in Leviticus. What is distinctive about the ascension offering? Why were ascension offerings made?

5. Make a copy of Leviticus 1. Go through the text and highlight all the verbs that explain what the worshipper is to do. With a different color highlighter mark what the priests are to do. What strikes you?

6. Imagine yourself enacting the procedure highlighted in the previous question. What impact do you think performing those actions would have on you?

7. What do you think the phrase 'an aroma pleasing to the Lord' means?

Questions to help apply the passage

1. List some ways that you have experienced God's mercy and kindness. How often do you thank Him for these things?

2. Describe the picture of God that emerges from Leviticus 1. How does this fit with how you think of Him? Are there things you need to add or adjust?

3. Leviticus 1 speaks about offering bulls, sheep, and goats. Considering what such an animal would have meant to an Israelite peasant farmer, what might be a modern equivalent? What do you think it would be like for you to turn that thing 'into smoke on the altar'?

4. The woman in Matthew 26:6-13 honored Jesus in a way that was scornfully dismissed by others as being too generous, too wasteful. Have you ever

seen someone act similarly? How do you think that kind of selfless devotion might be developed in you? Are there obstacles that would prevent you from emulating the woman's example?

5. What does it mean to be a 'living sacrifice' (Rom. 12:1)? List some ways that your life would look different next week if you lived in light of this identity.

2.

Table Fellowship

(Leviticus 2–3)

Introduction

Eating with God! That is the tantalizing prospect that Leviticus 2–3 presents, as themes of food and table fellowship are foregrounded. In view are ritualized or cultic meals that God and His people share. Accordingly, these chapters combine with Leviticus 1 to portray an incredible picture of restored union between Yahweh and people. A rich seam of ideas – access, devotion, adoration, eating, fellowship – is mined to present the ideal. This is the tangible, blessed experience of restored relationship with God that is on offer to anyone.

Leviticus 2–3 continues the focus on sacrifice that dominates chapters 1–7 by introducing the tribute (2:1-16) and fellowship (3:1-17) offerings. As with ascension offerings in Leviticus 1, there is a notable lack of imperatives commanding that these sacrifices be made. The result is that both tribute and fellowship offerings are portrayed as being offered to God voluntarily. The focus of the passage is instead concerned with regulating *how* such offerings are to be made so that they might become 'an aroma pleasing to the Lord' (2:2, 9; 3:5, 16; cf. 1:9).

Also absent is the terminology of atonement. While making atonement is explicitly connected to the ascension offering (see 1:4), the language next appears in 4:20 with respect to the purification offering. Thus, Leviticus 2–3 further nuances the concept of sacrifice. In the Old Testament, 'sacrifice' functions as an umbrella term for many different types of offering, each with its own distinctive function(s). Some sacrifices were for making atonement, others were not. Some sacrifices involved the blood of an animal, others did not. Sacrificial practice in ancient Israel was richly complex. Getting to grips with the distinctions pays dividends when it comes to both biblical theology and exegesis, as much for the New Testament as for the Old.

Listening to the text

Context and structure

The material in Leviticus 2–3 divides neatly between tribute offerings (2:1-16) and fellowship offerings (3:1-17). In a similar manner to Leviticus 1, each section can be further subdivided into grades or subtypes of offering, with attendant notes:

> Tribute offerings (2:1-16)
>> Of raw flour (2:1-3)
>> Of cooked flour (2:4-10)
>> Regarding yeast, honey, and salt (2:11-13)
>> Of firstfruits of new grain (2:14-16)
>
> Fellowship offerings (3:1-17)
>> From the herd (3:1-5)
>> From the flock (3:6-16a)
>>> Lambs (3:7-11)
>>> Goats (3:12-16a)
>> Regarding fat and blood (3:16b-17)

Leviticus 2–3 works as a unit with Leviticus 1. All three chapters are governed by the same introduction to divine speech in 1:2 ('Speak to the Israelites and say to them'; cf. 4:2) and each offering is presented as voluntary (contrast the language used for purification and reparation offerings in 4:1–6:7). The material in Leviticus 1–3 is also arranged in an ABA structure: offerings of meat (Lev. 1) – offerings of grain (Lev. 2) – offerings of meat (Lev. 3). This sort of structuring device is important in Leviticus and is part of the artistic arrangement of the text. The effect is to create emphasis, as well as inviting comparison between similar sections. ABA patterning (technically called palistrophic arrangement) appears at different levels in Leviticus: between chapters (e.g., Lev. 1–3 or 18–20), between verses (e.g., 16:29-31), and even within a single verse (e.g., 2:13).[1]

Working through the text

Tribute offerings (2:1-16)

The opening phrase of Leviticus 2 ('When a person [*nephesh*; literally 'life' or 'soul'] offers an offering of tribute to Yahweh' [my translation]) echoes the wording of 1:2 ('When a person ['*adam*] offers an offering to Yahweh' [my translation]). This creates continuity of theme while also marking out a new section. The Hebrew term for this offering (*minhah*), often translated 'grain offering' (so NIV,

---

1. Palistrophic patterning creates emphasis at several points. In the sequence A B C B' A', for example, attention is drawn to the central, pivot point (C). The beginning and end points are also highlighted (A and A'). James Watts further notes that for audiences who *hear* the text read, the emphasis falls on the section immediately following the conclusion of the palistrophe (in this case, whatever text follows A'). See James W. Watts, *Leviticus 1–10* (HCOT; Leuven: Peeters, 2013), 17.

ESV; NLT has only 'grain'), has connotations of showing respect, paying homage, or expressing veneration to a superior – hence, 'tribute offering'. In the Old Testament, 'tribute' can be offered to both divine (e.g., Lev. 2) and human figures (e.g., to Eglon in Judg. 3:15) and may be vegetarian or meat-based (in Gen. 4:4-5, *minhah* is used to describe both Cain and Abel's offerings). The tribute offering therefore presumes a power differential between giver and receiver, and functions as an act of homage.

In Leviticus 2, the tribute offerings are vegetarian. 'Fine flour' (2:1) was of better quality than the more common coarse-ground variety and was correspondingly more costly. Tributes to Yahweh must be of the *best* flour (cf. the 'male without defect' in 1:3). The fine flour was presented to the priests mixed with oil and accompanied by incense. Then, in contrast to the ascension offering, which was wholly burnt on the altar, a representative *handful* of the flour and oil mixture, together with the incense, was burned by the priest as a 'fire offering', becoming an 'aroma pleasing to the LORD' (2:2). The addition of incense (better: 'frankincense') seems to be to aid the 'pleasing aroma' dimension of the sacrifice (burning raw flour does not smell nice, in contrast to meat or even the baked goods outlined in 2:4-7).

Another notable difference occurs in 2:3, where we read that the remainder of the tribute offering (in this case, fine flour mixed with oil) belongs to Aaron and his sons. This portion was considered a most holy part of the fire offering made to Yahweh. The priests were to use the flour to prepare food and eat it in the LORD's presence in the courtyard of the tabernacle (see 6:16). This was a vital source of sustenance for the priests, who did not receive an allotment of land along with other tribes (cf. Josh. 14:3-4). In this way, the priests functioned as a spiritual barometer of Israel's faithfulness: lots of tribute offerings coming from a worshipping and God-acknowledging community would mean a well-provisioned priesthood. Priests going hungry or looking for alternative income streams, however, would signal the opposite (cf. Judg. 17:7-13; Neh. 13:10-11).

The next section, 2:4-10, follows a similar logic. Here, the tribute offerings consist of items cooked from fine flour. There are several options: flour could be made into cakes and wafers or cooked in a griddle or pan (2:4-7). Again, oil was to be either mixed with the flour or spread on the cooked goods (but note the absence of incense). All the items were also to be unleavened (see further below). The procedure at the tabernacle was the same as for raw flour: the cooked goods were presented to the LORD by giving them to the priest, who burned a representative portion on the altar to create an aroma pleasing to Yahweh (2:8-9). The remainder belonged to Aaron and his sons as their most holy portion of the fire offering (2:10). Once again, the priests enjoy the privilege of sharing Yahweh's meal.

The remainder of the chapter discusses ancillary points. First, no tribute offering may contain yeast or honey. Indeed, no offering destined for the altar may contain these items (2:11). While the prohibition is clear, the reason behind it is not. The text remains silent regarding rationale (here and elsewhere). Many commentators suggest that yeast and honey are connected with fermentation and decay and for this reason were unfit for offering to God. Yet, as 2:12 indicates, both yeast and honey *could* be presented to Yahweh, but only as a firstfruits offering (cf. 23:17). The ban applies only to burning upon the altar as a pleasing aroma. It is difficult to decide whether this had a practical or symbolic function.

Salt, on the other hand, must be added to all tribute offerings (2:13). The force of the command is strengthened through repetition and palistrophic arrangement. Three times (twice positive: 'add salt'; once negative: 'do not leave salt out') the reader is told to include salt. The arrangement of 2:13 draws attention to the central component with its unusual phrase: 'the salt of the covenant of your God'. Wenham notes that salt is connected with covenants on two occasions (Num. 18:19; 2 Chron. 13:5). In both contexts, the language of 'permanent' or 'eternal' (Heb.: 'olam) appears. He concludes, 'Salt was something that could not be destroyed by fire or time or any other means in antiquity. To add salt to the offering was a reminder that the worshipper was in an eternal covenant relationship with his God.'[2]

The final subsection considers firstfruits of grain offered as tribute (2:14-16). Firstfruits offerings comprised the first portion of a crop harvested and were presented to Yahweh in grateful anticipation of the remainder of the bounty to come (cf. 23:9-14). In such cases, heads of grain were roasted, crushed, and offered with oil and incense (2:14-15). The return to tribute offerings made with incense forms a frame with the opening section (2:1-3). The succinct nature of 2:14-16 is a reminder that Leviticus does not merely repeat instructions verbatim. The text is full of nuances and artistic variation – of things left unsaid, as much as said. Here, for example, readers are meant to understand that tribute offerings of firstfruits are also an aroma pleasing to Yahweh and that the portion unburned

---

2. Wenham, *Leviticus*, 71.

belongs to the priests, even though those things are not stated explicitly.

Fellowship offerings (3:1-17)

The offering outlined in Leviticus 3 is the only one that explicitly employs the term 'sacrifice' (*zebach*) in its name. The resulting phrase (*zebach shelamim*) has been variously translated. The KJV, followed by ESV, has 'sacrifice of peace offering', picking up on the use of the *shlm* root (think *shalom*, 'peace'). The NIV and HCSB have 'fellowship offering', emphasizing the communal nature of this offering (see further below). The Greek translation of the Old Testament (the LXX) has 'sacrifice of deliverance' (NETS). It is tricky to decide between the options; again, one is faced with the difficulty of finding a single English term that does justice to the Hebrew. Each of the above options captures something important: this offering is a result of the deliverance worked by Yahweh; it celebrates the peace that now exists between Him and His people, and it is deeply communal in nature. While I use the phrase 'fellowship offering' (one must pick something), it is important to remember the rich matrix of ideas associated with this type of sacrifice.

Fellowship offerings consisted of male or female animals from either herd (3:1-5) or flock (3:6-16a). The procedure is almost identical in all cases. The animal must be 'without defect' (the word means 'complete' or 'blameless' when used of people) (3:1, 6; cf. 1:3, 10; 22:21-22). The offerer was to lay his or her hand on the animal's head as a means of identification before slaughtering it at the entrance to the tabernacle (3:2, 8, 13). The priests then carried the blood to the altar to splash it on all four sides (3:2, 8, 13). As with the tribute offering, a portion was removed and set aside as Yahweh's share. In this case it is the fat: all the fat that covers the internal organs together with the kidneys and liver covering. For sheep, the 'fat tail' was also included (3:11). This last instruction accentuates the Middle Eastern provenance of the text where, in contrast to European and North American ovine varieties, sheep had a large fatty tail. This too was to be collected with the rest of the fat and burned on the altar (3:5, 11, 16).

The closing exhortation drives home the point concerning Yahweh's share. Leviticus 3:16b reads, 'All fat is Yahweh's!' (my translation). The fat of fellowship offerings belonged exclusively to Him. The command in 3:17 (cf. 7:23-27; 19:26) adds further force: 'You must never eat any fat or blood', a stipulation to be observed at all times ('a lasting ordinance') and in all places ('wherever you live'). The rationale for not eating blood is outlined in Leviticus 17 (see discussion at 17:10-12). The reason fat was offered to Yahweh seems to be twofold. First, and contrary to current Western sentiments, the fatty portions of an animal were considered the prime cuts. These instructions thus further amplify a now repeated theme: the best portions (rightly) belong to Yahweh. But, second, there is also a practical consideration. Meat is not easily consumed by fire. A stack of T-bone steaks and lamb cutlets would take a long time to burn through, potentially clogging up the altar. Fat presents no such problem and, if anything, aids the incineration of other items (for instance, the ascension offering that is assumed to already be on the altar, 3:5; cf. Exod. 29:38-42).

What of the rest of the animal? Although Leviticus 3 does not specify, original readers would have known exactly what happened (another reminder that this is

not meant to be read as a step-by-step manual). Leviticus
7 fills in the picture: the remainder of the meat was to
be eaten by the worshipper – that same day, if a thank
offering; by the end of the following day if in fulfillment
of a vow (7:15-16; cf. 19:5-8). There are three things worth
noting. First, Leviticus 3 outlines the normal procedure
for obtaining meat (at least meat derived from herd or
flock animals). Leviticus demands that all such animals be
ritually slaughtered at the tabernacle (see 17:3-4). Second,
there is a lot of meat. Imagine sitting down to eat an entire
cow, by nightfall! Implied is the *communal* nature of the
eating. A person's entire family, maybe even village, would
need to assist. This was a meal to be shared. Third, we need
to remember that in the ancient world, eating meat was a
rarity, a luxury enjoyed by only the wealthiest. The best
lens through which to view fellowship offerings, therefore,
is that of celebration or feast rather than grocery shopping.
These were special occasions to eat luxury food with
friends and family (end even with outcasts and foreigners).
And, as the usual practice was to present baked goods
alongside fellowship offerings, part of which was given to
the officiating priest (7:12-14), laity and priests essentially
shared the same meal.

Even more incredible is that table fellowship is with
Yahweh. Twice in Leviticus 3 we read that the priest
is to burn the fatty portions *as food* (3:11, 16). An un-
sophisticated reading might understand the Israelites to be
feeding Yahweh just as other religions feed their idols. Not
so. The Old Testament is strikingly countercultural in that
regard: it is Yahweh who feeds people and determines what
they may eat (see, foundationally, Gen. 1:29-30; 2:15-17).
The fire on the altar transfers the fat portions to God's

realm. The worshipper (and his or her extended family) eat the remainder. The picture that emerges is one of God eating *with people*. And not in some austere manner; this is celebration time. Yahweh wants to party with those gathered around Him! This is exactly what Deuteronomy 12:12 imagines: 'You must celebrate there *in the presence of the* LORD *your God* with your sons and daughters and all your servants. And remember to include the Levites who live in your towns, for they will receive no allotment of land among you' (NLT; emphasis added).

Here, we must remember that the language of atonement is absent in Leviticus 3. These sacrifices are not for making peace with God; rather, they celebrate and actualize a peace with God that already exists. This logic can be glimpsed in the usual order in which sacrifices were made: first, a purification offering to restore relationship; second, an ascension offering to express selfless devotion; third, a fellowship offering as a tangible expression of having been made right with God.

And all of this was to occur at the tent of meeting, the ostensible palace where Yahweh dwelt, a building constructed from gold, silver, and other precious materials. Leviticus 3 is nothing short of an invitation to dine with royalty, at their home! Thus, the ultimate privilege enjoyed by the people is not culinary, but relational: table fellowship with the King.

From text to message

The theological importance of these chapters should not be underestimated. At one level, Leviticus 2–3 contains procedural details pertaining to tribute and fellowship offerings. Yet, as noted earlier, this is not a how-to manual;

too many details are missing for that. Instead, these chapters are, once again, aimed at forming a picture of the ideal and inviting participation: voluntary acts of homage (tribute offerings) which rightly recognize Yahweh's greatness; celebratory, communal meals (fellowship offerings) that are the very embodiment of restored relationship – with God and neighbor. In the beginning, in the sacred place of the Garden, Adam and Eve enjoyed plentiful food in the presence of God. Subsequent to Genesis 3, however, eating with God occurs only in strange, sporadic, unrepeatable ways (e.g. Abraham in Gen. 18, or the seventy elders in Exod. 24:9-11). Leviticus 2–3 initiates *regular* table fellowship. In fact, this is a privilege that one can enjoy as often as one pleases. Creation blessings are being recovered as a foretaste of the messianic banquet on the day the world is remade (cf. Isa. 25:6-8; Matt. 8:11; 22:2-10; Luke 14:12-24).

Getting the message clear: the theme

Yahweh is King and tribute is rightly offered to honor and venerate Him. Yet, Yahweh also extends an open invitation to all His people, priest and layperson alike, to come and eat at His table, enjoying communion with Him and with one another as a foretaste of cosmic renewal.

Getting the message clear: the aim

At the heart of this passage lies the expectation that God's people will naturally formalize their subservience by paying homage, and that they will gather around the table of their King to enjoy food in His presence. Thus, the text assumes and portrays deep relational connections between God and His people: He is their God and they publicly acknowledge His majesty. And they are His people, blessed by His presence. That blessing is not left as an abstract idea, but becomes concrete in the context of a shared meal. In this way, the text also seeks to inspire readers: this is how good it can be to dwell with God. Again, we discover that Israel's worship system is about much more than mere mechanics. Instead, it functions as a ritualized teaching aid.

A way in

The Beatles famously sang, 'All you need is love'. Certainly, love is important: we treasure its presence and we mourn its loss. But what does 'love' mean? Hearing someone say, 'I love you', is nice, and words are important. Yet, on its own, 'I love you' can remain a somewhat abstract idea. But love can be made concrete: a hug, words of affirmation, a gift, or dedicated time help make love tangible. In a similar manner, 'relationship with God' can remain an abstract concept – something that we *talk* about. Leviticus 2–3 helped Israel make relationship with God *experiential*. Touching one's gift as it was passed to the priest, the sight of smoke spiraling upwards, the smell of meat and cakes cooking, the taste of freshly prepared food – all tangible signs and reminders of peace with God and the physical, palpable goodness of life in His presence.

Food and intimacy belong together. All of us experience this – from both sides. Sitting down to eat with people you have fallen out with is excruciating. Feeling lonely or isolated is only compounded when you must also eat by yourself. But, on the other hand, a long dinner with a group of close friends is a delight. Shared food establishes a context in which relationship thrives. The writer of Proverbs 15:17 saw this reality keenly: 'Better a small serving of vegetables with love than a fattened calf with hatred.' Leviticus 2–3 celebrates the restoration of peace between God and people and presents a picture of intimacy, closeness, and the benefits of fellowship, all through the lens of food.

Ideas for application

- Tribute offerings, made to a king, should rightly consist of the very best. Giving anything less suggests a heart that is not willing to fully honor and venerate the recipient (cf. Mal. 1:6-8).

- Intimacy with God is possible, but only on His terms and according to the means He has provided.

- God loves celebration and commanded Israel to act accordingly (e.g., Lev. 23; Deut. 12:5-12; 14:22-26). There is something right and fitting about rejoicing in God's presence in thankful acknowledgment for what He has done. This can be a helpful lens through which to evaluate the tone of our church gatherings and annual calendar.

- Table fellowship was a hallmark of faithful Israel. It was also a dominant feature of the early church: 'Every day they continued to meet together in the temple courts. They broke bread in their homes and ate together with glad and sincere hearts' (Acts 2:46). Unsurprisingly, hospitality is a vital trait for Christian individuals and communities to foster (e.g., Rom. 12:13; Titus 1:8; 1 Pet. 4:9).

- Material blessings we receive from God are not only for ourselves but are to be shared with others, especially those in need within the household of God (e.g., 2 Cor. 8:10-15; James 2:15-16).

- Themes of mutual fellowship, eating, and celebrating peace with God permeate Paul's discussion of the Lord's Supper in 1 Corinthians 11. The conceptual parallels with Leviticus 3 are worth exploring. In both cases, there is a ritualized meal, eaten not to achieve atonement, but based on atonement already made. Each actualizes faith, offering tangible, physical participation with God. Both also presume that restoration of fellowship with God must also involve fellowship with people. In fact, it was some (probably wealthy) Corinthians not considering 'the body' (that is, fellow believers; 1 Cor. 11:29[3]) that provoked the apostle's ire.

Suggestions for preaching

Sermon 1

One of the real opportunities these chapters afford the preacher is to help a congregation gain a more rounded appreciation of the biblical concept of sacrifice. The New Testament writers understood the nuances clearly, as did their first readers. Those less familiar with the distinctions and subtleties, however, are more liable to misread and misunderstand (in both Testaments). This is a valuable opportunity to fill in essential background. At the same time, this passage has its own intentions above and beyond merely making people better informed. Like all Scripture, this part also aims at the heart and is designed to provoke transformation.

- **Celebrate good times!** Our impulse to celebrate important events and achievements – birthdays, Christmas, anniversaries, graduations – is right and

---

3. Although NIV and NLT read 'the body of Christ' in 1 Cor. 11:29, 'of Christ' is not in the original Greek text.

good. Yet celebration can become self-interested and self-congratulatory. Leviticus 2–3 helps to re-orient our thinking by placing celebration in its right theological context: a proper understanding of who God is and the kind provision He has made for His people. What better way to remember these things than by involving God in the party or, in Old Testament parlance, 'rejoic[ing] before the LORD'?

- **Offering tribute.** Israel had a new King who had come to dwell in His royal palace (i.e., the tabernacle) in the middle of the camp. Presenting one's sovereign with tribute was expected; everyone in the ancient world knew that. Yahweh was no different. The relatively low cost of the offerings meant anyone could express their loyalty and respect by bringing a tribute of flour, part of which would ascend before God as a pleasing aroma. The focus here is on the individual; each Israelite is invited (and expected) to perform *public* acts of homage, visible indicators of subservience to Yahweh. This is an implicit call to perform outward signs of an inward faith.

- **Fellowship with God and neighbor.** Here, again, we start with an individual Israelite who brings his or her animal to the tabernacle and offers the best portions to Yahweh. This too becomes a pleasing aroma. Yet the remainder of the animal is shared with the wider community and eaten publicly before the LORD in joyous testimony to, and celebration of, the peace that now exists between God and His people. What a contrast to the Israel who grumbled for food in the desert. What recapitulation of creation blessing.

What a glorious anticipation of the eschatological feast to come: contentedness and satiety in the presence of the King. The New Testament develops and deepens these themes and ultimately links them to the blessing that Jesus makes possible. Little surprise, then, that Jesus requires His followers to come *together* to remember Him in the context of a shared meal.

Sermon 2

An alternative sermon might take Leviticus 1–3 as a unit. Doing so would limit the preacher's time for digging into the details. However, it would facilitate the drawing out of the idealized picture that emerges from the book's opening chapters. The problems of sin and separation are muted themes (they will come to the fore later in the book). Instead, the three offerings, as they are portrayed in this unit, focus on *maintaining* and *participating* in ongoing relationship with Yahweh (rather than on initiating or restoring). Here is the ideal: faithful Israelites, motivated only by thankfulness, approaching the tabernacle to offer gifts of devotion and adoration and to take up the invitation to share food with their Master and with one another. This is a portrait of a worshipping community that is worth preaching.

Suggestions for teaching

Questions to help understand the passage

1. What connotations does the phrase 'to offer tribute' have (in the Bible and outside of it)? What normally provokes such an action?

2. What role is played by Aaron's sons, the priests? Why did they need to do these things?

3. The portion of the offerings given to the priests is called 'most holy' (2:3, 10). What does this mean and why were they given it?

4. Discuss the roles of incense, yeast, honey, salt, fat, and blood in Leviticus 2–3.

5. Why do you think food and friendship belong so closely together?

6. Why does 3:16 say, 'All fat is Yahweh's' (my translation)?

7. Why do you think neither of these offerings is commanded, but rather desired?

8. How is God portrayed in Leviticus 2–3?

Questions to help apply the passage

1. In what ways do you think you get the Master-servant balance right when it comes to your relationship with God? In what ways do you think you get it wrong?

2. Israelites could perform a tribute offering as a demonstrable way of paying homage to God. What could you do to achieve the same purpose?

3. Does the idea of God telling Israel, 'You must party!' fit with how you think of Him? Which of your preconceptions or expectations might need to change?

4. Leviticus 2 portrays sacrifice without blood. Leviticus 3 portrays blood sacrifice without atonement. How does this make you rethink/redefine the concepts of sacrifice and atonement?

5. Do you have relationships with other believers that require some work to get them to table fellowship readiness? What will you do about it?

6. Can Christians eat fat and blood (3:17)?

3.
Purification for Sin
(Leviticus 4:1–5:13)

Introduction

What happens when God's people sin? What becomes of the adoration, veneration, and table fellowship that Leviticus 1–3 so richly portrays? Leviticus is not naïve. Indeed, the book operates on the assumption that human fault, whether accidental or deliberate, will damage relationship with both God and neighbor. With that reality in view, the final two offerings outlined in Leviticus 1:1–6:7 have *restoration* as their primary function. Each initiates a procedure to bring about cleansing, atonement, and forgiveness, and thus becomes essential for the long-term potential of God dwelling with His people.

The first of these, the purification offering, is the topic of 4:1–5:13. In contrast to the ascension, tribute, and fellow-ship offerings in Leviticus 1–3, the purification offering is accompanied by imperatives: 'When anyone sins ... he *must* bring' (4:2-3; emphasis added). The command under-scores the importance of making purification. Dealing properly with sin and impurity is not an optional extra, or something to be done only when it suits. There is an urgency and immediacy that pervades this passage. The reason is twofold: Israel had been chosen to become a kingdom of priests and a holy nation (Exod. 19:6) and therefore ought increasingly to reflect God's holiness (Lev. 11:44-45; 19:2; 20:26); and, secondly, sin and impurity *endanger*, especially when a holy God resides in close proximity (Lev. 10:1-2; 15:31; 20:1-27).

Also important to note is that, once again, these instructions come directly from Yahweh (see 4:1-2). Thus, the underlying premise in Leviticus 4:1–5:13 is divine grace and kindness. In the face of inevitable human failure, with all its potential to jeopardize unfolding restoration, Yahweh provides means to overcome sin and its effects. Will human sin be the final word? No! God has made a way.

Listening to the text

Context and structure

The purification offering is the fourth of the five major offerings covered in Leviticus 1–7. Leviticus 4:1–5:13 comprises the book's second block of divine speech, which marks it off as a discrete unit (4:1-2; cf. 1:1-2; 5:14). The section divides into two major panels, each beginning with the same clause: 'When a person' (*nephesh ki*; 4:2; 5:1; cf. 2:1). The focus of the first panel is inadvertent or unintentional sins (4:2-35); the second deals with sins of omission (5:1-13). The two panels are further punctuated by the particles 'if' or 'when' (4:3, 13, 22, 27, 32; 5:5, 7, 11), which mark out subsections. The chapter can be laid out as follows:

> Narrative introduction (4:1-2a)
>
> Unintentional sins (4:2b-35)
>> If the anointed priest sins (4:3-12)

> If the whole community sins (4:13-21)
> If a tribal leader sins (4:22-26)
> If a common person sins (4:27-35)

Sins of omission (5:1-13)
> Four representative sins (5:1-4)
> If offering from the flock (5:5-6)
> If offering birds (5:7-10)
> If offering flour (5:11-13)

Working through the text

Unintentional sins (4:2b-35)

The first panel outlines what must be done when a person 'sins unintentionally' by doing something Yahweh had forbidden (4:2b). The command may or may not have been known by the perpetrator. Either way, the person sins by violating God's order even if unaware of having done so.

Unintentional sins committed by the 'anointed priest' are dealt with first (4:3-12). 'Anointed priest' refers to the high priest who was set apart by being smeared with oil (Exod. 29:5-7; Lev. 21:10). (Thus, in the Old Testament, 'anointed one' could refer to either a priestly or kingly figure.) Because he represented the people, a high priest's sin had *communal* ramifications. The phrase, 'bringing guilt on the people' (4:3; NIV, ESV, HCSB), is best understood in the sense of causing the people to 'suffer guilt's consequences' (similarly, 4:13, 22, 27).[1] It is not stated what those consequences are,

---

1. In this, I follow Jay Sklar (*Sin, Impurity, Sacrifice, Atonement*, 24-41) who argues that 'suffering guilt's consequences' is the best contextual reading of the Hebrew verb *'shm*. James Greenberg has recently proposed the translation 'compelled by guilt' (*A New Look at Atonement in Leviticus: The Meaning and Purpose of* Kipper *Revisited* [BBRSup 23; University Park: Eisenbrauns, 2019], 26, fn. 56).

but the implied agent is God, and the result is that the sinner is provoked to make restitution. Human prompting or rebuke may also be in view. Leviticus 4:22-23 says, regarding a tribal leader becoming aware of sin, that 'he suffers guilt's consequences or *it is made known to him*' (my translation; similarly, 4:14, 28). In these ways hidden sin, otherwise unknown to the perpetrator, is brought to light, either by Yahweh or one's neighbor.

Uncovered sin must be met with sacrifice in order to secure atonement and forgiveness. In the case of the anointed priest, a young bull without defect must be presented as a 'purification offering' (*hatta't*). While the Hebrew term *hatta't* can mean 'sin' (hence, 'sin offering', as NIV, ESV, HCSB), this type of sacrifice was also used in contexts of ritual impurity where sin was not a factor (e.g., 12:6-8). The common denominator is that both sin and impurity defile and, hence, require purification.[2] Therefore, the term 'purification offering' may cause less confusion when reading other parts of Leviticus.

The procedure for achieving purification has elements familiar from Leviticus 1–3: presentation of the animal at the entrance to the tabernacle (4:4; cf. 1:3), the hand-pressing rite (4:4; cf. 1:4), ritual slaughter and use of the blood (4:4-5; cf. 1:5), and removal of the fat followed by its incineration upon the altar (4:8-10; cf. 3:3-5). Other elements are unique. For sins of communal consequence, for example, blood was carried into the tent of meeting and sprinkled seven times on the curtain separating the holy

---

2. The Hebrew noun *hatta't* can be translated as 'sin', 'punishment for sin', and 'offering for sin'. Likewise, the associated verb can mean 'to (commit a) sin' (as in Lev. 4:3) or 'to purify, cleanse from sin'. There is rich potential here for wordplays and puns which Leviticus utilizes with aplomb.

place from the most holy (4:5-6, 17) and was smeared on
the horns of the incense altar (4:7, 18). Leftover blood was
disposed of at the base of the altar in the courtyard (4:7,
18) with the rest of the animal being burned outside the
camp in a pure place (4:11-12, 21) (see *Figure 3.1*).

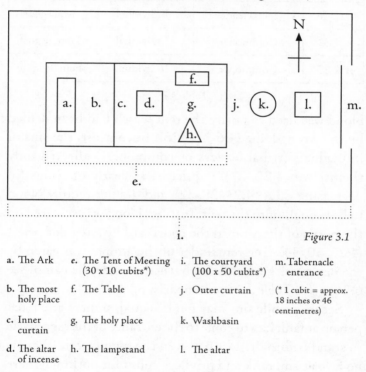

Figure 3.1

a. The Ark	e. The Tent of Meeting (30 x 10 cubits*)	i. The courtyard (100 x 50 cubits*)	m. Tabernacle entrance
b. The most holy place	f. The Table	j. Outer curtain	(* 1 cubit = approx. 18 inches or 46 centimetres)
c. Inner curtain	g. The holy place	k. Washbasin	
d. The altar of incense	h. The lampstand	l. The altar	

There are several important things to note. First, not all
sins are equal (despite the adage that tells us they are). The
sin of the anointed priest or the whole assembly was of
greater consequence than that of individuals. As a result,
the entire community suffered sin's consequences (4:3, 13).
Moreover, the sacrifice required was the costliest (a bull,
4:3, 14), only the high priest could officiate (4:4, 16), and

	Culpable person	Suffering guilt's consequences	Offering
4:3-12	High priest	Community	Bull
4:13-21	Whole community	Community	Bull
4:22-26	Tribal leader	Individual	Male goat
4:27-31	Commoner	Individual	Female goat
4:32-35	Commoner	Individual	Female lamb

Table 3.1

blood was used to purify the tent which had been defiled by the wrongdoing (4:6-7, 17-18). In contrast, the sins of individuals (tribal leaders or commoners) affected only themselves (4:22, 27), required less costly offerings (in decreasing value: 4:23, 28, 32), and did not require blood to be brought into the tent. Instead, blood was smeared on the horns of the altar in the courtyard by a regular priest (4:25, 30, 34). The remainder of the animal was eaten by the priests instead of being burned outside the camp (see 6:26). (See *Table 3.1* for comparison.)

Second, while sins may not be equal, sinners are. Each person at fault had to come to the entrance of the tabernacle to stand before the LORD – even the high priest. There is no favoritism; rank and privilege count for nothing. There is a personal interaction that must occur between offender and the one offended.[3]

Third, the results are the same, no matter the cost of the offering. In each case (left unstated for the high priest),

---

3. In the case of community sin, the entire assembly gathers at the tabernacle (4:14) even if the elders enact the hand-pressing rite on behalf of the people and an unspecified person slaughters the animal (4:15).

Officiant	Blood use	Remainder of animal
High priest	Curtain and incense altar	Burnt (4:12)
High priest	Curtain and incense altar	Burnt (4:21)
Priest	Altar of the ascension offering	Eaten (6:26)
Priest	Altar of the ascension offering	Eaten (6:26)
Priest	Altar of the ascension offering	Eaten (6:26)

Table 3.1 cont.

atonement is made (4:20, 26, 31, 35). Both senses of the verb *kpr* ('to make atonement') are operational (see discussion at 1:3-17): the blood of the purification offering *purifies* both guilty party and defiled tabernacle and functions as a *ransom* payment. In this way, divine wrath is averted. The positive result of making atonement is captured by the phrase 'it will be forgiven them/him' (my translation) (4:20, 26, 31, 35). The verb is passive, with Yahweh as the implied subject (i.e., it will be forgiven *by Yahweh*). This is important theologically. Forgiveness is granted by Yahweh, not the officiating priest. Furthermore, as God presumably grants forgiveness based on the inner disposition of the supplicant, this is no mere mechanical process (for counterexamples, see Isa. 1:11-20; Amos 5:21-27). At the same time, the divine verdict of 'forgiven' was not audible. The offender had to go away simply *believing* that Yahweh had forgiven, premised on His prior promise to do so for genuinely penitent people. This is salvation by grace, through faith, Leviticus-style.

Fourth, forgiveness is granted only *when the entire procedure is complete*. Care is needed here, because the point is often missed. James Hamilton, for instance, says that

'the death of the beast ... cleanses the worshipper of sin'.[4]
If this were the case, there would be no procedure after the
slaughtering of the animal. But there is. The death of the
animal is necessary, but not by itself sufficient. The entire
process, with all its various elements, agents, and blood
uses is required for forgiveness to be pronounced.

Sins of omission (5:1-13)

The second panel continues discussion of purification offerings, but with a slight shift of focus. The sins remedied in
4:3-35 were acts of *commission*, albeit done unintentionally
(4:2). Leviticus 5:1-4 lists four (representative) sins that are
perhaps best labelled acts of *omission* – that is, something a
person knowingly should have done, but did not. The first
is a refusal to respond to an injunction for witnesses to
come forward, even though the person knew something
about the case (5:1). The second and third examples relate
to contact with impurity, whether of animal (5:2) or human
(5:3) origin. However, touching something impure is not
by itself sinful, as chapters 11–15 make clear. So, what is
the problem? The ESV captures the sense of the Hebrew:
'If anyone touches an unclean thing ... and it is hidden
from him' (5:2). In other words, it is hidden from his own
memory.[5] Thus, the issue is not touching an impure thing
per se, but rather touching it only to forget the matter
carelessly before enacting proper cleansing procedures.
The last case concerns an oath made rashly which is also
subsequently forgotten ('hidden from him', 5:4 ESV).

---

4. James M. Hamilton Jr., *God's Glory in Salvation through Judgment: A
   Biblical Theology* (Wheaton: Crossway, 2010), 111.

5. Following Sklar, *Leviticus*, 116.

In all four cases, the sinner must be prompted to make restitution. The idea of 'suffering guilt's consequences' (my translation) appears again (5:2, 3, 4; cf. 4:3, 13, etc.) as does the potential for human prompting ('when he comes to know it', 5:3, 4 ESV; cf. 4:23). Either way, sin, once realized, had to be dealt with and not forgotten again. 'He is to confess he has committed that sin' (Lev. 5:5 HCSB) – a *specific* and *public* declaration of wrongdoing. Even though there may be human fallout (especially in 5:1), it is 'to the LORD' that a female lamb or goat must be brought as a purification offering to make atonement (5:6; cf. 4:28, 32). If someone could not afford a lamb or goat, then a pair of birds or even a small quantity of flour (approximately 1 kg) could be brought instead. Thus, all could heed the demand to make restitution. Atonement and forgiveness were possibilities for *everyone*.

Leviticus 4:1–5:13 provides a valuable window into the biblical concept of sin. The Old Testament knows three grades of wrongdoing: (1) unintentional sins; (2) deliberate, but minor, sins (including sins of omission); and (3) what are often termed 'high-handed' sins – namely, serious acts of rebellion and unfaithfulness (see Num. 15:22-31). The sacrificial procedures outlined in Leviticus address only unintentional (4:3-35) and minor (5:1-13) sins. There was no cultic remedy for 'high-handed' sins. Instead, the guilty individual or group faced death or being 'cut off' (e.g. Lev. 10:1-2; 24:23; Josh. 7:19-26).[6]

---

6. To be 'cut off' (Heb. *krt*) is frequently used in the Old Testament to convey punishment. This is a divine sanction, not one the community had authority to determine. One may be 'cut off' from one's people (e.g. Exod. 30:33; Lev. 17:4), from the nation (e.g. Num. 19:13), or from the presence of Yahweh (e.g. Lev. 22:3). While being 'cut off' sometimes occasioned immediate death (e.g. Num. 15:30-35), it could also denote banishment.

The only remaining possibility was to cry out to Yahweh for mercy (e.g. Exod. 32:7-14). This is what David does in Psalm 51. Following his 'high-handed' acts of adultery and arranged murder, David pleaded for cleansing, washing, and restoration (Ps. 51:7, 12) but never offers to make a purification offering. In fact, he recognized that all he could bring to God was a 'broken and contrite heart' (Ps. 51:17). And God, in mercy, forgave (2 Sam. 12:13).

Leviticus 4:1–5:13 also paints a wonderful picture of Yahweh. He knows His people will sin, wittingly or unwittingly. He knows His glory will simply consume any vestige of unholiness (Lev. 10:1-2). Yet, God desires to dwell with His people and be their God (26:12). So, He provides a way. This passage is deeply personal, even tender: God's people come to Him to receive the purification they need to continue living in His presence and enjoying His blessing. Owen Strachan captures the essence well:

> So far from the mere observance of arcane rituals, the Levites acted out the very story of redemption before the people of God. They showed the people who they were, drawing their attention to their uncleanness and to the bloody solution to this problem. They showed the people, most importantly, who Yahweh was. He had not left his people in their impurity. Instead, Yahweh stipulated sacrifices so that they could stand in his presence and represent him to the nations.[7]

However, banishment is still synonymous with death, as separation from Yahweh's presence, away from the source of life, is effectively a living death (cf. Lev. 13:45-46). Wenham (*Leviticus*, 242) suggests being cut off from one's people may also signify *eternal* separation.

7. Kevin J. Vanhoozer and Owen Strachan, *The Pastor as Public Theologian: Reclaiming a Lost Vision* (Grand Rapids: Baker, 2015), 43.

From text to message

A key danger to avoid when teaching this passage is to minimize what it portrays. A careless handling of the text may end up declaring (wittingly or not) that the rituals in this passage merely *symbolized* atonement and forgiveness or only *pointed to* a reality still to come. Yet, to assert something like this would be to profoundly misread Leviticus 4:1–5:13, which explicitly makes it clear (six times!) that penitent Israelites *did* know and receive Yahweh's forgiveness. Yes, there is a sense in which forgiveness for God's people in all times and places is inextricably bound up with the cross of Christ, but that is not to say that what was available to Israel was unreal or mere pretense. Did David not declare precisely the opposite?

> Then I acknowledged my sin to you
>> and did not cover up my iniquity.
> I said, 'I will confess
>> my transgressions to the LORD.'
> And you forgave
>> the guilt of my sin. (Ps. 32:5)

Getting the message clear: the theme

Because of His character and the prevalence of sin, Yahweh provides a means of atonement and forgiveness that is open to anyone. Sinners, without distinction, must come, trusting God regarding the provision He has made to be purified and rendered fit for His presence.

Getting the message clear: the aim

In dictating the means by which Israelites could address the rupture in divine-human relationship caused by sin, this passage deals with the reality of fallen humanity. There is a subtle warning generated about the likelihood of sin in the lives of God's people (especially when one considers that unintended sins and acts of omission are also culpable). Yahweh's driving desire is that His people be characterized by holiness, so much so that He will bring even hidden, minor sins to light. Thus, at heart, the passage portrays the mercy and kindness of Yahweh towards His people and His commitment to their transformation. There is a resultant call for sincere repentance, evidenced in word and deed, which is, in turn, met with provision of purification and forgiveness.

A way in

We are used to procedures being set up to help if things go wrong. Ships must have adequate lifeboats. Cars and houses need to be insured. There are *vice*-presidents and *vice*-principals – just in case. We make similar provisions in relational contexts. In our home, there is an ideal (that we at least aspire to): when one person wrongs another and realizes what they have done they ought to name the wrongful act and say, 'I'm sorry for x'. The person wronged should then respond, 'I forgive you for x' (not 'It's all right' or 'It doesn't matter', because wrongdoing is wrong and does matter). This process is not designed to encourage wrongdoing (no such encouragement is required!) but is meant to provide a means for restoration *if* (when!) something should happen. In a similar manner, Yahweh fully recognizes that things may arise that will disrupt relational harmony with His people and has accordingly put procedures in place if (when!) something should happen.

Our past sin can leave us with feelings of guilt and shame. In honest moments, we may even sense our potential to repeat the very same mistakes. The questions posed by our fallen nature are captured well by the lyrics of a song by Christian band, DC Talk: 'What if I stumble, what if I fall? ... Will the love continue when my walk becomes a crawl?' Leviticus 4:1–5:13 not only answers that question, but points us to the wider scriptural testimony of the means God has provided for His people to be fully and truly forgiven.

Ideas for application

- The holiness of God's people is important. Therefore, sin must be dealt with quickly and not ignored.

- We should learn to be sensitive to the Lord's discipline and the work of His Holy Spirit. The New Testament teaches that God continues to use suffering to highlight sin and prompt repentance (e.g., 1 Cor. 11:29-32; 1 Tim. 1:20; James 5:14-16).

- We have a responsibility to uncover sin in the lives of fellow believers, motivated not by revenge or pride, but by a deep concern for the corporate holiness of God's people (Lev. 19:17; Matt. 18:15-17). Of course, our own sin must be dealt with first (Matt. 7:3-5).

- There are sins of individual consequence and there are sins of corporate consequence. Repentance and confession need to be commensurate. Accordingly, the New Testament urges both individuals (e.g., Acts 8:22) and whole churches (e.g., Rev. 2:5) to repent.

- When we sin, our first impulse should be *to go to the Lord* in order to find mercy and forgiveness. If we rightly understand who He is, our actions will follow suit.

- God has no favorites. Whether rich and influential, or poor and vulnerable, all must stand before Him to plead mercy.

- In the Old Testament, true repentance is evidenced by a rich variety of inward (humility, contrition) and outward expressions (confession, sacrifice, tearing clothes, fasting, weeping). We must be careful to guard against glib sorrow for sin and hollow repentance.

- The New Testament repeatedly adopts the language and concepts of Leviticus 4:1–5:13 to explain what Jesus accomplished (e.g., Heb. 13:10-14; 1 John 1:17; Rev. 7:14). Two passages explicitly refer to Him as a *hamartia* ('sin offering') (Rom. 8:3; 2 Cor. 5:21 NIV margin). We must understand Jesus as God's ultimate means of dealing with sin and of securing purification and forgiveness.

Suggestions for preaching

Sermon 1

- **Sin matters.** There is little that provokes as much ire for modern people as injustice. The notion that people (at least *other* people) could act to suit themselves, cause indiscriminate harm in the process, and get away with it, jars. The Bible affirms being affronted like this but then deftly turns the table. God's holiness is exacting. The sin of His people, whether known or unknown to them, is an affront to God and cannot merely be swept under the proverbial carpet. Sin must be reckoned with. Purification is needed if relationship is to thrive. The good news is that God has made a way to deal with sin and restore relationship with His wayward people.

- **Sins of corporate consequence.** The more serious nature of communal sin is signaled in Leviticus 4:1-21 by the need to bring the blood of the purification sacrifice into the holy place and to burn the animal's carcass outside the camp. This makes perfect sense in cultures (like ancient Israel) that prioritize the group over the individual. Christians in the Western world have something to learn here about how God views corporate sins and why the New Testament has so much to say to *churches* (note the preponderance of 'you' plural in the epistles).

- **Sins of individual consequence.** Individuals also have a propensity to sin and thereby rupture relationship with God. One cannot simply blame 'society' or 'family'. The biblical solution is remarkably egalitarian. There is no difference: when convicted of wrongdoing, each person must come before God exercising sincere repentance and faith. Moreover, the route to restoration is available to anyone. From the prosperous leader who could afford a male goat to the pauper with his or her handful of flour, forgiveness and reconciliation were on offer. Thus, God's program of transformation extends to every person who enters into relationship with Him. Sin will be expunged.

- **Jesus is the final offering for sin.** Leviticus 4:1–5:13 is vital for understanding the significance of Jesus. There is a biblical trajectory that He completes. By the sacrifice of Himself and the shedding of His blood, people are redeemed. In Jesus, God's final

'No' to sin is sounded, justice is done, and complete forgiveness flows to the people of God. There is a finality to this offering, a once-for-all dimension, which means that now, apart from Christ, there is no atonement or forgiveness for sin. God has made a way – and that way is Jesus.

Sermon 2

Another sermon on the same passage might explore the two aspects of sin that the text alludes to. The first part would treat 'unintentional sins of commission' (corporate and individual) based on 4:1-35. The second part would then address 'sins of omission' in 5:1-13. The same points concerning God's gracious provision of means and the appropriate human response can be made. At the same time, structuring the sermon in this way allows the preacher to tease out a biblical doctrine of sin by exploring dimensions that rarely get much airtime (much of our focus lies on individual, deliberate acts of commission).

Suggestions for teaching

Questions to help understand the passage

1. Define 'unintentional sin'.

2. What does it mean to 'suffer guilt's consequences'? Can you think of examples (biblical or otherwise) of this happening?

3. Why is uncovering or becoming aware of hidden sin so important?

4. What sorts of ways might the 'whole Israelite community' (4:13) sin unintentionally?

5. Why is the blood of the sacrifice sprinkled in the holy place (on curtain and incense altar) in cases of high priestly or whole community sin?

6. How does an offering of flour for sin (5:11-13) fit with the statement in Hebrews 9:22 that 'without the shedding of blood there is no forgiveness'?

7. What do we learn about the nature of sin from Leviticus 4:1–5:13?

8. How does Leviticus 4:1–5:13 help you better understand the ministry of Jesus?

Questions to help apply the passage

1. This passage portrays people coming to the LORD to receive forgiveness for sin. When you sin, do you find it easy to come to God, or do you tend to withdraw from Him? What view of God is operative behind your actions?

2. What might it look like for you to rebuke others for sin? Or, on the other hand, to be rebuked? Are either of these a part of your experience? Why do you think that is the case?

3. Describe what repentance looks like in Leviticus 4:1–5:13. How does your repentance compare?

4. What might Christian 'sins of omission' look like (cf. 5:1-4)?

5. Does your church think much about corporate sin? What would it look like if it did?

6. When was the last time you thanked Jesus for offering Himself as a once-for-all sacrifice for sin?

4.

Making Restitution

(Leviticus 5:14–6:7)

Introduction

Wrongdoing has a negative impact on our relationship with God. But it can also impact relationship with other people. The vertical and horizontal results of sin are not easily untangled. Moreover, when it comes to addressing wrongdoing, is it enough to simply say sorry, or does reconciliation require more than just words? This is the complex territory that Leviticus 5:14–6:7 ventures into, providing much to reflect upon with respect to contemporary Christian application.

Like the purification offering of 4:1–5:13, reparation offerings are a mandatory means of addressing breaches in a person's relationship with Yahweh. The degrees of fault are also similar: unintentional violations of covenant fidelity (5:14-19) and deliberate sins of a minor nature (6:1-7).[1] So-called 'high handed' sins like apostasy and willful rebellion are beyond the scope of the legislation. In addition, reparation offerings also have an explicit interpersonal

---

1. Those working on the Hebrew text will notice that the verse numbering differs from that of English versions (Heb.: 5:14-26). I follow English conventions for verse numbering throughout.

dimension. Whether at fault with God and/or people, there is a sense of urgency to rectify problems as soon as they become apparent.

In contrast to previous sacrifices, reparation offerings do not have different types or grades (compare, e.g., the bull, sheep, and bird options for the ascension offering in Lev. 1). In each instance, the required payment is the same: a ram without blemish (5:15, 18; 6:6). The relatively high cost of the sacrifice (positioned between bull and male goat) underscores the seriousness of the errors outlined. These are not mere trifles or matters of little consequence. Rather, even seemingly minor misdeeds have the potential to disrupt harmonious relationship with both Yahweh and neighbor. Thus, this passage accords well with the broader biblical estimation of sin. Wrongdoing and evil – of any kind – are abhorrent to God. Leviticus 5:14–6:7 therefore helps readers appreciate the depth of the problem facing humanity, but also the extent of God's restorative plan that will one day refashion a cosmos without sin.

Listening to the text

Context and structure

The divine speech formula in 5:14 ('The LORD said to Moses') marks 5:14–6:7 out as a separate section (see the use of the formula and change of topic at 6:8). A second introduction of divine speech in 6:1 serves to divide the unit into two panels. The first focuses on unintentional sins (5:14-19); the second considers intentional acts of wrongdoing against one's neighbor (6:1-7). The passage thus displays the same movement from unintentional to intentional sins as did the purification offering. The text can be laid out as follows:

> Reparation for unintentional sins (5:14-19)
>> Narrative introduction (5:14)
>> Sin against holy things (5:15-16)
>> Sin against Yahweh's commands (5:17-19)
>
> Reparation for intentional sins (6:1-7)
>> Narrative introduction (6:1)
>> Sin against one's neighbor (6:2-7)

Although justifiably split into two panels, the text of 5:14–6:7 also displays an ABA arrangement. The first and third subsections (5:15-16; 6:2-7) include interpersonal implications and incorporate a 20 per cent additional payment that must accompany the offering; the middle section (5:17-19) does not have these features.

Working through the text

Reparation for unintentional sins (5:14-19)

Each subsection in 5:14–6:7 opens by specifying the preconditions which necessitate a reparation offering. When any of the sins described become manifest, there is an obligatory process to enact. This follows the pattern established for purification offerings which similarly began by stating preconditions (see 4:3, 13, 22, 27; 5:1, 2, 3, 4, 5). Thus, the reparation and purification offerings mark a contrast to ascension, tribute, and fellowship offerings which, in Leviticus 1–3 at least, have no stated reasons requiring that they be made. One of the ways this functions for readers is to expose the human tendency *not* to deal with sin properly, but rather to hide or mitigate it in some way. Divine commands become necessary: 'If someone sins … he must bring' (5:17-18 HCSB). This strongly asserts Yahweh's aversion to sin and invites God's people to develop the same attitude (as well as warning those who may be less concerned). In this way, the opening chapters of Leviticus construct a portrait of the ideal Israelite: a man or woman who worships Yahweh without compulsion (Lev. 1–3) and who quickly deals with sin, no matter how seemingly trivial (Lev. 4:1–6:7).

The first issue addressed, in 5:15-16, is unintentional sin with respect to Yahweh's 'holy things'. In Leviticus, *qodashim* ('holy things') primarily refers to the priestly portions of the sacrifices. The word appears with this sense nine times in 21:22–22:16, where the priests are warned by Yahweh to be careful with respect to 'the holy things of the people of Israel, which they dedicate to me' (Lev. 22:2 ESV). God had granted these 'holy things' as food for the officiating priests (6:14–7:10; 21:22), but it was *holy* food. Hence, special precautions were needed to prevent Yahweh's name from being dishonored through wrongful eating (22:2). Leviticus 22:14 gives an example of what unlawful eating might look like, which correlates closely with what 5:15-16 has in mind: 'If anyone eats of a holy thing unintentionally' (ESV). It is not hard to imagine a concrete scenario. Perhaps, in the busyness of the tabernacle precincts, a person thought they were eating a portion of a fellowship offering (perfectly allowable) but had accidentally picked up meat from a purification offering (which belonged exclusively to the priests). The error is unintended, devoid of willful transgression. But even though unwitting, Leviticus 5 makes it clear that the sin is nevertheless serious (cf. 22:3, 9). A violation has occurred. The ESV captures the force of the Hebrew well: 'If anyone *commits a breach of faith* and sins unintentionally in any of the holy things' (5:15; emphasis added). Ignorance is not the same as innocence.

When the unintended violation becomes known, the person responsible is commanded to bring a perfect (NIV 'without defect') ram from the flock as an 'asham to Yahweh (5:15).[2] The underlying root ('shm) is used to connote guilt and its consequences, hence the usual rendering, 'guilt offering' (KJV has 'trespass offering'). Yet, 'guilt offering' is potentially confusing because other sacrifices (especially the purification offering) also deal with sin and guilt. But 'asham can also refer to the recompense or debt that one owed because of guilt (accordingly, in 5:6, 'asham is translated 'penalty' [NIV] or 'compensation' [ESV]). In Leviticus 5:14–6:7 this concept of repayment is central. For this reason, many recent commentators prefer the term 'reparation offering' (i.e., 'compensation offering'), which I also adopt.[3]

Leviticus 5:15-16 elaborates how repayment worked. The guilty party had to bring a ram as a reparation offering 'to the LORD', a fitting act considering it was the 'LORD's holy things' that had been (unintentionally) tampered with (5:15). The ram must be a prime animal – that is, without defect and valued at the going rate ('of the proper value in silver'). There was to be no room for dodging or

---

2. The ritual prescriptions in 5:14–6:7 are noticeably abbreviated. Leviticus often simply takes as granted items that are covered in prior passages in order to avoid needless repetition (a dimension of the text we have already encountered). Reader familiarity is simply assumed with respect to filling in the blanks.

3. See, similarly, Sklar, *Leviticus*, 118; Wenham, *Leviticus*, 104; Roy E. Gane, *Leviticus, Numbers* (NIVAC; Grand Rapids: Zondervan, 2004), 132.

lessening the fine owed. In addition, the guilty person also
had to repay ('make restitution' NIV) what had been taken
from the 'holy things' *and* add a further 20 per cent of
its value (5:16). This repayment (including the additional
20 per cent) was to be given 'to the priest', again fitting,
considering it was the priest's food ('holy things') that had
been diminished.

Two things are vital to notice. First, the fine in Leviticus
5:15-16 (120 per cent plus ram) is substantially less than
the 200 to 500 per cent penalties prescribed elsewhere (e.g.,
Exod. 22:1-9). The difference seems to be that, in Exodus,
the guilty party is found out, whereas in Leviticus, the
guilty party comes forward of their own accord. Leviticus
is rhetorically geared to encourage *voluntary* exposure of
sin and appropriate redress.[4] Second, repayment to the
priest (the wronged party on the human axis) *preceded*
the offering of a ram to Yahweh (the wronged party on
the divine axis). Only after being duly compensated did
the priest use the ram to make atonement for the offender
(5:16). I consider the implications of this below. The end
result is that the offender is forgiven (literally 'it is forgiven
him'; cf. discussion at 4:2b-35).

No details are provided for how the slaughter of the
ram was to proceed or what was to happen with its blood
(compare 1:5; 3:2; 4:4-7). Leviticus 7:1-5 indicates that a
similar procedure to the fellowship offering was followed:
the blood was splashed around the altar and the fat
removed and burned (cf. 3:2-5). In the case of the reparation
offering, however, only the priests were permitted to eat
the remainder of the meat (7:6; compare 7:12-18).

4. Wenham, *Leviticus*, 109.

The second subsection (5:17-19) continues to address unintentional sins. This time, however, the exact nature of the sin remains unspecified. The person 'does not know' which of Yahweh's commands had been broken. Furthermore – and unlike 4:14, 23, and 28 – there is no statement that someone else makes them aware. How then could such a person ever know they needed to offer a reparation offering?

The key phrase in 5:17 involves another instance of the verb *'shm*. Translation, however, is tricky. The NIV's wording implies the person is objectively guilty ('he is guilty'; also, NASB). Yet, while undoubtedly true, this does not explain why the person would then make an offering, for they remain unaware of their guilty status. The ESV suggests cognition, presumably in relation to the act committed ('[he] realizes his guilt'). But, again, this is problematic because the text explicitly states the offender is *not* aware of any wrongdoing ('does not know') and so could never realize guilt no matter how much time elapsed. Jay Sklar suggests an alternate reading that resolves the difficulty. Picking up on the penalty/consequence dimension of *'shm*, Sklar argues for the meaning 'suffers guilt's consequences' in 5:17.[5] Leviticus 5:17-18 reads accordingly: 'And if a person, when s/he sins and does one of any of Yahweh's commands which s/he should not do, and does not know [about it], but suffers guilt's consequences and bears his/her iniquity, s/he must bring ...' (my translation).

Once more, a ram is used by the priest to make atonement for the offerer and forgiveness is assured (5:18). However, in this instance no repayment is required. The best way

---

5. Sklar, *Leviticus*, 122.

to understand this is that the precise nature of the violation against Yahweh's commands *never* becomes known. Thus, compensation is impossible. Nevertheless, the experience of suffering guilt's consequences (presumably brought about by Yahweh) serves to indicate a hidden fault which provokes remedial action to restore the damaged relationship with God.[6] The wordplay in 5:19 (three of the verse's five words in Hebrew are derived from *'ashm*) drives home the confidence the offerer has: 'It is a reparation offering; s/he has certainly made reparation to Yahweh' (my translation).[7]

Reparation for intentional sins (6:1-7)

The third subsection in this unit turns to consider intentional sins of an interpersonal nature. Yet, even though various wrongs against one's neighbor are itemized, 6:2 is careful to state that such acts nevertheless constitute 'a breach of faith against the LORD' (ESV). One cannot simply put 'sin against neighbor' and 'sin against God' into mutually exclusive boxes. The vertical and horizontal are intimately connected. Intentional wrong done to one's neighbor harms relationship with God (as well as with one's/the neighbor). Thus, the sins articulated in 6:1-7 are just as serious as those of 5:14-19. All are considered breaches of faith (5:15; 6:1) and require the same penalty: a ram brought as a reparation offering (5:15, 18; 6:6). At the same time, Leviticus 5:14–6:7 has no category for sins intentionally and directly committed *against Yahweh*. Perhaps the force conveyed to readers is that such a thing cannot even be contemplated.

---

6. For this reason, Greenberg (*A New Look at Atonement*, 25) translates *'ashm* in 5:17 as 'compelled by guilt' to pick up on the idea that this process (whatever exactly it looked like) provokes the offender to act.

7. Likewise, Wenham, *Leviticus*, 108.

Five representative misdemeanors are listed in 6:2-3 (each marked by the word 'or'): (1) deception regarding a deposit or (2) a security; (3) robbery; (4) oppression; and (5) lying about lost property and swearing falsely about it. The final phrase in 6:3 – 'one from anything a person might do to sin thereby' (my translation) – suggests the list is representative rather than exhaustive. The phrase 'swearing falsely' is important and probably extends to all the sins listed. Such an oath would likely have been made in connection with Yahweh's name. Thus, in each instance, there is a wrong committed against one's neighbor that is intentionally hidden and further compounded with a dishonoring of God's name by taking an oath of innocence.

The best reading of 6:4 incorporates the discussion of *'ashm* above: 'When s/he sins and suffers guilt's consequences, s/he must return ...' (my translation). The nature of the sin is known to the offender; each of the examples in 6:2-3 is a deliberate act. But, while the offender knows they are guilty, they nonetheless opt to do nothing *until compelled to do so* by some sort of divine intervention.

When that happens, repayment, again, becomes crucial. Whatever material gain the offender made must be returned to the person to whom it belonged: 'They must make restitution in full' (6:5). Moreover, they must also add 20 per cent of the value and give this to the owner (cf. 5:16). Although the text does not specify, repayment must therefore presumably involve confession of the wrongdoing which was, to this point, kept secret (the parallel passage in Num. 5:5-10 makes confession explicit). Furthermore, like 5:15-16, repayment to the one wronged must *precede* presentation of the ram and the making of atonement by the priest (6:5-6). Restating that the ram must be of 'the proper value' (6:6; cf. 5:16) takes on added rhetorical force in the immediate context of a person with a penchant for *financial* misdemeanor. Leviticus, it seems, can be tongue-in-cheek.

The ritual order in 5:14–6:7 is instructive:

- A sin is committed
- The sin remains hidden
- God acts to compel the offender by causing them to suffer guilt's consequences
- The offender confesses their misdeed (implied)
- Repayment is made to the original owner (when it could be quantified)
- An additional 20 per cent is added as a fine
- A perfect ram is brought as a reparation offering to Yahweh
- The ram is slaughtered, making atonement
- Divine forgiveness is secured

What is interesting to note is that divine forgiveness is reserved until the *end* of the process. In this way, reconciliation with one's neighbor becomes a necessary step to securing divine forgiveness. Admission of fault, repayment, and additional 20 per cent fine all function as outward signs of genuine contrition. Yahweh forgives those who truly repent and that repentance is borne out in word and deed – towards Him and towards others. Vertical and horizontal dimensions are once more brought together. The restoration that Leviticus portrays extends to God *and* neighbor. Relationships at both levels will be repaired in the world Yahweh is remaking.

From text to message

As with Leviticus 4:1–5:13, this unit deals with sin, its consequences, and remedial measures. The wrongdoing in view is, likewise, relatively minor or unintended, but nevertheless culpable. At the same time, there are differences worth exploring. In Leviticus 4:1–5:13, the focus is on purification. Leviticus 5:14–6:7, on the other hand, deals with the debt incurred by various transgressions. Paying heed to the nuances enables the teacher to build up a more rounded view of sin and its remedy (and, ultimately, of what Christ has accomplished). Of note in this passage is its explicit interpersonal dimension. The *social* aspect of sin is frequently lacking in Western Christian thinking, where one's personal relationship with God is viewed as being of primary (or even sole) importance. The result can be a lack of serious biblical reflection on interpersonal wrongdoing and forgiveness and the bearing this has on knowing God. Leviticus 5:14–6:7 can help to fill that deficit and provoke further investigation.[8]

Getting the message clear: the theme

Some sins constitute a breach of faithfulness which creates a debt obligation to God and one's neighbor. Such debt demands that restitution be made as a demonstrable act of repentance which allows atonement and forgiveness to occur and opens a path towards reconciliation with God and others.

---

8. For exploration of the biblical, theological, and pastoral issues at stake, see Kit Barker and G. Geoffrey Harper, eds., *Gospel Shaped Forgiveness: Forgiving One Another as God Has Forgiven Us* (ACTMS; Eugene: Wipf&Stock, [forthcoming]).

Getting the message clear: the aim

Leviticus 5:14–6:7 exposes human proclivity to sin without knowing, or to conceal wrongdoing for personal benefit at the expense of others. It therefore sounds a warning regarding the insidious potential sin has to infiltrate God's people, to remain unrecognized or ignored while all the time impacting relationship with God and others. Thus, the passage testifies to our deep dependence upon God to reveal sin, provoke His people to action, and provide means that can lead to forgiveness and restoration with both God and neighbor. Accordingly, we should even be moved to invite exposure of sin, to cry out in unison with the psalmist:

> Search me, God, and know my heart;
>   test me and know my anxious thoughts.
> See if there is any offensive way in me,
>   and lead me in the way everlasting.

> (Ps. 139:23-24)

A way in

As humans, we tend to display a profound desire to downplay or evade the seriousness of sin, especially our own. Examples are not hard to come by. Just think back to the last public apology you heard on the radio or read about in the paper, from a public figure who was caught doing something illicit. When you ponder their words, how much genuine ownership of the misdeed was there? Then again, how much genuine ownership was there the last time you were at fault? So often, we expend energy trying to convey that things are not as bad as they seem. Leviticus 5 does the opposite. This passage exposes our tendency to hide sin, warns us of its seriousness, but then invites and encourages us to appropriate the means God has provided in order to experience true reconciliation and forgiveness.

Making pizza with children is fun: weighing out the ingredients; mixing the flour, oil, water, and yeast together; setting the dough aside to rise. The palpable change in volume never ceases to amaze: 'How did the dough get so big?' That is the effectiveness of yeast. Just a few grains are enough to affect a whole bowl of flour. Sin has the same potential. Left unaddressed, it has a disturbing ability to penetrate, to infiltrate, to embed itself in the deepest recesses of our lives and cause chaos. God knows this. So, in mercy, He acts to expose and deal with sin so that His people might know the blessedness of being forgiven.

Ideas for application

- No sin is too small or unimportant for God to be concerned about. Even a little yeast spreads throughout the dough (1 Cor. 5:6; Gal. 5:9).

- Sin against people constitutes unfaithfulness towards God. We must not think that wronging our neighbor has no effect on our relationship with God.

- God is active in His people to bring conviction of sin – a key role of the Holy Spirit (John 16:7-8). We must develop a sensitivity to His prompting.

- Ignorance is not the same as innocence. Even though Paul sinned ignorantly, he was still culpable and needed divine mercy (1 Tim. 1:13).

- Divine forgiveness is intertwined with interpersonal forgiveness. Even in the Lord's Prayer, we ask God to 'forgive us our debts, as we also have forgiven our debtors' (Matt. 6:12).

- Being restored to one's neighbor may still need to precede coming before God. As Jesus taught, '[I]f you are offering your gift at the altar and there remember that your brother or sister has something against you, leave your gift there in front of the altar. First go and be reconciled to them; then come and offer your gift' (Matt. 5:23-24).

- God's people are ideally marked by an increasing willingness to have sin exposed in order to rectify quickly any issues that are causing relational harm with God and neighbor.

- What we do in relation to material possessions reveals our inner disposition. Ananias and Sapphira were struck dead for fraud in relation to dedicated property (Acts 5:1-11).[9] On the other hand, Zacchaeus *spontaneously* offered to repay those he had defrauded, up to four times what was taken (Luke 19:8). He thus demonstrated what the prophets had hoped for: the day Yahweh would write His law on the hearts of His people and move them to obedience by His Spirit (Jer. 31:33; Ezek. 36:26-27).

Suggestions for preaching

Sermon 1

- **Exposing the problem.** Leviticus 5:14–6:7 reveals the extent of the problem caused by sin. People can sin without meaning to. They can err without ever knowing. They can falsely swear innocence to

---

9. Gane, *Leviticus, Numbers*, 138.

cover up hidden misdeeds. Thus, this passage not only reveals the nature of sin, it also exposes the nature of the human heart and mind. It will not be straightforward for God's people to become a 'holy nation' and live out their calling to be a light and witness in the world (Exod. 19:4-6; 1 Pet. 2:9-12).

- **Warning of danger.** Sin can infiltrate God's people. Yet, ignorance and deliberate concealment mean that sin can go unnoticed by others – and even by ourselves. But God sees. Therefore, even unintentional and unknown sins endanger, because they too constitute a breach of faith against God. This is true, even when acts are committed against another person. When we dishonor God by sinning against Him and others, we are left with a debt to pay.

- **Provoking right action.** God, in His kindness and mercy, acts in the lives of His people to provoke awareness of sin. He causes them to suffer guilt's consequences, not as punishment, but as discipline – to compel them to make restitution. Hidden sins are thus brought to light. Moreover, His people are not left in the dark about what to do. Whether the sin is unintentional, unknown, or even deliberate, Leviticus 5:14–6:7 outlines a way forward which involves confession, repayment, compensation, and an offering presented to Yahweh. However, to ignore God's prompting and appointed means would signify stubborn defiance, leading to a worse fate.

- **Guaranteeing God's forgiveness.** For those in Israel who heeded God's prompting, who evidenced sincere repentance in word and deed, there was assurance of forgiveness. The penitent Israelite could go away restored to God and neighbor. The same is true now. Through His Holy Spirit, God convicts the world of sin. He acts to discipline His children (Heb. 12:5-11). The goal is identical: to prompt sincere repentance, to encourage reconciliation with others where necessary, and to instill a deep confidence that, in Christ, the penalty we owe to God has been paid in full.

Sermon 2

In a shorter series, a preacher could cover Leviticus 4:1–6:7 in one sermon. There is a conceptual commonality that ties the wider section together: both the purification and reparation offerings deal with *restoring* relationship with God (and possibly neighbor) in the wake of sin. When we preached this unit at our church, we included both sacrifices under the rubric of 'God has made a way'. At the same time, any preacher wanting to tackle 4:1–6:7 as a whole will need to be careful not to collapse the two offerings into one another and so obscure their differences (which are theologically valuable and worth teasing out).

Sermon 3

In 'Ideas for a Preaching or Teaching Series in Leviticus', I suggested several topical sermons that could be preached, based on the book. The five offerings of 1:1–6:7 are germane for a sermon that explores the biblical theme of sacrifice. Careful consideration of the similarities and differences between Israel's major offerings pays dividends for understanding how sacrificial language and concepts are employed throughout the rest of the canon, in often quite subtle or unexpected ways (e.g., the well-known passage in

Isaiah 53:10 speaks of the servant becoming a *reparation* offering ['*asham*], not a 'sin offering' as is often assumed). This sermon could also be preached in conjunction with an expository series to tie together elements arising from talks based on Leviticus 1–7.

Suggestions for teaching

Questions to help understand the passage

1. What are the 'Lord's holy things' (5:15)?

2. What does the penalty of a ram convey? (Compare with the range of other offerings listed in Lev. 1–5.)

3. What term best translates '*asham*: 'guilt offering' (NIV), 'trespass offering' (KJV), 'restitution offering' (HCSB), 'reparation offering', or something else?

4. What do Leviticus 7:1-10 and Numbers 5:5-10 add to our understanding of the reparation offering?

5. What does this passage teach about material sin and material restitution?

6. Why is there such a strong correlation between human and divine restoration in the passage?

7. Is forgiveness in Leviticus 5:14–6:7 based on faith?

8. The New Testament does not make explicit reference to the reparation offering. Nevertheless, are there passages you can think of which draw on the *concepts* which underlie Leviticus 5:14–6:7?

Questions to help apply the passage

1. Do you view unintentional sin as serious? Why is that the case?

2. In 5:17, God provokes an offender to action by causing them to 'suffer guilt's consequences'. Has this ever been your experience? What did you do about it?

3. Are you a person who welcomes sin being exposed in your life? How do you think you might grow in this virtue?

4. Jesus talks about a person leaving their gift in front of the altar while they go to be reconciled with someone who had something against them (Matt. 5:23-24). Does this apply to any relationships in your life?

5. Do you have assurance of the Lord's forgiveness? If not, how does Leviticus 5:14–6:7 (as well as any other biblical passages you can think of) speak to that circumstance?

5.
The Lord of Worship
(Leviticus 6:8–7:38)

Introduction

At first glance, Leviticus 6:8–7:38 appears odd.[1] Perhaps this seeming appendix of miscellaneous items related to sacrifice was tagged on to the end of 1:1–6:7 because, in the days before word processors, who would want to go back and rewrite the whole thing. However, that would be a premature conclusion. It would also make the assumption that those responsible for the text as we have it were incompetent. Instead, a careful reading of the passage reveals that this part of Leviticus has its own persuasive aims. Working out what those aims are is the primary task for any who want to preach and teach this section well.

Although 6:8–7:38 continues to explore the topic of sacrifice, there is a subtle shift in focus. Earlier chapters were primarily concerned with correct process. Here, that is less important. Instead, attention turns to what happens after the offering is presented. The correct allocation and

---

1. Those working on the Hebrew text will notice that the verse numbering differs from that of English versions (Heb.: 6:1–7:38). I follow English conventions for verse numbering throughout.

use of prebends are dominant themes – in particular, who should acquire which portion of a sacrifice when it is offered, whether it be God, priest, or layperson.[2]

The section is also marked by a stronger statement of divine authority. The divine speech formula ('The LORD said to Moses') appears only four times throughout 1:1–6:7 (1:1; 4:1; 5:14; 6:1). It appears *five times* in 6:8–7:38 (6:8, 19, 24; 7:22, 28). This increased frequency has the effect of highlighting the divine origin, and hence authority, of the instructions in this section. That aim is helped by the introduction of the term *torah* ('law, instruction') for the first time in Leviticus and by repeating it six times (6:9, 14, 25; 7:1, 11, 37). Leviticus 6:8–7:38 is shaped to be received as the authoritative *torah* of Yahweh. I will suggest some thoughts below regarding *why* such an emphasis needs to be made.

Listening to the text

Context and structure

Use of the divine speech formula in 6:8, coupled with the change of topic, marks the beginning of a new unit. Summary statements in 7:7-10 and 7:37-38 suggest a division into two main sections. The first focuses on sacrifices which may have priestly portions (but none for laypeople); the second deals with fellowship offerings which had assigned portions for priests and laity. Leviticus 7:37-38 serves to summarize all of 6:8–7:36. Furthermore, the repeated phrase 'this is the *torah*' (my

---

2. A prebend is the technical word for a stipend or wage that is derived from religious funds. In a Christian context, a minister or pastor usually receives a prebend (i.e., wage) from the monies given by the congregation.

translation; 6:9, 14, 25; 7:1, 11) is an important structural marker which, in combination with the divine speech formula, implies five major subdivisions. All of this can be laid out as follows:

> Allocations for priests (6:8–7:10)
>> The ascension offering (6:8-13)
>> The tribute offering (6:14-23)
>> The purification offering (6:24-30)
>> The reparation offering (7:1-6)
>> Summary statement (7:7-10)
>
> Allocations for priests and laity (7:11-38)
>> The fellowship offering (7:11-36)
>> Summary statement (7:37-38)

Working through the text

Allocations for priests (6:8–7:10)

The first panel revisits the ascension, tribute, purification, and reparation offerings (notably in the same order as Leviticus 1:1–6:7).[3] The fellowship offering is treated separately in the second panel (7:11-36). Each subsection in 6:8–7:10 adds clarification or further instruction, with the predominant focus being allocation of duties and prebends for the priests.

Discussion of the ascension offering in 6:8-13 is primarily centered on the idea of *permanence*. In contrast to spontaneous ascension offerings from the community (Lev. 1), the *daily* ascension offering made by the priests (see Exod. 29:38-42) was to remain burning continuously, day and night. Accordingly, three times there is a demand that the fire on the altar 'must be kept burning' (6:9, 12,

---

3. For discussion of offering names, see at Lev. 1:1–6:7.

13), and twice more that 'it must not go out' (6:12, 13). In fact, the last thing said in the subsection is exactly that: 'The fire must be kept burning on the altar continuously; it must not go out' (6:13). The reason for this continual burning is twofold. First, 9:24 makes it clear that the fire which consumed the offerings on the first day of tabernacle operation *came from Yahweh*. It was this divine fire that was to be kept burning in perpetuity. Second, a continually smoldering ascension offering meant a continually rising 'aroma pleasing to the Lord' (cf. 1:9). Twenty-four hours a day, the ascension offering would placate Yahweh's wrath and allow Israel to dwell in His favor.

Practical considerations are outlined. The altar fire was to burn through the night (6:9). Then, in the morning, the ashes were to be removed to a pure location outside the camp (6:10-11). New firewood and a fresh ascension offering were to be arranged on the fire, to be fueled by the fat of fellowship offerings throughout the day (6:12). There is no need to discuss priestly portions of meat, because the ascension offering was *wholly* burned (except for the hide which did belong to the priest; see 7:8).

The second subsection begins in 6:14: 'This is the *torah* of the tribute offering' (my translation). The opening verses summarize the procedure from Leviticus 2. The offerer was to give his or her tribute to the priest who presented it to Yahweh at the altar (6:14; cf. 2:2, 8, 16). A 'memorial portion' from the flour and oil mixture, plus any incense (literally 'frankincense'), was burnt on the altar, causing a pleasing aroma to ascend before Yahweh (6:15; cf. 2:2, 9, 16). The declaration in Leviticus 2:3 and 10, that the remainder of the offering belonged to Aaron and his sons, is clarified in 6:16-18. The flour and oil were to be cooked (without yeast) and eaten by the priests as food. However, as this effectively meant sharing in Yahweh's 'meal' ('I have given it as their share of the food offerings presented to me'), the food was 'most holy' (6:17). It therefore had to be eaten in a 'holy place' – that is, 'in the courtyard of the tent of meeting' (6:16). The location of the meal makes sense of the following limitation: 'Any male descendant of Aaron may eat it' (6:18). As the priests were exclusively male, there would only ever be men in the tabernacle precincts. Their wives and children would be at home (regarding their provision, see discussion at 22:1-16; see also Num. 18). In one sense, then, this was effectively like a modern workplace providing lunch or dinner for its staff. When on duty, the priests would simply eat at work.

The concept of holiness requires clarification. Although often regarded as a *moral* descriptor, that simply does not work in Leviticus. Even in the present passage we have *objects* (food) and *places* (the courtyard) which are holy. Leviticus 23 will introduce the idea of holy *time*. Holiness, therefore, is a broader category which often has a *non*-moral sense. Fundamentally, in the Old Testament, holiness describes God – it is a descriptor of 'God-ness' (see especially Isa. 6:3). Thus, as people, objects, places, and times are made holy, they are made fit for God's presence and are set apart for His use. Hence, holiness is 'by invitation only'. God alone is intrinsically holy; anything and anyone else needs to become holy through the means God provides. Accordingly, the closer one gets to God, the greater the degree of holiness required (which will also include ethics and character). This reality is mapped by the layout of the tabernacle with its zones of increasing holiness (see *Figure 5.1*).

Zone	Access
A. The camp	All people (unless otherwise excluded)
B. The courtyard	Priests (and ritually pure Israelites at the entrance)
C. The holy place	Only priests
D. The most holy place	Only the high priest

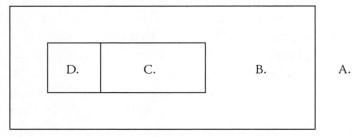

Figure 5.1

Perhaps the best analogy for holiness is radiation. The closer one gets to a nuclear reactor (the source of the radioactivity) the higher the radiation and the greater its impact. Safety measures need to be commensurate. There are boundaries (think 'containment lines') that must be maintained. In a nuclear power plant, there is a world of difference between sweeping the floor of the canteen and sweeping the floor of the reactor room.

The remainder of the subsection (6:19-23) considers the tribute Aaron and his sons were to present, beginning on the day of their anointing. A similar procedure is followed involving goods baked from flour and oil (hence, no incense; see discussion at Lev. 2:1-16) which were subsequently burnt on the altar. Leviticus 6:23 introduces the key principle that a person must not derive benefit from their own offering: 'Every tribute offering of a priest will be wholly burned; it must not be eaten' (my translation). Instead, this was to be 'the LORD's perpetual share' (6:22).

The '*torah* of the purification offering' (6:25, my translation) focuses primarily on priestly dues. Thus, the legislation fills in what is missing in 4:22–5:13 (although, see 5:13) – namely, what was to happen with the unused portion of the sacrifice. (In the purification offering for high priest and nation the remainder of the bull was burned outside the camp; see 4:11-12, 21.) Leviticus 6:26 states that the 'priest who offers it shall eat it'. Moreover, the meal could be shared with any male in his family (6:29) so long as this 'most holy' food was eaten in the tabernacle courtyard (6:26). The exception again is any sacrifice that the priest benefits from personally. Such meat must be burned (6:30; cf. 4:3-21).

Translation of 6:27a is tricky (similarly, 6:18). The phrase literally reads, 'Anything (or anyone) which touches its flesh will be holy' (my translation). Many English versions understand this as a reference to contagious holiness; that is, whoever or whatever touches the flesh *becomes* holy (SO NIV, NASB, HCSB, NLT). However, the text could also be read as a demand that whatever makes contact *must (already) be* holy (see NIV margin; ESV, following KJV, is ambiguous).[4] Considering the following instructions about

---

4. Commentators, ancient and modern, are divided on the point. Correspondence between this phrase ('Anything which touches X will be holy') and the syntactically similar, 'Anything touching X will be impure' (e.g. 11:24, 26, 27, etc.), suggests they ought to be read with similar force: i.e. as conveying status change due to contact.

washing garments and breaking or scouring pots (6:27-28), the former reading seems the more likely. Just as impurity must be kept away from the place where God dwells (see Lev. 11–15) so, likewise, holiness must be confined within the tabernacle. Like sodium and water, holiness and impurity are fine in their respective environments. But if they mix, disaster ensues.

In contrast to the ascension, tribute, and purification offerings, treatment of the reparation offering (7:1-6) fills in procedural details that were formerly left out. Leviticus 7:2-4 clarifies where the ram was to be slaughtered (same place as ascension offerings), where its blood was to be splashed (around the altar on all sides), and what portion of the animal was to be given to God by burning (the fatty parts). The remainder of the ram was 'most holy' and, like the purification offering, became food for the officiating priest (7:6). Any male from that priest's family could eat it, but only in a holy place (i.e., the tabernacle courtyard).

The panel concludes with a summary statement in 7:7-10, which neatly summarizes the priestly prebends stipulated in 6:8–7:6 (see *Table 5.1*, page 139).

Allocations for priests and laity (7:11-38)

The second panel is entirely devoted to discussion of the fellowship offering. Again, the major point of emphasis is on who receives which portion of the sacrifice (for each of the variant types introduced). In contrast to tribute, purification, and reparation offerings, meat from fellowship offerings is not described as 'most holy' (cf. 6:17). Nor must it be eaten in a holy place (contrast 6:16, 26; 7:6). This is fitting considering most of the animal was consumed by the offerer (with his or her extended family). Not being priests, ordinary people had no straightforward access to the tabernacle courtyard. Nevertheless, 7:20 establishes that 'flesh from the fellowship offering ... *belongs to Yahweh*' (my translation, emphasis added). As discussed at 3:1-17, this offering enacted table fellowship between God and His people. Yahweh is the King who extends hospitality to His subjects and, as befitting any ruler, He decides who gets what (cf. Gen. 43:34).

Leviticus 7:12-18 considers three variant fellowship offerings. The first is made as a tangible expression of thanksgiving (7:12; cf. Ps. 56:12b-13). The concept of 'meal' is immediately evident. The meat was to be accompanied by bread (and wine; see Num. 6:17; 15:8-10): unleavened loaves, wafers, and cakes (7:12), and, with them, more cakes made with yeast (7:13). One of each kind became Yahweh's portion – along with the animal's fatty parts (3:3-5) – and was in turn given to the officiating priest as his share (7:14). The remaining meat belonged to the offerer who had to eat it all before morning (7:15).

The second and third variants were fellowship offerings made in connection with a vow or as a freewill offering (7:16; cf. Lev. 22:21-23; Ps. 66:13-15). No bread or cakes are mentioned, perhaps because they are assumed, or because the thanksgiving fellowship offering (7:12-15) was deemed more important. The key difference is that, this time, meat may be eaten on the same day *or the next* (7:16). Anything remaining on day three had to be burned up (7:17). The reason given is that, by day three, the meat is 'tainted' (ESV) or 'repulsive' (HCSB) (7:18). Eating a tainted sacrifice would mean 'he who offers it shall not be accepted, neither shall it be credited to him' (7:18 ESV). Rather, 'the person who eats from it will bear their iniquity' (my translation).

The prospect of bearing iniquity in 7:18 becomes a segue to the middle section of the panel (7:19-27), which elaborates other potential faults and consequences. As the meat of fellowship offerings belonged to Yahweh (7:20), it had to be kept separate from anything impure (for discussion of the category, see at 11:2b-23). If meat touched something impure, it had to be burned (7:19). If any person became impure, they were excluded (7:21). Otherwise, they would violate Yahweh's holiness. The penalty is stated twice for effect: 'that person must be cut off from his people' (7:20-21 HCSB). To be 'cut off' meant removal from the camp and banishment from Yahweh's presence. It was synonymous with death (see also discussion at 5:1-13). The same penalty applied to anyone who ate the fat of cattle, sheep, or goats, or who ate blood (7:26-27; cf. 3:17; 17:10-14). The rationale again flows from the central theme of the unit: the fat of herd and flock animals was Yahweh's share. For anyone else to eat this would be akin to stealing from the king – an overt act of rebellion. Other animal fat, however, was open to use (7:24).

The final subsection in the second panel (7:28-36) considers the priestly portion of fellowship offerings. In addition to the fat which belonged to Yahweh, the offerer also had to present the breast of the animal by waving (or elevating) it (7:30). Once presented, the fat was burned on the altar and the breast was given to 'Aaron and his sons' – that is, to all the priests (7:31). The officiating priest also received a select cut from the offering: the animal's right thigh (7:32-33). Portions given to the officiating priest *and* to all the sons of Aaron (cf. 7:10) ensured that the whole priesthood was taken care of, not just the 'favorite' or 'popular' priests. Equal provision was the goal. The

following verse highlights once again that all of this is
Yahweh's declared will: 'I have taken from the sons of
Israel ... and I have given them to Aaron the priest and
his sons' (7:34; my translation, emphasis added).

Sacrifice	Yahweh's portion	Officiating priest's portion	Portion for 'all Aaron's sons'	Layperson's portion
Ascension offering (6:8-13)	The whole animal (minus hide)	The hide (7:8)	None	None
Tribute offering (6:14-23)	A 'memorial' handful plus any incense	All baked goods (7:9)	Raw flour (7:10)	None
Purification offering (6:24-30)	Fatty portions	Remainder of the animal (7:7), unless offered for the priest (6:30)	None	None
Reparation offering (7:1-6)	Fatty portions	Remainder of the animal (7:7)	None	None
Fellowship offering (7:11-36)	Fatty portions	Right thigh (7:32)	Breast (7:31)	Remainder of meat

Table 5.1

The final verses of the unit function as a summary for
Leviticus 6:8–7:38. In contrast to the instructions in
1:1–6:7, which originated 'from the tent of meeting' (1:1),
the material in 6:8–7:38 was given to Moses 'on Mount
Sinai' (7:38 ESV). This is another reminder that preserving

chronology was not of foremost importance for the author. Rather, theological and rhetorical concerns drive the arrangement.

Leviticus 6:8–7:38, with its focus on correct handling and dissemination of sacrificial portions, is repeatedly punctuated with the statements, 'Yahweh said to Moses' (6:8, 19, 24; 7:22, 28) and 'this is the *torah*' (6:9, 14, 25; 7:1, 11, 37). The question is *why*? Why is this passage delivered with such force? The implication is that the Israelites were likely to resist these instructions. They were likely to avoid sharing with the priests who ministered on their behalf; to ignore sacred boundaries; to experience being 'cut off'. Perhaps even the priests were prone to abuse their authority and make improper claims (cf. 1 Sam. 2:12-17). All must therefore come to realize that it is Yahweh, the Lord of worship, who apportions each person's share. Obedience is required. The result would be a happy ideal: priests serving the people and people serving the priests, enabling all of God's people to live in harmony with Him.

From text to message

With this unit, there is a real danger of getting lost in the details (for the teacher as much as the audience). Two panels, five subsections, and six offerings (note the addition of the ordination offering in 7:37 [cf. 8:22-29]) make clear communication tricky. The teacher will therefore need to draw out the connecting themes so that the overarching purposes of the text can be seen. The goal of this passage was not simply to make Israelites better informed about the sacrificial system (even though it does add new information). Its primary aim is to move readers towards obedience and transformation and so further the purpose of the book: to fashion a community of Yahweh worshippers. Leviticus, as always, is aimed at the heart.

Getting the message clear: the theme

Yahweh is the Lord of worship who delivers authoritative instructions which dictate duties, allocations, and sacred boundaries in relation to the tabernacle sacrifices. Obedience will lead to a community of people, made up of priests and laity, gathered around its God in safety and mutual service.

Getting the message clear: the aim

At the heart of this passage lies the desire for an obedient and worshipping community to come into being. But that desire is tempered by realism. Change will not simply happen by itself; the Israelites were used to doing things their own way (see 17:1-5). Accordingly, Yahweh speaks authoritatively to warn regarding potential infringements of sacred boundaries that will endanger and separate. Care must be exercised now that a holy God resides close by. Furthermore, divine declarations are made regarding priestly duties, and priests and laity are persuaded to correctly apportion sacrificial elements. Only by so doing will Yahweh, priest, and layperson receive their respective dues and thus begin to realize the ideal of rich fellowship marked by provision and blessing for all.

A way in

The failure of Christian leaders is as damaging as it is common. Whether a high-profile case that dominates the media or a less noticed situation in a local church, the results can be devastating for the individual(s) involved as well as for the wider community. Likewise, for Israel's priesthood to go bad would have been catastrophic. Without priestly mediation, the tabernacle would cease to function, sin and impurity would go unremedied, and the people would face the inevitability of divine wrath. Much hung on the priests' proper fulfillment of sacred duties; relationship with God was at stake. Accordingly, maintaining a functioning and well-provisioned priesthood lies at the heart of Leviticus 6:8–7:38. Generous allocation of material provisions would allow Israel's priests to focus on completing their God-given role.

Do you help pay for your pastor or minister? Do you give to global mission? Jesus and Paul agreed that you should. Those who preach the gospel should receive their living from the gospel. Their rationale was straightforward: 'Don't you know that those who serve in the temple get their food from the temple, and that those who serve at the altar share in what is offered on the altar?' (1 Cor. 9:13). Paul seems to think that Israel's cultic rituals inform Christian attitudes and practice. In fact, he says they speak directly to the exercise of gospel ministry. Why would he say that? What lies behind the analogy he makes? To answer those questions, Leviticus 6:8–7:38 is essential.

Ideas for application

- We are totally dependent upon God to initiate, instruct, and preserve access to Him.

- God dictates how He is to be worshipped. Obedience is better than tradition or innovation (cf. Deut. 12:1-14; John 4:21-24).

- With Jesus, the daily system of animal sacrifice comes to an end (Heb. 7:27). All prospects for forgiveness, cleansing, and fellowship now center upon Him.

- For Israel, sacrifice meant participating in the altar and with God. Building on this logic, Paul cautions Christians about partaking in pagan sacrifices which would mean joining with demons, thereby arousing God's anger (1 Cor. 10:18-22).

- Heeding God's instruction is necessary to avoid being cut off. Jesus repeats the same idea in John 15:1-17 in relation to obeying His commands. Spirit-empowered obedience is the expected mark of New Covenant faith.

- God is holy and therefore dangerous for anything or anyone impure or unholy. The New Testament reaffirms the warning this sounds (e.g. 2 Cor. 6:14–7:1; Jude 5–16) as well as pointing to the all-surpassing accomplishment of Christ, who has opened a way for people to enter the very presence of God (e.g. Heb. 10:19-22; Rev. 22:1-5). Sanctification and doxology are intrinsic to Christian faith.

- Drawing on the analogy of priestly prebends, Paul reiterates Jesus's command that those who preach the gospel should receive their living from the gospel (1 Cor. 9:13-14; cf. 1 Tim. 5:17-18). Generosity is expected towards those who serve in this way (the need for command exposes our natural disinclination to be open-handed).

Suggestions for preaching

Sermon 1

- **Learning from priestly duties and prebends (6:8–7:10).** The tribe of Levi received no inheritance of land. Priests and their families were therefore dependent upon the offerings made at the tabernacle for their livelihood. In this opening section, Yahweh dictates priestly duties in relation to ascension, tribute, purification, and reparation offerings. And, at the same time, God states categorically that those who serve in these ways ought to receive material remuneration for their work. Hence, Yahweh shares offerings made to Him with the priests, assigning them a portion from each type of sacrifice.

- **Learning from fellowship offerings (7:11-38).** Fellowship offerings were a primary way for Israelites to source meat; eating such food was a rare treat. Yet, the example of Yahweh sharing His 'meal' with the priests in 6:8–7:10 now becomes the model for Israelite offerers. They too must be generous towards the priests who minister on their behalf. Portions are assigned to priest and layperson alike to ensure that all share equally in the provision made possible by God.

- **Learning from the Lord of worship.** Leviticus 6:8–7:38 portrays the potential of a community gathered around Yahweh in mutual worship and service with each participant receiving their allotted share. But that happy ideal would not simply emerge of its own accord. Yahweh therefore asserts His authority to dictate the terms of proper worship. He speaks and delivers His *torah* so that the entire community might learn to worship together in a *God-directed* way. Obedience becomes the key to safe worship that is pleasing to God. Even though Jesus has provided the once-for-all sacrifice of Himself (Heb. 10:11-14), there is much here to stimulate Christian reflection: worship of the triune

God is still on His terms (John 4:21-24); safe boundaries around holiness are ongoing (Heb. 12:14-29);
God continues to appoint duties through His Holy
Spirit (1 Cor. 12:4-11); the open-handed generosity of
God in Christ functions as the model for emulation
(2 Cor. 8:8-9); and ministers of the gospel must still
receive their living from the gospel (1 Cor. 9:1-14).

Sermon 2

In 'Ideas for a Preaching or Teaching Series in Leviticus',
I suggested a bird's-eye view series that could survey
the book in five sermons. The first sermon ('The LORD's
sacrifices') covers Leviticus 1–7. The challenge here is to
convey the depth and richness of the Israelite sacrificial
system without losing the congregation on the way.
A robust framework is needed. One suggestion would
be to focus on the overarching purposes of sacrifice with
respect to relationship with God (and tease out their New
Testament equivalents). This would give three major points:

1. Sacrifice that *initiates* (ordination offering)

2. Sacrifice that *maintains* (ascension, tribute, and fellowship offerings)

3. Sacrifice that *restores* (purification and reparation offerings)

Alternatively, one could structure a talk around the primary
ways that different cultures conceive of sin and its effects.
One advantage of this approach is that utilizing a diversity
of ways the Bible speaks of sin and its remedy means
that we might better address the 'felt needs' of different
people. Anthropologists tell us there are three overarching

categories of sin which have particular traction in distinct parts of the world. Leviticus 1–7 speaks to each one:

1. Addressing sin which defiles and separates us from a holy God (especially the Middle East)

2. Addressing sin which dishonors God and renders us shameful (especially Asia)

3. Addressing sin which makes us guilty and subject to judgment (especially the Western world)

Suggestions for teaching

Questions to help understand the passage

1. Skim over Leviticus 1–7. For each of the five major types of sacrifice, articulate its purpose in one sentence.

2. How were the priests supported by the sacrificial system? Why was this necessary?

3. Are pastors the New Testament equivalent of priests? What is the same? What is different?

4. Why were fat and blood off limits (7:22-27)?

5. What does holiness mean?

6. What does it mean to be 'cut off' (7:20, 21, 25, 27)? Does this concept have any overlap with church discipline (cf. Matt. 18:15-17; 1 Cor. 5:1-2)?

7. How do you think 6:8–7:38 connects with and furthers the aims of the book?

8. Why does this passage need to be conveyed with such force ('The LORD said' and 'This is the *torah*')?

Questions to help apply the passage

1. How much consideration do you give to God's holiness? Are there ways in which you have changed, or need to change, because He is holy?

2. What might it mean for you and your church to consider God as the Lord of worship?

3. Should Christians eat fat and blood (cf. 7:22-27)?

4. Are there ways in which the biblical language and concept of sacrifice need to become more a part of your Christian thinking and faith?

5. How well do you financially support those who preach the Gospel?

6. Leviticus 6:8–7:38 portrays the ideal of God's people united in material generosity and mutual service. Acts 2:42-47 sounds similar notes for the Jerusalem church. How does your faith community compare?

6.

Priests Who Need a Priest
(Leviticus 8–10)

Introduction

Priests are essential to the operation of the tabernacle. Without them, there would be no sacrifice, no atonement, and no prospect of approaching God safely. Thus, following discussion of sacrifice in chapters 1–7, Leviticus 8–10 focuses on the inauguration of Israel's priesthood. This block of material is crucial for understanding not only Leviticus, but also New Testament descriptions of Jesus's priestly ministry.

With Leviticus 8–10, there is a notable shift of genre from ritual instruction (Lev. 1–7) to narrative. Apart from 24:10-23, this is the only narrative material in Leviticus (one of the reasons people find the book hard to read) and arguably helps with discerning the macrostructure of the book (for further discussion, see 'Getting Our Bearings in Leviticus'). The use of narrative explicitly anchors events described within the broader storyline of the Pentateuch (narrator comments, e.g. 1:1, achieve the same end). Leviticus 8–10 thus invites readers to situate this material in the immediate context

149

of the exodus and Mount Sinai (more on this below). In
fact, overt connections to Exodus 29, which outlines the
process for ordaining priests, cement the link. Leviticus
8 narrates the enactment of what Exodus 29 prescribed,
in almost verbatim terms.

Once more, it becomes apparent that preserving chronology is not the driving concern behind the arrangement of material in Leviticus. If it were, then one would
expect the account in Leviticus 8 to follow immediately
after the completion of the tabernacle in Exodus 35–
40 (compare the order of material in Exod. 25–29).
Instead, the author of Leviticus delays the expected
account of priestly inauguration by inserting material
pertaining to sacrifice (Lev. 1–7), which already
assumes a functioning priesthood (e.g. 1:5, 7, 8, etc.).
While discerning the reasons for this arrangement must
remain speculative, it does allow Yahweh's first words
from the tabernacle to be an invitation to perform spontaneous acts of adoration (see discussion at Lev. 1). It
also allows the description of priestly failure and subsequent instruction (Lev. 10) to function as a segue to
the next major section (Lev. 11–15; cf. 10:10). Whatever the case may be, there is still a logic to the order:
Leviticus 1:1–6:7 outlines the process for various sacrifices; Leviticus 6:8–7:38 revisits each sacrifice but with
a particular focus on priestly dues; Leviticus 8–10 then
turns to consider the priesthood itself.

Listening to the text
Context and structure
Leviticus 8–10 is marked out as a unit by genre (narrative) and by the divine speech formula in 8:1 ('The

LORD said to Moses'; cf. 11:1). The unit consists of three blocks of material which align with the chapter divisions. Each can be further subdivided. Leviticus 8 is punctuated by a sevenfold repetition of 'as the LORD commanded' (8:4, 9, 13, 17, 21, 29, 34), which marks out seven paragraphs. In Leviticus 9, the newly ordained priests begin to perform their duties and the chapter divides into three sections related to the preparation, performance, and results of sacrifice. In Leviticus 10, the shift from the Nadab and Abihu episode to further instruction is marked by a unique variation to the divine speech formula, 'The LORD said to *Aaron*' (10:8; emphasis added). The various sections and subsections can be outlined thus:

The priesthood is ordained (8:1-36)
    Ritual preparation (8:1-4)
    Ritual enactment (8:5-29)
        Dressing Aaron (8:5-9)
        Anointing the tabernacle and Aaron
           (8:10-13)
        The purification offering (8:14-17)
        The ascension offering (8:18-21)
        The ordination offering (8:22-29)
    Ritual completion (8:30-36)

The priesthood begins to function (9:1-24)
    Preparations for sacrifice (9:1-6)
    Performance of sacrifice (9:7-21)
    Results of sacrifice (9:22-24)

The priesthood fails and is reinstated (10:1-20)
    Nadab and Abihu (10:1-7)
    Further instruction (10:8-20)

Working through the text

The priesthood is ordained (8:1-36)

Leviticus 8 enacts the ordination ceremony prescribed in Exodus 29. The procedure utilizes offerings discussed in Leviticus 1–7, sometimes with variations. Notable throughout is the role played by Moses, who acts in a quasi-priestly manner to establish Israel's first priests (by comparison, the priests-to-be only do what laypeople could do – e.g., pressing hands on animal heads [8:14, 18, 22]). Moses's involvement makes the occasion unique and unrepeatable. All of Israel's future priests must trace their ancestry to this moment (hence, the importance of genealogies in the postexilic period; see, e.g., 1 Chron. 6; Ezra 2 [especially 2:61-63]).

The ceremony itself moves through three phases. The first outlines ritual preparations (8:1-4). Yahweh commands Moses to gather the necessary people, animals, and materials (8:2). The entire assembly is summoned as witness (8:3).[1] This was to be a public act of ordination; everyone must know who the rightful priests are. And Moses did 'as the LORD commanded' (8:4).

In the second phase, the ritual process is enacted (8:5-29). Moses reminds the assembly that this is what God ordered (8:5; cf. Exod. 29). The aim of the ritual is twofold: (1) to *consecrate* the tabernacle as a suitable place of priestly ministration (see 8:10-11, 15); and (2) to *consecrate* Aaron and his sons (see 8:12, 30). Consecration is the act of making persons or objects holy so they may exist and serve in proximity to God's presence.[2] Fittingly, the ritual

---

1. Regarding what 'assembly' refers to, see Wenham, *Leviticus*, 97-99.

2. On the concept of holiness, see discussion at 6:14-23. See also *Figure 11.1*.

begins with washing, a common rite of passage that marks transition from one state to another (8:6). Having been washed, Aaron is dressed in clothing suited to his new (high priestly) status, 'just as Yahweh commanded' (8:7-9, my translation; cf. Exod. 28).

Next, the 'sacred anointing oil' specified in Exodus 30:22-25 is applied to tabernacle, altar, basin, utensils (8:10-11), and to Aaron (8:12) (his sons are anointed later in 8:30). The oil consecrates tabernacle equipment, making it 'most holy' (Exod. 30:29). It also consecrates persons, rendering them fit to serve as priests (Exod. 30:30). Aaron's sons don their (less ornate) priestly garments, again 'as the LORD commanded' (8:13).

Sacrifices follow. First, a bull is presented as a purification offering (see also discussion at 4:1–5:13). Moses again acts as priest to perform the slaughter and utilize the blood. The result is threefold: the altar is purified, consecrated, and atoned for (8:15).[3] An ascension offering of a ram comes next (8:18-21; see also discussion at Lev. 1). The procedure for both sacrifices carefully adheres to the respective instructions in 4:3-12 and 1:10-13, thereby earning the verdict that all was done 'as the LORD commanded' (8:17, 21).

A second ram was then presented as 'the ram for the ordination' (8:22). The sacrifice follows the procedure for a fellowship offering: blood is splashed around the altar (8:24; cf. 3:8); the fat is removed and burned (8:25, 28; cf. 3:9-11); the offering is accompanied by bread (8:26; cf. 7:13-14); the right thigh and breast are removed and waved (or 'elevated') (8:27, 29; cf. 7:30); the breast becomes Moses's portion (8:29; cf. 7:31, 34); and the

---

3. For discussion of atonement, see at 1:3-17.

remainder of the animal is eaten by those offering it, on
the same day (8:31-32; cf. 7:15). Yet, there is a striking
difference. In all the offerings covered in Leviticus 1–7,
blood is never applied to the offerer. But here, blood from
the ordination ram is placed on the right-hand-side ears,
thumbs, and big toes of Aaron and his sons (8:23-24; cf.
14:14). Blood placed on the extremities acts as a visible
(remember the watching assembly) sign of a person's
entire dedication to Yahweh. Aaron and his sons are
henceforth marked as Yahweh's.

The final phase of the ceremony moves towards
ritual completion (8:30-36). One more act of sprinkling
completes the consecration of Aaron, his sons, and
their garments. They are then able to eat the meat of
the ordination offering 'at the entrance to the tent of
meeting' (8:31). The ordination, however, is not over. The
process will take seven days, during which Aaron and
sons are instructed not to leave the tabernacle's entrance
(8:33, 35). There is debate about whether the ceremony
outlined in Leviticus 8 was enacted once (on the first
day of the seven) or every day. Exodus 29:36 required at
least a bull to be offered daily. Either way, 'Aaron and
his sons did everything the LORD commanded through
Moses' (8:36).

The heartbeat of this section is obedience. Yahweh's
instructions from Exodus 28–30 are enacted precisely. The
sevenfold repetition of 'just as Yahweh commanded' (my
translation) drives the point home for readers. Priests are
no mere human innovation; they serve a divine purpose.
Moreover, it is Aaron and sons who are chosen and set
apart for the task, again at divine behest. This is a strong
statement regarding legitimacy.

The priesthood begins to function (9:1-24)

Leviticus 9 proceeds in three movements. The first describes preparations for sacrifice (9:1-6). A list of required people, animals, and other materials are gathered (9:2-4; cf. 8:2-3). Obedience is, again, a keynote (9:5). This is a crucial instance in the life of the fledgling nation. Reference to the 'eighth day' (9:1) signals a new beginning, the first day of a new order brought about through the processes enacted over the preceding week (with potential allusion to the seven days of creation[4]). The significance of the moment is made clear in 9:4 – 'Today the LORD will appear to you'. This is Yahweh's express wish. In fact, He commanded these things *'so that* the glory of the LORD may appear' (9:6; emphasis added). Re-creation themes begin to bubble to the surface.

The second movement records the performance of sacrifice (9:5-21). A sequence unfolds, beginning with the priests' own sacrifices (9:5-14) and then moving to those of the people (9:15-21). The verdict is, as in Leviticus 8, that each is carried out as commanded (9:10, 21).[5] However,

---

4. Thematic and lexical connections between the building of the world (Gen. 1) and the building of the tabernacle (Exod. 25–40) are widely recognized. Moreover, following the seven-day ordering of the world, Adam is appointed to 'serve' and 'guard' in the garden (Gen. 2:15), terms used elsewhere to describe Levitical duties (e.g., Num. 3:7). Leviticus 8 presents a striking parallel: following the seven-day consecration of the tabernacle and altar (Exod. 29:44), Aaron and sons begin to 'guard' and to 'serve' at the tabernacle (cf. Num. 18:7).

   Elsewhere in Leviticus, 7 + 1-day patterns are evident in relation to circumcision (Lev. 12:2-3; cf. Gen. 17:12) and cleansing (Lev. 14:8-10; 15:13-14).

5. There are, however, some subtle differences: (1) no pressing of hands on animal heads is described; (2) the language of 'pleasing aroma' does not appear; and (3) the animal combinations are unusual. It is possible

while Moses continues to direct affairs (e.g. 9:5), there is a vital difference: *Aaron and his sons* perform the sacrifices. In Leviticus 8, these men were set apart to be priests; now, they begin to function as priests.

The results of sacrifice are outlined in 9:22-24. Aaron lifts his hands and blesses the people. Numbers 6:23-27, as well as providing the possible words used, indicates that the high priest's blessing of the people was the means of securing Yahweh's favor towards them (Num. 6:27). Following this, Moses and Aaron entered the tent of meeting (9:23). And they survived! This is a huge moment in the storyline of the Pentateuch.[6] At the end of Exodus, Yahweh's glory filled the tabernacle and all, including Moses, were excluded (Exod. 40:34-35). Now, entry is reestablished; priests and sacrifice are the means. When Moses and Aaron exit, Yahweh's glory appears, as promised (9:23; cf. 9:6; Exod. 29:43-46). Moreover, fire comes out from before Yahweh and consumes the sacrifices on the altar (cf. discussion at 6:8-13) and all the people shout for joy and fall prostrate in worship (9:24).

These final verses are vital for the force of the text as they address a crucial question: How do you know the priests are sanctioned? Sure, they have gone through a ceremony, but does ritual change anything? Does it affect reality? Divine fire is proof that it does. Consuming fire

---

that the sacrifices in Leviticus 9 are unique variants suited to the first day of priestly mediation.

6. Benjamin Kilchör (in a pre-publication draft kindly shared with me) suggests this episode indicates that sacrificing is not the essence of priestly duty. Rather, sacrifice enables the priests to enter the tent of meeting in order to concentrate on the true core of their task: to serve before the face of Yahweh.

signals not only Yahweh's acceptance of the offerings but also of those who presented them. This is a green stamp of approval on the whole cultic enterprise. The point could not be more emphatic.

Again, the question is *why?* Why did this point need to be made so strongly? Remember the narrative setting. Israel had just left Egypt and was being inducted into a whole new system of worship, one the people were unused to. There was active resistance. In Numbers 16, for instance, Korah and his followers attempted a *coup d'état* against Aaron and Moses. Some of the rebels even had their own censers, perhaps indicating former employment as priests in Egypt.[7] Thus, underlying antipathy – even outright rebellion – needed to be quelled. The point remained just as valid for much of Israel's history, spotted as it is with alternative priesthoods (e.g., 1 Kings 12:26-33) and pagan officiants (e.g., 1 Kings 18:19-24). Leviticus 9 makes a firm statement for all times: *this* is the priesthood Yahweh desires.

The priesthood fails and is reinstated (10:1-20)

The rapturous scene at the end of Leviticus 9 quickly evaporates in 10:1-7. Two of Aaron's sons, Nadab and Abihu, offered 'unauthorized fire' (literally 'foreign' or 'strange' fire) before Yahweh. In striking contrast to the repeated refrain through Leviticus 8–9, the men did what the LORD 'had *not* commanded' (10:1, my translation, emphasis added). Then, repeating the language of 9:24 verbatim, 10:2 states

---

7. For details, see James K. Hoffmeier, 'Egyptian Religious Influences on the Early Hebrews,' in *'Did I Not Bring Israel Out of Egypt?': Biblical, Archaeological, and Egyptological Perspectives on the Exodus Narratives* (ed. James K. Hoffmeier, Alan R. Millard, and Gary A. Rendsburg; BBRSup 13; Winona Lake: Eisenbrauns, 2016), 27-31.

that 'fire came out from before Yahweh and consumed [Nadab and Abihu]' (my translation). Moses provides the reason: Yahweh will prove Himself holy in the sight of the people (10:3). The episode thus becomes a visceral reminder of the danger that holiness poses. It is endangerment which explains the subsequent verses. Corpses defile (see Num. 19) and therefore must be removed immediately to avoid further wrath (10:4-5). Aaron and his remaining sons are commanded not to mourn lest they die (10:6). Grieving might communicate disapproval of Yahweh's righteous judgment. Besides, they still bear the anointing oil from their ordination and so must remain in the tabernacle (10:7). Further breach of holiness boundaries would also occasion death.

The incident raises several questions. First, *what* exactly did Nadab and Abihu do and *where* did they do it? Was theirs an act of commission, or omission? Did they attempt entry to the holy of holies? Opinions vary. The ancient rabbis listed twelve possibilities.[8] In the end, certainty is not possible. However, the ambiguous nature of the violation serves the interests of the text. Lack of clarity concerning the details encourages even more meticulous care when approaching God's presence. This is dangerous business, so tread carefully, unless you want to be the next smoldering ruin. It also reiterates the point that (obedient) priests are a necessary layer of protection for the people.

Second, *why* did Nadab and Abihu act this way? Again, certainty is elusive. However, Leviticus 9 potentially provides clues. Although Nadab and Abihu were ordained as

---

8. For a helpful survey of the options, see John E. Hartley, *Leviticus* (WBC 4; Dallas: Word Books, 1992), 132-33.

priests (8:33-36) and took part in the ordination offerings
(8:14, 18, 22, 27, 31), Aaron alone performed the sacrifices on
the eighth day and only he entered the tent of meeting with
Moses (9:23). His sons served no more than a supporting
role (9:9, 12, 18). It is possible that Nadab and Abihu, in
entering before the LORD (10:1), were attempting to assert
their right to do more important tasks.[9]

But then, third, how could the tabernacle function
again? Not only have newly-inducted priests rebelled and
brought down the very anger they were meant to assuage,
but the bodies of Nadab and Abihu now defile consecrated
precincts (cf. Lev. 8:10-11). The whole cultic system is in
jeopardy. Leviticus delays dealing with the problem until
chapter 16, the Day of Atonement (see discussion there).

The Nadab and Abihu incident provokes further
instruction in 10:8-20, which signals that the priesthood
will have a future. In 10:8, 'Yahweh spoke to Aaron' (my
translation), a unique variation on the divine speech
formula which occurs only here. The direct address is
appropriate considering Aaron's installment as high priest.
It also signals that the high priest would functionally begin
to take on Moses's role as teacher (10:11) and interpreter
(10:16-20) of divine commands.

In light of 10:1-7, Leviticus 10:10 adds a crucial role
descriptor for Israel's priests: they were required 'to
separate between the holy and the common and between
the impure and the pure' (my translation; cf. Ezek. 44:23),
distinctions which are elaborated in Leviticus 11–15 and
18–22 (for discussion of the terms, see at Lev. 11). The
verb 'to separate' in 10:10 echoes the language of Genesis

---

9. Greenberg, *A New Look at Atonement*, 141-42.

1, where God performs multiple acts of 'separation' in His ordering of the world (Gen. 1:4, 6, 7, 14, 18). Israel's priests are tasked with participating in and promoting God's (re) ordering work, motivated by their all-too-real experience of failure (10:1-2). Their service would ensure the people did not suffer the fate of Nadab and Abihu.

The remainder of chapter 10 has the air of cautious reinstatement. The devastating failure of Nadab and Abihu, on the very day of their inauguration, seems to prompt Moses to supervise proceedings carefully. Reminders are given concerning priestly portions (10:12-15) and Aaron's remaining sons are rebuked for not eating the purification offering (10:16-18). Aaron, however, assures Moses that there are valid reasons (10:19-20). The section ends on a positive note: 'he [Moses] was satisfied' (10:20).

From text to message

The power of this unit is best felt by taking it as a whole. This is often the case with Old Testament narratives: important themes generally emerge only after several chapters. Therefore, reading narrative in a piecemeal fashion can lead to distortion or missing the higher-level functions of the text. The challenge, of course, is having more material to work through in a Bible study or sermon. However, the advantages outweigh the disadvantages. While it would undoubtedly be valuable to work through the details of Leviticus 8–10 in smaller chunks, the shock of 10:1-2 would be missed if not read against the building rhythm of the preceding chapters and the climax of 9:23-24. With narrative, helping an audience sense the broader story arc is vital and is usually a more dependable route for discerning the theological message.

Getting the message clear: the theme

In fulfillment of Yahweh's commands, priests are ordained and begin to serve before God on behalf of the Israelites. Yet, interaction with the holy remains dangerous. Heeding God's instruction leads to a joyous theophany. Disobedience, however, brings death and silence. Yahweh will be honored.

Getting the message clear: the aim

The narrative of Leviticus 8–10 depicts events surrounding the establishment of Israel's priesthood. However, the text is doing more than simply recalling the past or providing information for readers. By repeatedly asserting fulfillment of divine instruction ('as the LORD commanded'), Yahweh's definitive stamp of approval is given, and the priesthood is validated by heavenly mandate. This endorsement of Aaron and his sons is affirmed by describing the appearance of fiery glory in response to their cultic activities. Even the shocking eruption of additional fire in 10:2, while also instructing about Yahweh's holiness, emphasizes that, most of the time, the priests get it right. Taken together, these chapters of Leviticus are a forceful statement concerning the legitimacy of the Aaronide priesthood. There is a warning here to anyone who would dismiss or trivialize the importance of appointed priests for God's people.

A way in

Priests are either villains or dupes. At least, that is how they are popularly portrayed. From the novels of Jane Austen to *Father Ted* to Dan Brown's *The Da Vinci Code*, priests are viewed with an air of suspicion or scorn. For many Christians too, particularly following the Reformation,

the whole notion of having priests seems dubious, wrong
even: 'We don't need someone to stand between us and
God!' When you add to this a strong Protestant aversion
to ritual, the die is cast. All this colors how we read the
Old Testament, especially a section like Leviticus 8–10,
which sustains an unswerving focus on priests and the
rituals they perform. But, before we protest about time
spent thinking through this passage, we should know that,
in it, God voices a warning to anyone who would downplay
or ignore the significance of priests.

Do you consider yourself a priest? If not, why not? John
tells us that Jesus has made all believers 'priests to his God
and Father' (Rev. 1:6 esv). That should influence how we
view ourselves and our ministry. Moreover, Peter tells us
that Christians are 'a chosen people, a royal priesthood'
(1 Pet. 2:9). So, individually and corporately, Christians are
priests. Unsurprisingly, we are tasked with performing certain
priestly duties. But there is more than just our identity at
stake. The author of Hebrews informs us that Jesus is a high
priest who, even now, ministers on our behalf in the heavenly
tabernacle. To understand what these New Testament
passages are getting at, we need to turn to Leviticus 8–10.

Ideas for application

- Priests are divinely validated and are essential to
  God's purposes, both then and now.

- Leviticus 10:1-3 graphically portrays the reality that
  God is 'a consuming fire' (Exod. 24:17; Deut. 4:24;
  Heb. 12:29). Holiness ought to make us tremble.

- The Israelites were priests (Exod. 19:6) who needed
  priests (Lev. 8–9). In the same way, Christians are

also priests (1 Pet. 2:9; Rev. 1:6) who need a priest (Jesus) to serve on their behalf.

- Jesus is our high priest. Yet this describes His heavenly, rather than earthly role. As Hebrews 8:4 asserts, Jesus could not be a priest on earth. Instead, Jesus's priestly lineage is of a different line (that of Melchizedek, Heb. 7:1-28) and His permanent (Heb. 7:24) ministry relates to the greater, heavenly tabernacle (Heb. 8:1-2; 9:11-12, 24-26). Because Jesus serves as high priest, we find sympathy for our weakness and gain confidence to approach God's glory (Heb. 4:14-16; 10:19-22).

- The earthly tabernacle was consecrated with blood (Lev. 8). Hebrews 9:21-24 asserts that Jesus has consecrated the heavenly tabernacle with the better blood of His own sacrifice.

- Serving God is the essence of human identity, both past (Gen. 2:15) and future (Rev. 22:3-4). The imagery in Genesis 2 and Revelation 22 denotes temple service. Unsurprisingly, Christians are called to a priestly ministry (individually and corporately). We should therefore be people who represent God well to onlookers (1 Pet. 2:9-12; cf. Exod. 19:4-6), offer various kinds of sacrifice (Acts 10:4; Rom. 12:1; Phil. 4:18; Heb. 13:15), engage in the priestly task of evangelism (Rom. 15:16), and teach others the ways of God (cf. Lev. 10:11; Deut. 31:9-13).

- We must be content with our God-assigned role (cf. 1 Cor. 12:4-31), learning from the negative example of Nadab and Abihu, who sought more than their lot.

Suggestions for preaching

Sermon 1

- **The priesthood begins (8:1-36).** The constant refrain of this section is obedience. Yahweh had prescribed a method to consecrate priests and tabernacle (Exod. 28–31), which is here enacted. Accordingly, the narrator notes seven times that all was done 'just as Yahweh commanded' (my translation). The rituals function as a rite of inauguration which transforms Aaron and his sons from ordinary men into a holy priesthood. In this way, they are wholly and uniquely set apart for divine service on behalf of Israel. All is completed as per Yahweh's command.

- **The priesthood functions (9:1-24).** The key shift here is signaled by a change in grammatical subject. In Leviticus 8, Moses performs all the actions (and is the subject of the verbs). In Leviticus 9, Aaron takes over as primary subject. The inauguration ceremony is therefore deemed successful and legitimizes Aaron and his sons to do the actions they now perform. The ritual results climax in 9:22-24 with blessing, joy, entry to the tent of meeting, and public theophany. The people experience a manifestation of Yahweh's glory as a direct result of priestly mediation, sealing its effectiveness and authenticity.

- **The priesthood fails (10:1-20).** The notes of joy and celebration are quickly undone, and new tensions are raised. Use of verbatim repetition drives home the stark contrast between 9:24 and the actions of Nadab and Abihu. Thus, God's holy nature is proclaimed and a note of warning sounded for all future generations. Approaching Yahweh must be carried out with utter carefulness and in line with His parameters, lest disaster ensue. Moreover, the failure of Nadab and Abihu invites the further instruction which follows (10:8-20) and the clarification of essential priestly duty, that of separating between the holy and the common and between the impure and the pure (10:10).

- **The priesthood continues.** The Israelites were priests who needed a priest – a person to act on their behalf and do the things it was unsafe for them to do. In a similar manner, Christians are priests who need a priest. The role and description of Old Testament priests is mined by the New Testament writers to make assertions about the identity and practice of followers of Jesus. Even more importantly, Jesus Himself is pictured as the superlative high priest who offers His own blood to open access to the heavenly tabernacle, from where He unendingly serves on behalf of His people.

Sermon 2

Leviticus 8–10 is an excellent foundation upon which to build a topical exploration of priesthood. The inauguration described reaches back to prior instruction in Exodus and paves the way forward for Old Testament theology. Thus, the text already invites further canonical reflection. The importance of priestly conceptions for New Testament theology and practice is often underappreciated. Hence, helping a congregation put the pieces together leads to an increased understanding of a vital biblical theme. Regarding helpful resources for the preacher, Andrew

Malone's book is the best on the topic.[10] Not only is it written in an accessible way, but it comes packed with insightful comments and a valuable framework for holding the data together.

Suggestions for teaching

Questions to help understand the passage

1. How is the word 'priest' normally understood? To what degree does that definition correlate with Leviticus 8–10?

2. Bearing chapters 1–7 in mind, what do the sacrifices in Leviticus 8–9 accomplish? Is there any significance to the different order of offerings?

3. What role does Moses play in Leviticus 8 and why does he do this?

4. Are there other examples of a 7 + 1 pattern in the Old Testament? How might these bear on reading 9:1 ('On the eighth day')?

5. Explain the canonical importance of 9:23 ('the glory of the LORD appeared to all the people').

6. Describe the function of ritual in Leviticus 8–9.

7. Why were Nadab and Abihu consumed by fire (10:2)?

8. What does 10:10-11 contribute to understanding the purpose of priests?

9. What do you learn about God's nature and character from Leviticus 8–10?

---

10. Andrew S. Malone, *God's Mediators: A Biblical Theology of Priesthood* (NSBT 43; Downers Grove: IVP, 2017).

Questions to help apply the passage

1. When asked to describe God, do you ever say, 'He is a consuming fire'? Why or why not?

2. Are you in any danger of being dissatisfied with your Spirit-appointed role among God's people?

3. In thinking about the person and work of Jesus, what does His description as 'high priest' add to your understanding?

4. When was the last time you thanked Jesus for being your high priest?

5. What would it mean for you to consider yourself a priest (cf. Rev. 1:6)? What kinds of priestly things ought you to be doing?

6. In what ways should being identified as a 'royal priesthood' (1 Pet. 2:9-12) impact your church community?

7. What practical steps will you take to grow in your knowledge of the biblical theme of priesthood?

7.
Time for a New Diet?
(Leviticus 11)

Introduction

Does it matter what a person eats? Or, more sharply, does God care about what a person eats? Leviticus 11 tackles these questions head on as it constructs a theology of food. At the same time, Leviticus 11 is as engaging as it is theologically rich. This is a carefully crafted and artistically brilliant piece of literature, full of wordplays and biblical allusions designed to capture the attention of God's people.

Yet, with Leviticus 11–15, we also come to what is, for many Christian people, the strangest and least familiar portion of the book. The regulations contained here seem pedantic to the extreme and so far removed from normal life that it is hard to find reason to even read these chapters, let alone preach or teach them. In addition, the categories used – pure and impure, defilement and cleansing, holy and common – are so frequently misunderstood that, even for those who do attempt to engage with the text, the result can simply be confusion.

Understandably, then, Leviticus 11 has not fared well in Christian thinking. While kosher laws remain fundamental for many Jewish people, dietary restrictions, at least theologically motivated dietary restrictions, are anathema for Christians. That has been the case throughout church history. Texts like Mark 7 and Acts 10–11 provided a basis for the dismissal of Israel's food regulations. The legacy of the Reformation also bears heavily for Protestants.[1] From its earliest days, the church wrestled with how best to read and apply Old Testament law. Different approaches emerged. What the Reformation succeeded in doing was to make one of these approaches – the so-called tripartite division of the law into civil, ceremonial, and moral commands – a confessional matter. Texts like Leviticus 11, obviously either ceremonial or civil, were understood as 'abrogated' in Christ.[2] However, even if this were to be a helpful approach for reading Old Testament law, it still leaves a crucial question entirely unaddressed: How does Leviticus 11 (as well as chapters 12–15) function as Christian Scripture? What is God *continuing to do* with this passage?

The answer may not be as straightforward as hoped. While texts like Mark 7 and Acts 10–11 might appear at first glance to imply that Leviticus 11 has served its time, the apostle Peter quotes 11:44-45 and applies the twice-repeated command to be holy directly to his Christian readers: 'Be holy, because I am holy' (1 Pet. 1:16). It seems that simply adopting Leviticus 11 wholesale or fully dismissing it are both ruled out of court. There is a complexity that must be grappled with to teach this passage well.

---

1. I explore the issues further in '"Do Not Eat the Owl": Hearing Leviticus 11 as Christian Scripture,' *Hiphil Novum* 6 (2020), 20-32.

2. See the *Westminster Confession*, 19.3–5. See also my earlier discussion under 'Preaching and Teaching Old Testament Law'.

Listening to the text

Context and structure

Leviticus 11–15 forms the next major block of material after 1–7 (sacrifice) and 8–10 (priests). The shift from Leviticus 8–10 to 11–15 is marked by a change of genre (narrative to ritual instruction) and the divine speech formula in 11:1 ('The LORD said to Moses'; cf. 8:1). Leviticus 11–15 is united by a sustained focus on the topic of purity/impurity (the associated words appear more frequently here than anywhere else in the Old Testament). However, while belonging to the wider unit, Leviticus 11 also stands apart. Its regulations relate to *preventable* impurity; those of 12–15 concern impurity which is largely *unpreventable*. Accordingly, Leviticus 11 contains avoidance commands that are missing from chapters 12–15.

Leviticus 11 divides into two main sections (11:2b-23, 24-40) followed by a concluding paragraph (11:41-45). A narrated introduction (11:1-2a) and closing postscript (11:46-47) round out the unit. The main sections also contain several subdivisions. As the structure of Leviticus 11 is important for discerning its theological message (see below), the following outline is a little more detailed than for other chapters.

> Narrative introduction (11:1-2a)
>
> Categories of pure and impure animals (11:2b-23)
> > Land creatures (11:2b-8)
> > Aquatic creatures (11:9-12)
> > > Aquatic swarmers[3] (11:10)

---

3. 'Swarmers' is a translation of the Hebrew *sherets*. The word is used as a catchall term for smaller creatures that tend to gather and move in groups or swarms (e.g., flies or krill).

Flying creatures (11:13-23)
Flying swarmers (11:20-23)

Defiling potential of death and land swarmers (11:24-40)
Defilement caused by carcasses of forbidden animals (11:24-28)
Defilement caused by land swarmers (11:29-38)
Defilement caused by carcasses of permissible animals (11:39-40)
Defilement versus holiness (11:41-45)

Postscript (11:46-47)

Working through the text

Narrative introduction (11:1-2a)

The chapter commences with the (now familiar) divine speech formula. However, in 11:1 Aaron is included with Moses for the first time ('The LORD said to Moses *and Aaron*' [emphasis added]). This recalls Yahweh's direct address to Aaron in 10:8 and is a reminder of Aaron's new role as high priest. This dual address is a unique feature of Leviticus 11–15 (11:1; 13:1; 14:33; 15:1) and draws special attention to Aaron's responsibility to supervise appropriate boundaries for priesthood and laity alike (see 10:10-11).

Categories of pure and impure animals (11:2b-23)

The first main section of the chapter deals in turn with different categories of creature, establishing which were permissible to be eaten or touched by the Israelites. The progression is systematic and orderly. Land animals are dealt with first (11:2b-8). Criteria are established: 'You may eat any animal that has a divided hoof and that chews the cud' (11:3). Four counterexamples follow: the camel, hyrax (or 'rock badger'), and rabbit (or 'hare') fail the first criterion (11:4-6); pigs fail the second (11:7).[4] The two stated criteria meant that permissible animals would primarily be drawn from flock and herd. This creates an affinity between the animals Israel ate and those that were offered to God upon the altar.[5] Anything falling outside these limitations was deemed 'impure' (*tame'*) and subsequently prohibited for dinner (11:8).

It is worth thinking about what the category of pure/impure means (the language is clustered in Lev. 11–15 but is important across the canon).[6] Two popular options simply do not work. The first supposes *hygiene* is in view – uncleanness or impurity is equated with dirtiness.[7] This, however, says more about our modern obsession with germs than it does about the text. A second approach regards purity/impurity as a *moral* category. This, likewise, quickly leads to problems. For instance, the perennial question concerning why giving birth in Leviticus 12:2 makes a

---

4. It should be remembered that Leviticus 11 is not meant to be a zoology text. While rabbits are not true ruminants, they nevertheless *appear* to chew the cud. Also, ancient Israelites knew as well as we do that insects have six legs, even though they are described as walking on 'all fours' (11:21). The text is phenomenological and idiomatic, not scientific.

5. Of course, the parallel is not exact. Israelites could also eat wild gazelle (cf. Deut. 14:4-5) or fish, which are nowhere said to have been offered in sacrifice.

6. For elaboration, see my forthcoming volume, *'You Shall Be Clean': A Biblical Theology of Defilement and Cleansing* (NSBT; Leicester: IVP).

7. The Hebrew terms can be translated as either 'clean'/'unclean' or 'pure'/'impure'. I will consistently utilize the more technically correct language of 'purity' and 'impurity'.

woman 'sinful' (the text says 'impure') demonstrates the
case. Leviticus 12:2 is not talking about moral fault.

So, what then does it mean to be impure? In Leviticus,
'pure' and 'impure', as well as 'holy' and 'common', denote
states of being (cf. 10:10; 11:47). A somewhat simplified
relationship between these categories can be diagrammed
as follows (see *Figure 11.1*).

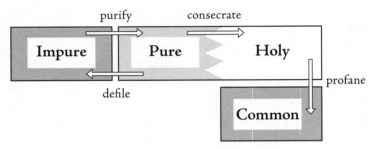

Figure 11.1

The default state of an object, place, or person is 'pure'.
Those who were pure had limited access to holy places
such as the entrance to the tabernacle (e.g., 1:3; 3:2;
etc.) – represented by the jagged line. Purity was thus a
prerequisite for offering sacrifice. More sustained contact
with the realm of holiness, however, required pure persons
and objects to be consecrated, to be made holy (as are the
priests and altar in Lev. 8). Conversely, holy things could
be profaned – that is, publicly diminished in reputation by
being treated as merely common (see further at Lev. 21–
22).[8] Pure persons or things could, likewise, be defiled.
Carcasses (11:24), giving birth (12:2), skin infection

---

8. Here I follow the analysis in Joshua D. Reeve, 'Blemished Bodies in
    Sacred Space: Disability in Leviticus 21:16-24' (PhD diss., Sydney
    Missionary and Bible College, 2018), 245-52.

(13:46), genital discharges (15:2-3), and menstruation (15:19) all conveyed ritual impurity which subsequently required purification. Stipulated rites varied (depending on the severity of the defilement) and could be *minor* (lasting only a day, e.g., 15:16) or *major* (lasting for longer periods, e.g., 12:5).

Most kinds of ritual impurity occurred naturally and were therefore unavoidable (which is why there are no commands to prevent impurity in Lev. 12–15).[9] Thus, by itself, becoming ritually impure was not a problem. However, ritual impurity was problematic if one came into proximity with the holy. Holiness destroys impurity. That potential becomes a serious threat when a holy God resides within the camp. Leviticus 15:31 elucidates: 'You must keep the Israelites separate from things that make them unclean, so they will not die in their uncleanness for defiling my dwelling place, which is among them' (cf. 22:2-9; Isa. 6:3-5). Thus, the concern of Leviticus 11–15 is partly avoidance (where possible), partly instructional (identifying sources and durations of impurity), and partly remedial (outlining purification rites). The priests' job, assigned in 10:10-11, was not to stamp out all forms of ritual impurity (which was impossible). Rather, they were to teach, diagnose, and purify, with the goal of ensuring people knew when they could approach the tabernacle. Aaron and sons had a life-preserving role.

---

9. In addition to ritual impurity, the Old Testament uses impurity terminology in connection with moral failures (see discussion at Lev. 18-20). In contrast to *ritual* impurity, however, *moral* impurity *is* avoidable and has no prescribed removal rites. The polluted person is simply banished from God's presence, usually through being 'cut off'.

Accordingly, when animals are labelled 'impure' in Leviticus 11, it is not a moral judgement. Nor is it a hygiene matter (as if some animals were healthier to eat than others). The pressing issue is maintaining relationship with Yahweh by avoiding sources of defilement. Wrongful eating or touching would result in (necessary) separation from God's tabernacle presence. The text is geared to prevent that result. The resulting dietary limitations are specific to Israel: 'they are unclean *for you*' (Lev. 11:8 [emphasis added]). Obedience would demarcate a nation set apart (cf. 20:25-26).

Following land animals, aquatic creatures come next (11:9-12). Again, criteria are stated: 'you may eat any that have fins and scales' (11:9). Any creature living in fresh or salt water that does not meet these criteria is 'detestable' (ESV) and therefore prohibited (11:10-12). The term 'detestable' (*sheqets*) is a stronger word than 'impure' (*tame'*), a point I will return to below.[10] It should also be noted that aquatic swarmers (NIV 'swarming things') are treated as a subset of creatures which live in water (11:10).

Leviticus 11:13-23 turns to flying creatures. No criteria are established this time. Instead, twenty prohibited examples are listed (11:13-19). Although correctly identifying each species is far from certain (see the variation in English translations), many are carnivorous. Perhaps underlying the list is avoidance of creatures that have consumed blood. Once more, swarmers are included as a subset (11:20-23). All flying swarmers are deemed off limits (11:20, 23) except for four varieties of locust (11:22). As with aquatic creatures, all prohibited flying creatures are deemed 'detestable' (11:13, 20, 23).

---

10. The 2011 NIV unfortunately obscures the shift by translating both Hebrew words (*tame'* and *sheqets*) as 'unclean'.

Although in many ways straightforward, Leviticus 11:2b-23 raises questions. One of the most common is, Why these animals? Why are some creatures 'pure' while others are 'impure'? Of course, the problem is that Leviticus 11 is silent regarding rationale – it simply states the case without explanation. That, however, has not prevented attempts to fill in the blanks; there are at least fourteen distinct proposals.[11] In the end, none accommodates all the data. That said, the most probable options are those which explore connections with creation and/or death. There are good reasons for this. Death looms large over Leviticus 11 (the word 'carcass' [x13] appears more frequently here than anywhere else in the Old Testament). Carnivores are not permitted for food. Contact with death defiles people and clothing (e.g. 11:25). The text creates strong associations between death and impurity.

Connections are also made to creation. Although not as immediately evident in English, Leviticus 11 is saturated with terms and phrases shared with Genesis 1. Some of the many examples include:[12]

- 'to separate' (Gen. 1:14, 18; Lev. 11:47)

- 'in the seas' (Gen. 1:22; Lev. 11:9, 10)

- 'to swarm' and 'to creep' used together
  (Gen. 1:21; Lev. 11:44, 46)

---

11. For those interested in pursuing the matter further, the following article is a good place to begin: Jiří Moskala, 'Categorization and Evaluation of Different Kinds of Interpretation of the Laws of Clean and Unclean Animals in Leviticus 11,' *BR* 46 (2001), 5-41.

12. Super keen readers can chase up my extended discussion in '*I Will Walk Among You*', 111-48.

- 'living creature' (Gen. 1:20, 21, 24, 30;
  Lev. 11:10, 46)
- 'according to its kind' (Gen. 1:11, 12, 21, 24, 25;
  Lev. 11:14, 15, 16, 19, 22, 29)

In addition, both passages divide animals into the same four categories: land, aquatic, aerial, and swarming creatures.[13] The spheres they inhabit are also identical: land, water, and air (note the reversal of order from Gen. 1 which has air, water, land). In these ways, Leviticus 11 repeatedly alludes to Genesis 1. I consider the theological importance of this below.

Defiling potential of death and land swarmers (11:24-40)

Themes of death and impurity saturate 11:24-40 (in seventeen verses, 'carcass' appears eleven times, 'to die' thrice, and 'to be impure' twenty-five times). Touching a dead animal makes one 'unclean till evening' (11:24). Carrying a carcass also makes one's clothes impure (11:25). Even animals otherwise permissible to eat and touch defile when they die from natural causes (11:39-40; cf. Deut. 14:21). Although the impurity is minor (lasting only until evening) and is straightforwardly dealt with (by washing and/or waiting), it nevertheless poses danger if sacred boundaries are transgressed (see 15:31). Ritually impure people cannot approach the tabernacle. Separation from Yahweh is therefore required, albeit limited in duration.

---

13. That four categories are envisioned is affirmed by the use of multiples of four throughout: *four* impure quadrupeds (11:4-7), *twenty* excluded birds (11:13-19), *four* acceptable locust varieties (11:22), and *eight* detestable land swarmers (11:29-30).

The defiling potential of death outlined in 11:24-28 (impure animals) and 11:39-40 (pure animals) also serves a literary function: it frames the verses in between (11:29-38) (see 'Context and structure' above). Leviticus 11:29-38 is the longest subsection in the chapter and focuses entirely on land swarming creatures. Eight representative examples are named (11:29-30). These are the most defiling of all creatures. They are both 'impure' (11:29) *and* 'detestable' (11:41). They defile not only people (e.g., 11:31) but also clothing (11:32), cooking utensils (11:33), food (11:34), and drink (11:34). If even 'part of their carcass' (my translation) falls upon something, it becomes impure (11:35). The arrangement of the chapter creates further emphasis on these animals. As noted above, aquatic and aerial swarmers are treated as subsets of their wider categories (see 11:10, 20-23). But land swarming creatures are not. Their unexpected placement in 11:29-38 (rather than following 11:8) makes them stand out. The question, of course, is why?

Defilement versus holiness (11:41-45)

The concluding paragraph brings together the various strands noted above. Land swarmers are the only creatures mentioned. Avoidance and consequence are made explicit: 'You shall not make yourselves detestable with any swarming thing that swarms, and you shall not defile yourselves with them, and become unclean through them' (11:43 ESV). Here are detestable creatures that can make *people* detestable *to God*. The warning is driven home through the use of another allusion to Genesis 1–3. The phrase in 11:42 ('moves on its belly') occurs in only one other place: Genesis 3:14, where the serpent is cursed and told, you will 'move on your belly'.

In this moment, the theology of the passage crystallizes. The unique phrase in 11:42 arrests attention and provokes reflection. In the Garden, Adam was given a food allotment ('you may eat'; Gen. 2:16) with accompanying restriction ('you must not eat'; Gen. 2:17). Danger came in the form of a serpent, a land swarming creature (Gen. 3:1-5). The penalty for disobedience was banishment from Garden and God's presence (Gen. 3:24). Now, in Leviticus 11, Yahweh gives Israel a food allotment ('you may eat'; 11:3) with accompanying restrictions ('you must not eat'; 11:8, etc.). Danger would come especially from land swarming creatures (11:29-38, 41-43). The penalty for disobedience was banishment from tabernacle and the presence of God therein (because one had become 'impure'; 11:24, etc.; cf. 7:20-21; 12:4; 15:31).

In this way, Leviticus 11 puts Israel into Adam's shoes. As in the Garden, food becomes the marker of fidelity. What one eats or does not eat is deemed vitally significant to God. Adam bore the penalty of ignoring that truth. Every Israelite (cf. 11:2) was now faced with a three-times-a-day choice: Will I disobey like Adam and Eve or heed the word of Yahweh and express faith through right eating? Worship of Yahweh intrudes into kitchen and dining room. Let there be no doubt: relationship with God is an all-of-life commitment.

Now Leviticus 11:44-45, an odd climax on a first reading, makes sense. Here is the chapter's concluding call to become like Yahweh, to share in His holiness. It is a plea to avoid everything that will result in defilement and banishment. Adam's example adds poignancy to the appeal and is intended to move the affections. Readers sense God's love for His people, His desire for a different outcome this time.

In fact, this is the very reason Yahweh brought Israel out of Egypt: to be holy as He is (11:45). Food would become an arena in which faithfulness was demonstrated (or not), a point given extra weight through a wordplay between the 'bringing up' of Israel from Egypt (11:45) and the 'bringing up' of cud by permitted animals (11:3).

Postscript (11:46-47)

Leviticus 11:46 summarizes the content of the chapter: this is the *torah* concerning animals, birds, water creatures, and land swarmers. Verse 47 explicitly recalls 10:10 and thereby connects all the material in Leviticus 11 to the priestly mandate to maintain correct boundaries. By doing so, it also brings to bear the narrative context of 10:10, the incineration of Nadab and Abihu. This adds considerable force to instructions about eating and touching. Boundaries between pure, impure, and holy are no mere matter of indifference. Life and death are at stake (cf. 15:31).

From text to message

A major obstacle facing anyone wanting to teach Leviticus 11 is the assumption of irrelevancy on the part of those being taught. People will, from the very start, assume this passage has nothing to say to them. That inertia must be overcome. How best to do that will depend on the given audience. Helping people to sense the theological import of the text is key. God cared deeply about what Israel ate – and He continues to care about what His people eat today. Indeed, Leviticus 11 reveals considerable persuasive intent towards convincing readers of that fact. Food is a marker of faithfulness and God wants His people to know it. Yet, many Christians have no developed theology of food, even though it constitutes a significant part of their lives. There is a gap in our thinking and theology that Leviticus 11 can begin to fill.

Getting the message clear: the theme

God establishes what is permissible for His people to eat. Eden and the consequences of disobedience are recalled to urge Israel to correctly separate animals so as to avoid defilement. The goal is to enable ongoing life with God by emulating His holiness.

Getting the message clear: the aim

Leviticus 11 makes assertions about which animals Israel were to regard as impure. However, when cast as divine speech (see 11:1-2a), assertions become demands that require obedience. Keeping these dietary restrictions became a mark of fidelity for Israel. Yet to conclude that Leviticus 11 has no ongoing relevance for Christian readers would constitute a very shallow reading of the text, because this passage does more than simply assert regulations and demand obedience. It also reminds readers of Eden. Recalling those events, in turn, sounds a warning for God's people regarding what happens when divine dietary regulations are ignored. Yet, the passage expects a different outcome. It invites readers to conform, urging them to become holy like God, rather than find themselves defiled and banished for ignoring His commands about eating. Hence, even if the demand to obey *these* food regulations is mitigated, the other things Leviticus 11 is doing continue to bear upon Christian readers.

A way in

As a society, we are very food conscious. Just type 'food' into Netflix and see what comes up. Or the next time you are at the bookshop, observe how many shelves are devoted to cookbooks (and requisite diet books!). We are a food-savvy culture. But are you a food-savvy Christian? Do you attend a food-savvy church? As Christians, we can pride ourselves on having a sound theology of forgiveness, an impeccable doctrine of justification, or a reasoned view of spiritual gifts. But do we have a theology of food, or is that a blind spot in our thinking, even though we eat multiple times a day? We are physical creatures; we need food to survive. But does God care what we eat? This is the very question Leviticus 11 wants us to consider. Here is a passage that has something to teach us.

A good diet is important. We have all seen and perhaps even experienced that reality. On the one hand, lack of food leads to stunted growth, malnutrition, even starvation. Yet, on the other hand, excess leads to a different set of problems. A balanced diet is essential. The analogy holds true for our biblical diet. If all the books in the Bible were an essential mineral, what would a health check reveal? Too much iron? Low on calcium? More vitamin B^{12} required? Chances are our 'Leviticus levels' may be low (perhaps dangerously low!). There might even be a complete absence of 'Vitamin L^{11}'. Yet God has placed this passage here for our benefit. He wants us to understand that there is an intimate connection between food and faith. What we eat matters to God.

Ideas for application

- God not only provides humans with food, but declares what may and may not be eaten.

- God cares deeply about what His people eat; food is a mark of fidelity.

- Food marked a sharp distinction between Jew and Gentile (e.g., John 4:9; Acts 10:28; Gal. 2:11-13). In Christ, the dividing wall is broken down, creating one new humanity reconciled to God through the cross (Eph. 2:14-18).

- Leviticus 11 outlines Israelite dietary regulations. But Christians have dietary regulations too. The New Testament is filled with examples. In fact, if anything, Christians may have a more restricted diet than ancient Israel. For instance, we must not eat (or drink):

  o to excess, because that is greed (1 Cor. 5:11; Col. 3:5-6)

  o all the time, so we can fast and pray (Matt. 6:16-18)

  o anything that will cause a fellow believer distress (Rom. 14:15) or cause someone to stumble (Rom. 14:20-21)

  o anything we regard as being impure (Rom. 14:14)

  o while ignoring someone who has no food (James 2:14-17)

  o all our food by ourselves, but must pursue hospitality (Heb. 13:2; 1 Pet. 4:9)

  o meat sacrificed to an idol (1 Cor. 10:18-22)

  o while judging another for their dietary choices (Rom. 14:2-4)

- Having a robust theology of food is essential for embodied life in this world.

- Cleansing is a key component of biblical hope. In Matthew 8:2, a skin-diseased man fell before Jesus saying, 'Lord, if you are willing, you can make me clean.' This was not a plea for forgiveness, but for purification. Jesus simply responded, 'Be clean!' (Matt. 8:3). Here is another facet of the good news: Jesus can make you *pure* – that is, fit to be in God's holy presence.

- In 2 Corinthians 7:1, Paul urges his readers: 'let us cleanse ourselves from every defilement of body and spirit, bringing holiness to completion in the fear of God.' Bodily defilement is an ongoing threat to Christians; what we do *physically* impacts relationship with God (see also Rom. 14:23; 1 Cor. 5:15-20; 11:29-32).

Suggestions for preaching

Sermon 1

- **To eat or not to eat (11:1-23).** Even a quick skim through Leviticus should be enough to tell us that God cares what His people eat. All these instructions are a direct word from God that clearly demarcates which animals Israel could and could not eat. Prohibited animals are declared 'impure' – not a moral or hygienic label, but rather one that indicates the status of a person or object. Becoming impure is not necessarily problematic unless one contacts the holy, because then disaster unfolds. These regulations are designed to keep Israel safe when interacting with a holy God. Diet matters.

- **Land swarmers and death (11:24-40).** Land swarmers are addressed in 11:29-38. However, the relative

length of treatment, their unexpected placement in
the chapter, being framed by discussions of death,
and a supremely defiling potential all highlight these
creatures. The question, of course, is why? Why draw
attention to these animals more than others?

- **Become holy, not defiled (11:41-47).** The question of
why is addressed in the final section. Land swarmers
are the only creatures mentioned. They are impure
and detestable and have the potential to make people
detestable (to God). They, more than any other
creature, can cause people to become impure, resulting
in banishment from the tabernacle. Land swarmers
can separate people from God. Now, the call to avoid
defilement and to embrace holiness becomes clearer.
This is an invitation to dwell with God, to become like
Him, and so avoid exclusion and removal.

- **Echoes of Eden?** At the climax of the passage, in
11:42, the author inserts a phrase ('move on its belly')
that creates an immediate connection to Genesis
3:14 and the cursed (land-swarming) serpent. A host
of other verbal and conceptual links with Genesis
1–3 emerge which together drive home the point:
Israel is Adam 2.0. The nation will face the same
test of faith (obedience) in relation to the same issue
(food). Adam and Eve's story is drawn upon to add
poignancy to the call for obedience. The dietary
regulations in Leviticus 11 will teach the nation to
heed the word of Yahweh, even in the small things.

- **Hearing Leviticus 11 as Christian Scripture.** Does
God care about what Christians eat? Leviticus 11
becomes 'useful' for teaching and (perhaps) correcting

(cf. 2 Tim. 3:15). Leviticus 11 clarifies that what is on our plate reveals what is in our hearts. In Eden and in Israel, God cared about what His people ate. Food was a mark of fidelity. And it continues to be. The New Testament is filled with instructions and commands aimed at teaching *Christians* that what and how they eat is important to God and impacts relationship with Him. We must have a sound theology of food. Perhaps it is time for a new diet.

Suggestions for teaching

Questions to help understand the passage

1. Why does 11:1 include Aaron?

2. Leviticus 11 is addressed to all Israelites (11:2a). Why do you think that is the case? What might this suggest about the *enculturation* of faith?

3. What does it mean to become 'impure'?

4. What remedial (removal) procedures does Leviticus 11 prescribe to make impure people and objects pure again?

5. Why are land swarmers so prominent in the passage (11:29-38, 41-45)?

6. What does it mean to become holy as God is holy (11:44-45)?

7. Read over Leviticus 11. What parallels to Genesis 1–3 do you notice? Why are they here?

8. What does Leviticus 11 contribute to a biblical understanding of death?

Questions to help apply the passage

1. Leviticus 11 says God is the one who decides what His people may eat (cf. Gen. 2–3). Can you think of biblical examples of times when that truth was forgotten? Are there times when you have forgotten it?

2. Can Christians eat pork?

3. How should the presence of allusion (e.g. between Lev. 11 and Gen. 1–3) and literary artistry (e.g. word-play) impact how you read the Pentateuch?

4. Does God still ask His people to be engaged in acts of (re)ordering the world (11:47; cf. 10:10)? What biblical insights can you bring to bear on the question?

5. For Israel, what they ate (or refused to eat) marked them out as God's people. Should that be the case for church communities?

6. What (theologically motivated) dietary changes do you need to make?

7. Sketch out a way that you might use the category of purity/impurity to explain the gospel to someone from a Muslim or Hindu background. You may want to imagine a specific context, perhaps a meal.

8. When you consider the concept of purity, do you think in physical or spiritual terms? How does 2 Corinthians 6:17–7:1 contribute to your thinking?

8.
Washing and Waiting
(Leviticus 12–15)

Introduction

The topic of ritual impurity dominates Leviticus 12–15. That alone makes this one of the least traveled parts of the Bible. Even for those who venture into these chapters, there is a growing sense that one is not in Kansas anymore. This is an alien world full of seemingly trivial prohibitions and bizarre rituals. Perceived gender disparity and an inexplicable fascination with bodily fluids can prove the final straw. If ever there was a part of the Old Testament that screamed, 'Let me back to the Gospels!', this is it.

And yet, the structure of Leviticus cautions against being overly hasty in one's dismissal. The shadow of 10:1-3 lies across Leviticus 11–15, that shocking moment of divine fire and the incineration of Nadab and Abihu. Even though the exact details of what happened are hazy (see discussion at 10:1-20), one thing is clear: the sons of Aaron committed a *ritual* fault. The brothers' fate remains a real possibility for anyone who might similarly fail to heed the limits set by Yahweh. Their death therefore becomes the basis for the priestly commission to carefully separate holy from common and pure from impure (10:10). Positioned after chapter 10, Leviticus 11–15 demands careful study. These instructions enable appropriate boundary-keeping that could literally be lifesaving.

Although Leviticus 12–15 belongs with chapter 11 and shares many affinities, the units are also distinct. Leviticus 11 deals with preventable impurity and, hence, contains avoidance commands. Leviticus 12–15, on the other hand, is concerned with *un*preventable impurity. The sources of impurity discussed usually occur naturally and are beyond a person's control. Accordingly, there are no avoidance commands. Instead, the focus lies on accurate diagnosis and remedial measures. Safeguarding life in Yahweh's holy presence is the goal.

Listening to the text

Context and structure

Along with chapter 11, Leviticus 12–15 constitutes the third major block of material in the book after 1–7 (sacrifice) and 8–10 (priests) and is united by genre (ritual instruction) and topic (impurity). Major transitions are marked by occurrences of the divine speech formula ('The LORD said to Moses [and Aaron]', 12:1; 13:1; 14:1, 33; 15:1) and summary conclusions (12:7b; 13:59; 14:32, 54-57; 15:32-33).

> Impurity related to childbirth (12:1-8)
>> Diagnosing impurity (12:1-5)
>> Remedying impurity (12:6-8)
> Impurity related to *tsara'at* (13:1–14:57)
>> Diagnosing *tsara'at* on persons (13:1-46)
>> Diagnosing and remedying *tsara'at* on fabrics (13:47-59)
>> Remedying *tsara'at* on persons (14:1-32)

Artistic arrangement is again evident. Chapters 13–14 alternate between persons and objects (ABAB). Leviticus 15 forms a palistrophe (chiasm) with 15:18 as the central pivot (ABCBA). The entire unit also displays an ABA pattern: the section dealing with surface infections (13:1–14:57) is bracketed by sections that focus on matters connected to reproduction (12:1-8; 15:1-33). Furthermore, several framing devices connect the beginning of Leviticus 12 with the end of Leviticus 15, tying the unit together: a woman experiences long-term impurity (12:2, 4; 15:25), cleansing involves a 7 + 1 pattern (12:2-3; 15:28-29), and a warning is levelled about transgressing sacred boundaries (12:4; 15:31).

Working through the text

Impurity related to childbirth (12:1-8)

Leviticus 12:1-5 outlines the nature and scope of impurity related to childbirth (for the meaning of 'impure', see discussion at 11:2b-23). The duration of post-partum impurity is the longest set period for defilement (compare the 'till evening' of 11:25 or 15:18). If the baby is a boy, the mother (not the child) becomes impure for forty days (7 + 33 days) (12:2, 4). If a girl, then the mother's impurity persists for eighty days (14 + 66 days) (12:5). The source of impurity is the same in both instances: 'her bleeding' (12:4, 5). It is not fully clear whether the impurity is transmissible. The phrase 'just as she is unclean during her monthly period' (12:2) may indicate that contact can transfer impurity (cf. 15:19-24). However, the reference may simply note the correspondence in seven-day waiting times.[1]

As with Leviticus 11 (and the rest of 13–15), Leviticus 12 does not provide a rationale for its instructions (much as we might wish it did). The text simply does not explain why childbirth produces impurity. However, it is important to remember that all cultures have pure/impure boundaries which adherents may not be able to rationalize. Even in the West this is true. Ask someone: Would you be okay to eat a sandwich while sitting on the toilet? Most people will immediately answer no. But explaining *why* is trickier. It is not morally wrong to do so. Nor is it unhygienic (hands are not touching anything). Yet instinctively we feel this action is off limits. I suspect we would even enforce these limits upon others (especially children!). Boundaries can exist apart from ability to rationalize.

Nor does the text answer another question that inevitably arises for readers: Why is the term of impurity following the birth of a girl twice that for a boy? A definitive answer has not been forthcoming. However, a common kneejerk

---

1. See also my more extended discussion in *'You Shall Be Clean'*, chapter 1.

reaction, that this demonstrates the devaluing of women in Israelite culture, is almost certainly incorrect. The only stated difference between male and female babies is that boys are circumcised on the eighth day (12:3). Hence, one possible rationale is that impurity following a boy's birth is *halved* (by circumcision) rather than being *doubled* for girls. Perhaps the most convincing argument for the discrepancy is the one recently proposed by Matthew Thiessen.[2] Based on a survey of ancient medical texts, Thiessen notes that female fetuses were believed to develop more slowly than their male counterparts and, accordingly, produced a greater quantity of impurity.

Irrespective of the underlying rationale, Leviticus 12:4 highlights the danger that ritual impurity poses (cf. 15:31). It is not the (unavoidable) impurity itself that threatens. Rather, it is potential contact with the holy while in an impure state. The requisite warning is sounded: 'She shall not touch anything holy, nor come into the sanctuary, until the days of her purifying are completed' (ESV). This instruction is for the mother's protection.

Leviticus 12:6-8 turns to remedial procedures. When the days of a woman's purification are over (either 40 or 80 days), she is to make two offerings at the tent of meeting: (1) an ascension offering of a year-old lamb and (2) a young pigeon or dove for a purification offering (12:6). The option of presenting two birds allowed poor people to make the required offerings (12:8; cf. Luke 2:22-24). Although the sequence is not specified, the purification offering likely came first (cf. 8:14-21; 9:8-14, 15-17). Referring to this as

---

2. Matthew Thiessen, 'The Legislation of Leviticus 12 in Light of Ancient Embryology,' *VT* 68 (2018), 297-319.

a 'sin offering' (so NIV, ESV, HCSB) is potentially confusing as no wrongdoing is in view (see discussion at 4:2b-35). Instead, 'purification offerings' *cleansed* the offerer from either sin or impurity. The latter function is in view here. The ascension offering was a concrete expression of homage to Yahweh (see discussion at 1:1-17). Thus, together, these offerings accomplish atonement (12:7) – that is, restoration with God. The barrier separating the woman from God is overcome: she is now pure and can approach the tabernacle (12:7; cf. 12:4). Moreover, her ascension offering indicates continuing devotion to Yahweh. The sacrifices are *restorative* in nature.

Impurity related to *tsara'at* (13:1–14:57)

The large block of material in Leviticus 13–14 is united by a singular concern: impurity arising from *tsara'at* (cf. the conclusion in 14:57, 'This is the *torah* of *tsara'at*'; my translation). Paying heed to the Hebrew is helpful, as English versions make it appear that different topics are being considered. For instance, the NIV variously translates *tsara'at* as 'defiling skin disease' (13:2), 'spreading mold' (14:34), and 'defiling molds' (14:55). Even the consistent rendering in the ESV ('leprous disease') or NASB ('leprosy') is problematic: In what sense can a woollen jumper or house contract 'leprosy' (13:47; 14:34)? Moreover, historical data suggest that leprosy (i.e., Hanson's Disease) did not exist in ancient Israel. Yet, when it comes to identifying *tsara'at*, certainty proves elusive. We simply do not know enough about the Ancient Near East to tie down a definitive meaning. It is quite likely that *tsara'at* is an umbrella term which includes several related phenomena. In Leviticus 13–14, *tsara'at* can afflict persons, fabrics, and buildings.

Nevertheless, commonalities are evident: *tsara'at* affects surfaces, penetrates below the surface, has ability to spread, and makes the afflicted person or object ritually impure.

As with Leviticus 12, the burden of Leviticus 13–14 is twofold: diagnosis and remedy. Leviticus 13:1-46 focuses on correctly identifying *tsara'at*-affected people. Leviticus 13:2 reveals why the following details are needed: a swelling, rash, or spot has 'become on the skin of his flesh like a mark of *tsara'at*' (my translation). A benign disease is thus suspected of having developed into something more sinister. The procedure involves priestly examination. Note the passive verb: 'he is to *be brought* to Aaron the priest or to one of his sons' (13:2 HCSB [emphasis added]). There is a communal responsibility at work, perhaps even against the wishes of the individual (who may prefer to hide his or her situation).

Leviticus 13:3-8 details how examination is to proceed. If the disease has turned the hair white and has penetrated below the skin, it is immediately deemed *tsara'at* and the person is declared impure (13:3). If not, then one or two seven-day periods of isolation followed by reexamination are enacted to determine if the disease is spreading (13:4-6). If the original sore fades the person is declared pure (13:6). However, if the disease reappears, the person must be examined again. If spread is established, it is *tsara'at* and the person becomes impure (13:7-8).

The remainder of the chapter outlines variant cases (with subsections marked by 'When' [*ki*]):

1. When a mark of *tsara'at* appears on a person (13:9-17)

2. When a boil appears (13:18-23)

3. When there is a burn (13:24-28)

4. When a person has a mark on their head (13:29-37)

5. When a person has white spots (13:38-39)

6. When a man has hair loss (13:40-44)

Each subsection contains a set of diagnostic criteria to determine whether *tsara'at* is present, utilizing isolation periods if needed.

The overriding concern is the capacity of *tsara'at* to penetrate the skin and expose the underlying 'flesh'. This explains 13:13, which seems so counter intuitive: a person *entirely covered* by skin disease is declared pure. Why? Because there is *no exposed flesh*. This is insightful: it is not the presence of disease that makes one impure; indeed, those declared 'pure' with respect to *tsara'at* (13:6, etc.) still have a skin infection of some description. Rather, it is the exposure of flesh that is problematic: 'whenever raw flesh appears on him, he will be unclean' (13:14 HCSB). Leviticus 13:15 clarifies the problem: 'The raw flesh [literally 'living flesh'] is unclean.' And, for however long *tsara'at* exposes 'living flesh', the person must live alone outside the camp, dressed as a mourner and crying out, 'Impure! Impure!' (13:45-46, my translation; cf. Num. 5:2). As in Leviticus 12, separating the impure from the holy is paramount (12:4; cf. 10:10; 11:47; 15:31).

Although the period of impurity for *tsara'at*-affected people is indefinite, Leviticus 14:1-32 recognizes the potential for cleansing and restoration. It is important to note that the procedure is not designed to heal an afflicted person, but to purify an *already healed* person so they might retake their place among the people.

The reinstatement procedure is complex (attesting to the severity of the defilement). First, healing must be verified (14:3). The subsequent purification ritual involving two birds can seem bizarre, but it makes sense within the conceptual world of Leviticus. Impurity is a quasi-physical substance that must be removed. The ritual items listed in 14:4 were understood in the ancient world to have absorbing qualities. The process thus absorbs impurity from the afflicted person by means of sprinkling with cedar wood, scarlet yarn, hyssop, and blood, and transfers the impurity to the second, living bird (14:5-7). The living bird's release carries the impurity away from the camp. Use of wordplay reveals the connections: the person made impure through exposure of 'living flesh' is purified using 'living water' (NIV 'fresh water') and removal of defilement by a 'living bird' (13:14; 14:5-6; my translation).

It is crucial to remember, here and elsewhere in Leviticus, that ritual is not constrained by cause and effect. To ask *how* scarlet thread could possibly remove impurity is as unanswerable as wondering how the donning of a gown and odd-looking hat can declare a person 'graduated'. The effectiveness of ritual goes beyond the mere sum of its parts. The proof of the pudding is in the eating. If the formerly *tsara'at*-affected person approaches holy space and is not struck dead, then the ritual is proven effective (even if one cannot rationalize how the various steps accomplish this).

After the bird ceremony, washing and shaving follow (14:8). Then, having spent seven days outside his or her tent, the person must wash and shave again (14:8-9). A seven-day preparation period often accompanies a significant transition of status (as with consecration of priests [8:33–9:1] or purification of people with major impurity [15:28-29]).

Climactically, 'on the eighth day' (14:10; cf. 9:1; 12:3), a final ritual procedure completes the person's purification.

The ceremony takes place 'before the LORD' at the entrance of the tent (14:11), reminding readers that required restoration is primarily with Yahweh. The ritual is also public – the entire community must know that the person has been purified (cf. Matt. 8:4, 'go, show yourself to the priest … as a testimony'). A sequence of three sacrifices is utilized. The first is a reparation offering (see discussion at Lev. 5:14–6:7), albeit with unique features. Blood from the slaughtered lamb is applied to the person's right-hand-side ear, thumb, and big toe (14:14; contrast 7:2). He or she is also anointed with oil (14:17-18). This should recall the similar rite of passage enacted for Aaron and sons (8:23-24, 30). The ceremony publicly changes the status of the beneficiary – in this case, from impure to pure. Purification and ascension offerings follow (see also discussion at Lev. 1:1-17; 4:1–5:13) and 14:20 summarizes the results: atonement is secured, reuniting the formerly separated person to Yahweh, and he or she is declared 'pure' (14:23-32 makes the same results achievable for the poor). The transition is completed: banishment has ended (cf. 13:46) and life among God's people is reenabled.

In addition to persons, fabrics (13:47-59) and buildings (14:33-53) can be affected by *tsara'at*.[3] The same concerns and remedial measures are evident: cases of suspected *tsara'at* must be examined by a priest (13:49; 14:35-37, 44, 48); seven-day isolation periods are utilized (13:50, 54; 14:38); diagnosing surface penetration and spread is important (13:51; 14:37, 44); objects declared impure are removed (including by destruction) (13:52, 55-57; 14:39-41, 45); when *already* 'healed' from *tsara'at*, fabrics and houses can be purified and reused (13:58; 14:49-52); the prescribed

---

3. Note that discussion of buildings looks forward to when the Israelites have entered the land (14:34).

ritual accomplishes atonement and cleansing (13:58; 14:53). Juxtaposed with the purification of persons, 13:47-59 and 14:33-53 are another indicator that Leviticus is concerned with more than only human restoration.

Leviticus 14:34 adds an important detail: 'When you enter the land … and *I* put a mark of *tsara'at* in a house' (my translation, emphasis added). Elsewhere in the Old Testament, *tsara'at* is frequently connected with judgment (Num. 12:10; 2 Sam. 3:29; 2 Kings 5:27; 15:5; 2 Chron. 26:19). Thus, Leviticus 14:34 hints at punitive action. Moreover, that a *tsara'at*-affected person must offer a reparation offering (14:12) suggests underlying wrongdoing (see discussion at 5:14–6:7). Either way, *tsara'at* affliction could be directly caused by Yahweh's agency. Perhaps *tsara'at*-affected persons and objects functioned as 'sign acts', visibly embodying the separation that impurity occasions. Seeing this would be a powerful motivator, either to avoid defilement or enact appropriate cleansing.

Impurity related to genital discharges (15:1-33)

Leviticus 15 details defilement related to genital discharges. The case is stated in 15:2b-3: a genital discharge is impure and makes a person impure. However, not all discharges are equally defiling, a point emphasized by the chiastic arrangement of the material (see 'Context and structure'). There is a spectrum of impurity from minor to major (see *Table 8.1* below).

Type of discharge	Degree of impurity	Direct trans-mission?	Indirect trans-mission?	Remedial measures
Abnormal male discharge (15:2b-15)	Major	?	Yes (people and objects)	Seven-day wait, washing, sacrifice

Type of discharge	Degree of impurity	Direct transmission?	Indirect transmission?	Remedial measures
Abnormal female discharge (15:25-30)	Major	?	Yes (people and objects)	Seven-day wait, washing, sacrifice
Normal menstruation (15:19-24)	Major	Yes (people)	Yes (people and objects)	Seven-day wait
Normal emission of semen (15:16-17)	Minor	Yes (people and objects)	No	Washing and waiting until evening
Sexual intercourse (15:18)	Minor	Yes (people)	No	Washing and waiting until evening

Table 8.1

Remedial measures incorporate a range of methods depending on the severity of impurity. Again, it should be emphasized that impurity and sin are different categories. It is not wrong to menstruate or have sexual intercourse. Indeed, sex and childbirth are part of God's good intention for humanity (cf. Gen. 1:28; 3:16). It is also worth noting that the legislation applies equally to men *and* women (this is more than simply a patriarchal aversion to menstruation, as some argue).[4] Regarding *why* genital discharges defile, the text does not say. However, one result of the legislation is to force a divide between sex and cult. Pagan fertility practices would

---

4. The text also presumes agency on the part of the woman. She would know when her period began and ended and hence bore the responsibility to protect others and to follow appropriate cleansing procedures.

find no analogy in Israel's worship system. There is also a correlation formed between major impurity and abnormality which, when added to the connection between defilement and death in Leviticus 11, suggests that increasing impurity was understood as a movement away from Yahweh.

Transmission is also problematic. Defilement from genital discharges could be conveyed to objects or other persons, either directly or indirectly. Once more, the severity of impurity is the key factor (see *Table 8.1*). Semen defiles by direct contact: the man himself (15:16), articles of clothing (15:17), or a woman engaged in intercourse (15:18). Likewise, menstrual blood defiles a person by direct contact (15:24), as does touching the menstruant (15:19-20).[5] In addition, *indirect* transmission is possible: touching a bed or seat made impure by a menstruating woman conveys impurity (15:21-23). Defilement arising from abnormal male (15:2b-15) and female (15:25-30) discharges exhibits the same potential for direct and indirect transmission. In all cases of indirect transmission, the defilement is of a lesser potency ('unclean till evening' 15:5, 6, 7, etc.) and cannot be passed on to a third party.

The summary statement in 15:31 reminds readers of the seriousness of the instructions (cf. 12:4): 'keep the Israelites separate from things that make them unclean, so they will not die in their uncleanness for defiling my dwelling place, which is among them.' Moreover, the specter of transmission adds a *social* dimension to the need for correct separation. Heeding Yahweh's instructions concerning impurity is not just about self-preservation; it is an act of love towards one's neighbor to prevent their endangerment.

---

5. It is important to note that a woman having her period is not thereby totally excluded from society. Touching her is not prohibited; one just needed to be mindful of the impurity transmitted.

One of the intriguing aspects of Leviticus 12–15 is the specificity of the instructions. Not all blood loss defiles, only that of childbirth. Not all disease defiles, only infestations which penetrate the surface and expose the flesh. Not all bodily discharges defile, only those issuing from genitals. Nothing is said about cut fingers, conjunctivitis, or runny noses. It thus becomes evident that the preeminent concern in Leviticus 12–15 is not public health but stemming the spread of ritual impurity.

What is the rationale for the sources of impurity listed? It is difficult to know. In many other cultures (ancient and modern), similar causes of defilement are commonplace. However, considering the creation theology that pervades Leviticus, resonances with Genesis 1–3 are worth contemplating (even if only tentatively). As noted in Leviticus 11, the wording of 11:42 ('moves on its belly') is uniquely shared with Genesis 3:14 (the curse on the serpent) and evokes the Garden scene for readers. Leviticus 12, beginning with 'A woman' (12:2b, my translation) and treating childbirth potentially continues recall of the Garden scene by alluding to Genesis 3:16. Leviticus 13, beginning with 'A man' (13:2b) completes the sequence (cf. Gen. 3:17). It is probably unwise to hang too much on this but alluding to the judgment scene in Genesis 3 may add force to the warning that impurity results in banishment from Yahweh's presence and must be taken seriously (11:47; 12:4; 15:31; cf. Gen. 3:24).

From text to message

This is a large body of text (157 verses!) which addresses a topic that many Christians have not spent any time thinking about (and can see no relevance for). The difficulties are self-evident. Nevertheless, Leviticus 12–15 (along with Lev. 11) is the place where the important biblical theme of purity/impurity is most systematically addressed. The rest of the canon will simply presume the categories enunciated here and utilize them in a range of ways. Numbers will supplement the material (e.g., Num. 19), Ezekiel will subvert it for rhetorical ends (e.g., Ezek. 9:7; 20:26), and the Gospels will use it to explain the significance of Jesus (e.g., Matt. 8:2-4; Mark 5). From Genesis to Revelation, purity/impurity is a common and theologically vital theme. For that reason alone, grappling with these chapters is essential.

Getting the message clear: the theme

Leviticus 12–15 articulates divine guidance concerning boundaries between pure and impure in relation to childbirth, *tsara'at* infection, and genital discharges. The text is diagnostic rather than preventative, but also presents remedial measures to remove impurity, allowing Israel to dwell safely with a holy God.

Getting the message clear: the aim

This passage functions as a call for Israel to take heed and to learn diligently about the things that make them impure, not because such things can necessarily be avoided, but because they endanger and bar access to sacred places. Correctly separating between pure and impure is essential. Thus, the text contributes to the picture of Yahweh presented by Leviticus. He is a holy God who must not be approached carelessly, but who nevertheless desires relational closeness with His people. Accordingly, Leviticus 12–15 enables accurate diagnosis and prescribes purification rites so that the people might not only recognize their susceptibility to impurity but might be encouraged to seek the cleansing God has provided.

A way in

COVID-19. At the beginning of 2020, that phrase meant nothing to most people. Now, due to the ensuing pandemic, COVID-19 is engrained in the memories of people across the world. Suddenly, we have all become very aware of disease and disease control measures (I am writing this chapter at home under lockdown conditions). While disease is *not* synonymous with the biblical concept of impurity, it does provide a valuable analogy that can help us appreciate the purpose of Leviticus 12–15. Like a virus, ritual impurity can affect one's life uninvited, without warning, and beyond one's control. Again, like a virus, potential transmission to others becomes an issue, especially with serious forms of defilement. Ultimately, impurity endangers. The result of an impure person transgressing sacred bounds could well be death. Thus, the primary danger in Leviticus 12–15 is theological and social, not biological. These instructions have one central purpose: to protect Israel from Yahweh's holiness.

Ideas for application

- It is impossible for people to make themselves fit for God. Like Israel, we are fully reliant on the procedures and personnel (think: Jesus) God provides for cleansing.

- Ezekiel 36:25-27 looked forward to the renewal of God's people. That renewal is pictured as cleansing from impurities and, in context, is intimately connected with the Holy Spirit ('my Spirit') that God would put in His people.

- Being pure before God is vitally important if we are to survive an encounter with the holy. People cannot simply co-exist with God 'just as I am'. Thus, at the heart of biblical faith, is the need for radical transformation and purification of our inner and outer selves (e.g., 1 Cor. 15:50-53; 2 Cor. 3:18; Eph. 4:22-24). Hebrews 10:22, drawing heavily on Leviticus, makes the point explicitly: 'Let us draw near to God with a sincere heart and with the full assurance that faith brings, having our *hearts sprinkled to cleanse us* from a guilty conscience and having our *bodies washed with pure water*' (emphasis added).

- In addition to the other metaphors drawn upon to explain the significance of Jesus's work (redemption, reconciliation, propitiation, victory, etc.), the New Testament emphasizes that Jesus is the one who purifies people and therefore makes them admissible to God's presence (Mark 1:40-42; John 13:10; 15:3; Heb. 9:13-14; Rev. 19:7-8). Even when those with transmittable (i.e., major) impurity touched Jesus, it was their defilement that was overcome (Mark 5:25-29, 41).

- Paul adopts the language of ritual purification to urge Christians to become fit for God's service: 'Therefore, if anyone cleanses himself from what is dishonorable, he will be a vessel for honorable use, set apart as holy, useful to the master of the house, ready for every good work' (2 Tim. 2:21 ESV).

- Leviticus 12–15, with its description of ritual washing to remove impurity, becomes the basis for the metaphor of washing away sin employed in Psalm 51:7 and Zechariah 13:1.

Suggestions for preaching

Sermon 1

- **Impurity and childbirth (Lev. 12).** Leviticus 12 describes the involuntary impurity that affected post-partum women in Israel. Becoming impure in this manner did not signify moral fault but did mean that the affected woman needed to stay away from sacred places like the tabernacle. Even though post-partum impurity was long-lasting, it was removable once the decreed time had elapsed. An impure woman could become pure again.

- **Impurity and *tsara'at* (Lev. 13–14).** *Tsara'at* could afflict people, fabrics, and buildings. Leviticus 13–14 provides diagnostic criteria to distinguish cases of *tsara'at* infection. When confirmed, infected people and objects became ritually impure. Such impurity was serious and resulted in either banishment (for people) or destruction (for objects). In addition, Leviticus 13–14 opens the possibility that *tsara'at* and its resulting impurity could be divinely apportioned, thus serving as both warning and deterrent. God's people must learn to separate pure from impure and to have due regard for the holy.

- **Impurity and discharges (Lev. 15).** Leviticus 15 considers the defilement pertaining to both normal and abnormal genital discharges. The degree of severity increases for abnormal discharges, requiring, in turn, more complex remedial measures. This chapter also emphasizes the potential to transmit impurity to persons and objects. Love for one's neighbor should therefore provoke great care with respect to Yahweh's instructions, lest that neighbor be endangered by unknown defilement. Love for God is displayed by submitting to the purification rites available which would make proximity with God possible once more.

- **Impurity and Christ.** When the woman in Mark 5:25-29 reached out to touch Jesus, a person with major impurity encountered the holy. Yet, instead of divine fire, she experienced healing, cleansing, and an end to twelve years of suffering. When Jesus touched the hand of a dead girl, He was not defiled but instead raised her to life (Mark 5:41). With these vignettes, Mark portrays the radical nature of Jesus's ministry: to reach out to the impure, the rejected, and the marginal to bring about their transformation and make them fit for the kingdom of God by overcoming sources of impurity.

Sermon 2

An alternate approach for preaching these chapters in a single sermon would be to work through one section in detail and then use this to understand the remainder. For example, Leviticus 12 is short (only eight verses) and easier for a congregation to get its head around, and yet raises the key issues concerning ritual impurity: its unavoidability, non-sin nature, spectrum of severity, possible countermeasures, and impact on approaching the sacred. Clarifying these matters gives people the necessary insight to better understand 13–15 (which can be covered in less detail). A three-part sermon (with points responding to frequently asked questions) is one possibility:

1. Is the Old Testament biased against women (Lev. 12)?
2. What do skin disease and bodily fluids have to do with anything (Lev. 13–15)?
3. How is Leviticus 12–15 possibly relevant to Christian faith and practice?

Sermon 3

For preachers with more time, or for those whose context would benefit from a more sustained exploration of impurity (e.g., for churches which either have or seek to reach people from Muslim or Hindu backgrounds), Leviticus 12–15 can be preached as three separate sermons. Chapters 12 and 15 are self-contained units and can be preached as such. Leviticus 13–14, connected by a focus on *tsara'at*, are chapters best taken together. Sermon outlines could follow the breakdown listed under 'Context and structure' above. Preaching Leviticus 12–15 as three talks would expand the overall series to twenty sermons in total, making it still possible to complete over two school terms.

Suggestions for teaching

Questions to help understand the passage

1. Explain the relationship between 10:10 and Leviticus 12–15.

2. In what ways is Leviticus 12–15 similar and dissimilar to chapter 11?

3. The Hebrew word translated as 'unclean' in many English versions can also be rendered 'impure'. Which do you think is better? Why?

4. Based on Leviticus 12–15, what are the consequences (personal, familial, social, theological) of becoming impure?

5. Construct a chart that conveys the spectrum of severity of impurity. What remedial processes were available?

6. Define the word 'ritual'? How do rituals work (you may want to think about a wedding, graduation, or church practice)?

7. What is the relationship between impurity and sin?

8. Why do you think such a large section of Leviticus is devoted to the topic of purity/impurity?

9. Is Leviticus 12–15 an expression of legalism or grace?

Questions to help apply the passage

1. What part of Leviticus 12–15 did you find strangest when you read it first? How would you now explain it to someone else?

2. Leviticus describes a God who is concerned about the intimate details of His people's lives – from pantry (Lev. 11) to boudoir (Lev. 15). How does that make you feel?

3. If you were an Israelite, do you think that becoming impure would be something to be concerned about? What understanding of people and God is influencing your answer?

4. Is 15:31 outdated or still relevant? Why do you think so?

5. The New Testament declares that Jesus makes people ritually pure. What does this contribute to your understanding of His person and work?

6. When John sees the New Jerusalem where God will dwell with people forever, he comments, 'Nothing impure will ever enter it' (Rev. 21:27). How should this picture of the end influence your life now?

7. Leviticus 12–15 testifies to the inner and outer transformation that should characterize those in relationship with God. What evidence of transformation is there in your life? Are there areas due for a 'makeover'?

9.

The Day of Atonement
(Leviticus 16)

Introduction

Human sin and impurity may well be unavoidable, yet these things nevertheless separate people from God. Is there any hope that relationship with God can survive long-term? Leviticus 16 says yes. Positioned at the heart of the book, this passage is a profound statement of divine grace and comes as amazingly good news.

Leviticus 16 presents the Day of Atonement (or Yom Kippur; cf. 23:27) as the means of dealing with the effects of sin and impurity left unaddressed by regular means. The explicit recall of Nadab and Abihu in 16:1 returns readers to Leviticus 10 and the shocking incineration that marred the first day of priestly activity. The brothers' fault was to do 'what [Yahweh] had *not* commanded' (10:1, my translation, emphasis added). The newly-consecrated tabernacle (cf. Lev. 8:10-11, 15) was thus defiled by both corpse contamination and rebellion, jeopardizing the whole cultic endeavor (see discussion at 10:1-20). Leviticus forestalls dealing with the problem until chapter 16. That delay serves two literary functions. First, it builds tension for readers. And, second, it creates space to address the topic of ritual purity/impurity (Lev. 11–15). However, while Leviticus 11–15 helpfully clarifies boundaries between pure and impure (cf. 10:10), a new problem emerges. It is difficult to read chapters 11–15 and not conclude that impurity is inescapable. Additionally, the potential for secondary transmission by people and objects raises the specter of *unknown* impurity. When 15:31 declares that impurity defiles Yahweh's dwelling place and thereby risks death, the rhetorical trap is sprung: *anyone* in Israel could end up like Nadab and Abihu. The ritual in Leviticus 16 exists to prevent that eventuality.

The central placement of this passage in Leviticus reflects the singular importance of Yom Kippur within the life of Israel. Here, the theme of increasing access to Yahweh's presence reaches a new high point. In contrast to the unique (and therefore unrepeatable) entry by Moses and Aaron in 9:23, Leviticus 16 makes regular, recurring admittance possible. The significance of the chapter is further accentuated by a wealth of literary devices. Instead of the normal divine speech formula ('The LORD said to Moses'), there is a *double* reference to Yahweh speaking (16:1-2a). Many key words and phrases occur in multiples of seven.[1] Other words are unique to this chapter.[2] All of these literary markers drive home the exceptional significance of the Day of Atonement.

---

1. For instance, '[most] holy place' (x7), 'clothes' (x7), 'atonement cover' (x7), 'sin' (x14), and 'goat' (x14).

2. Examples include the use of *haqqodesh* (literally 'the holy') to refer to the most holy place; the plural 'impurities' in 16:16; and the word *'aza'zel* (16:8, 10, 26; see NIV fn.).

Listening to the text

Context and structure

Leviticus 16 is a standalone unit marked out by the (double) speech formula in 16:1-2 (cf. 17:1). The chapter draws upon prior material and also anticipates the content of Leviticus 17–27. Looking back, Leviticus 16 assumes the sacrificial procedures and priestly operations of chapters 1–9. It also makes an explicit link to the death of Nadab and Abihu in 10:1-2 (16:1). Furthermore, by outlining a procedure for dealing with the impurities (plural) of Israel (16:16), the Day of Atonement continues the focus of Leviticus 11–15. At the same time, Leviticus 16 also deals with *moral* faults, anticipating chapters 18–20, and is connected to the annual calendar outlined in Leviticus 23. There are also strong verbal connections to the book's only other narrative in 24:10-23. Unsurprisingly, therefore, many conclude that Leviticus 16 forms the centerpiece of the book (see 'Getting Our Bearings in Leviticus').[3]

The main sections of the chapter are as follows:

> Narrative introduction (16:1-2a)
>
> Ritual overview (16:2b-10)
>
> Elaboration of key elements (16:11-28)
>
> Prescriptions for perpetual observance (16:29-34a)
>
> Narrative conclusion (16:34b)

The chapter also displays the palistrophic patterning that is so common in Leviticus. The arrangement further

---

3. Rolf Rendtorff even argues that Lev. 16 is the central point of the entire Pentateuch ('Leviticus 16 als Mitte der Tora,' *Biblical Interpretation* 11 [2003], 252-58).

emphasizes the unique purification offerings and entry to the most holy place at the center of the ritual.

> Narrative introduction (16:1-2a)
>> Timing (not at any time) (16:2b)
>>> Purification and ascension offerings (16:3)
>>>> Washing and dressing (16:4)
>>>>> Purification offerings for Aaron and people (16:5-22)[4]
>>>> Washing and dressing (16:23-24a)
>>> Ascension and purification offerings (16:24b-28)
>> Timing (once a year on the tenth day of the seventh month) (16:29-34a)
> Narrative conclusion (16:34b)

Working through the text

Narrative introduction (16:1-2a)

The unusual double introduction to divine speech has been noted above. This device marks the following material as especially noteworthy. Remembering Aaron's two sons who died when approaching Yahweh not only establishes the narrative context and exigency for the Day of Atonement but also adds pathos and urgency. As always, Leviticus is written to have an *affective* impact on readers. (For a schematic layout of the tabernacle see *Figure 3.1*.)

---

4. The so-called 'scapegoat' is part of the people's purification offering (see 16:5 where the two goats comprise *one* purification offering).

Ritual overview (16:2b-10)

The first main section of Leviticus 16 gives a bird's-eye view of the ceremony. The instructions, addressed to Aaron, begin with a warning. Aaron is forbidden to enter the inner sanctum, the holy of holies, 'at any time' (16:2 ESV).[5] The stated reason is that Yahweh appears there in a cloud (cf. Exod. 24:15-16). As with Nadab and Abihu, the consequences for inappropriate entry are stark: 'he will die' (16:2).

However, the ban is not total. Entry is invited, but Yahweh dictates the when and the how. Hence, 16:3 reads, 'This is how Aaron is to enter the Most Holy Place.' The necessary preparations involve exceptional elements. While the various sacrificial animals are as expected (16:3, 5; cf. 1:10; 4:3, 22-23), Aaron's attire is not.[6] Instead of his ornate high priestly vestments (cf. Exod. 28), Aaron, having bathed in water, is to dress in a plain linen garment (16:4). Plain clothing is fitting for the somber tone of the day (cf. 16:29) with its confession of sin (16:21). Also, linen garments are elsewhere associated with the divine realm (e.g., Ezek. 9:2-3; Dan. 5:5; 7:6-7; cf. Rev. 15:6) and are thus apt for Aaron to wear as he enters Yahweh's presence.

The remaining verses of the section provide a sketch of how the sacrificial animals will function. The bull for Aaron is unexceptional (16:6; cf. 4:3). However, the purification offering for the people is special. *Two goats*

---

5. Leviticus 16 consistently (and uniquely) uses *haqqodesh* ('the holy [place]') to refer to the innermost section of the tent where the ark was housed.

6. The sacrifice of a goat for the community rather than a bull (cf. 4:14) follows more closely the offering in 9:3 (Jacob Milgrom, *Leviticus 1–16: A New Translation with Introduction and Commentary* [AB 3; New York: The Anchor Bible, 1991], 1018).

constitute a singular purification sacrifice on the Day of Atonement. Lots are cast to determine which goat is to be slaughtered in the normal manner and which will be sent alive into the wilderness (16:8-10).[7]

Elaboration of key elements (16:11-28)

The bulk of Leviticus 16 revisits the sacrificial procedure skimmed in 16:6-10 in order to add detail. Aaron's purification offering is considered first (16:11-14). The procedure presumes many of the details outlined in 4:1–5:13 and does not repeat them here. Instead, the focus is on the unique-to-this-day use of blood. Having slaughtered the bull, Aaron must enter behind the curtain (i.e., into the holy of holies) with incense and censer in order to create a cloud of smoke (16:12-13). This smoke serves two purposes. First, it acts to conceal the ark and create a protective barrier between Yahweh's presence and Aaron 'so that he will not die' (16:13). (Note again how the threat of death pervades the passage. This is dangerous business. Cf. 16:1-2.) Second, the incense cloud evokes the cloud which conveys Yahweh's presence in

---

7. In 16:8 lots are cast for two goats, 'one lot for Yahweh and one lot for *'aza'zel'* (my translation). Who or what *'aza'zel* is, however, remains debated. There are three main options: (1) *'aza'zel* is the name of a demon (cf. 1 Enoch 8:1; 9:6); (2) *'aza'zel* is related to the Arabic *azazu* ('rough ground'), thus meaning 'rocky place' or 'precipice' (cf. 'cut-off land', 16:22 [my translation]); or (3) *'aza'zel* is derived from *'ez* ('goat') and *'azal* ('to go away'), hence 'go-away goat' or '(e)scape-goat'. Although each possibility has merit and conveys the idea of banishment from the camp to the wilderness, I think the third option has the least difficulties in context. Accordingly, I use 'scapegoat' throughout. Interested readers can consult the discussion in Wenham, *Leviticus*, 233-35; Sklar, *Leviticus*, 209-10; Milgrom, *Leviticus 1–16*, 1020-21.

the tabernacle (16:2) as it did on Mount Sinai (Exod. 19:9; 24:15-18). Next, Aaron is to take some of the bull's blood *into the most holy place*, the only occasion on which this happens, and sprinkle it seven times before the ark (16:14; contrast 4:5-7). In the Old Testament (and other Semitic cultures), seven is the number of perfection or completion. Sevenfold sprinkling accomplishes *complete* cleansing.

The next stage of the ceremony involves the purification offering for the people (16:15-17). Once more, the blood of the slaughtered animal (this time a goat) is carried into the most holy place and sprinkled seven times before the ark (16:14). Although less clear, 16:16 implies that Aaron, likewise, sprinkles blood in the holy place ('He is to do the same for the tent of meeting'; cf. Exod. 30:10). It is this sprinkling of blood, not the death of the animals, which makes atonement for Aaron, his household, and the whole community, for their impurity and rebellion (16:16-17). Strikingly, the blood of bull and goat is also said to atone for the most holy place itself (16:16). Here, we see that the sins and impurity of Israel defiled not only themselves, but the tabernacle too (cf. 15:31).

The same is true for the altar in the courtyard. Thus, the next stage of the ceremony addresses this contamination (16:18-19). Blood is smeared on the altar's horns and sprinkled upon it seven times to make atonement (16:18). In this way, the altar is purified and re-consecrated for future use (16:19). Jacob Milgrom calculates that on the Day of Atonement blood is sprinkled or smeared a total of forty-nine times (i.e., seven times seven), a literary device that signals comprehensive atonement.[8]

---

8. Milgrom, *Leviticus 1–16*, 1039.

What becomes clear from 16:16-19 is that both people and sancta (i.e., 'holy things') must be restored to God. The problem is the cumulative impact of Israel's 'impurities and rebellions' (both plural) (16:16, my translation). A raft of ritual and moral faults threatens the ongoing viability of the tabernacle. Whereas known impurity could be addressed by the means outlined in chapters 11–15, *unknown* defilement could not (especially major impurities which required active remedial procedures). Moreover, while unwitting sins or deliberate acts of a minor (i.e., person-to-person) nature could be remedied by the purification and reparation offerings (see discussion at Lev. 4:1–6:7), there was no cultic provision for 'high-handed' acts of rebellion (cf. 1 Sam. 3:13-14). Indeed, in cases like Nadab and Abihu, the culprits may already be dead or otherwise 'cut off' and therefore unable to make confession, restitution, or purification. It is this 'remainder' that the Day of Atonement is designed to deal with. The result is comprehensive: full atonement for people, tabernacle, and altar. Yom Kippur resets the stage.

Yet, the ritual has yet another unique element. Leviticus 16:20-22 expands on the role played by the 'scapegoat'. Three times this goat is referred to as the 'living goat' (16:10, 20, 21), emphasizing that it is not sacrificed as the first goat was, even though both constitute one purification offering (16:5). Instead, Aaron is to lay *both* hands on its head (16:21). In contrast to the *one*-handed pressing rite described elsewhere (1:4; 3:2, 8, etc.), the laying on of two hands functions as an act of transferal. Accordingly, Aaron is to 'confess over it all the wickedness and rebellion of the Israelites – all their sins – and *put them on* the goat's head' (16:21 [emphasis added]). This goat is then dispatched on a one-way journey to the wilderness (16:22).

What is the point of the second goat? Many commentators view the goat as a removal device (for sin or impurity or both). Similarities with the bird rite in Leviticus 14 are noted. There, one bird is killed while the other, living bird is released 'in the open fields' to remove impurity from the camp (14:7). However, parallels with the Leviticus 14 rite are not exact: (1) there is no mention of hyssop, cedar wood, or scarlet yarn (all understood to have absorbing qualities) (cf. 14:4); (2) the blood from the slaughtered goat does not contact the living goat (cf. 14:6); (3) the focus in 16:21 is *sins*, not ritual impurity (cf. 14:7); and (4) the bird rite is the initial step in a three-part ceremony (cf. 14:3-20), whereas the scapegoat ritual arguably constitutes the climax.[9]

Another, and I think better, way to view the second goat is to see it as substitutionally bearing the banishment Israel deserved.[10] Here, it is important to remember that, in biblical thinking, there is a distinction between sin and sin's consequences. Thus, one can be forgiven for sin but still suffer its aftereffects. Numbers 14 illustrates the case clearly. Following yet another bout of rebellion leading to threatened destruction, Moses intercedes on behalf of the people (Num. 14:10-19). Yahweh responds, 'I have forgiven them' (Num. 14:20). However, in the following verses Yahweh proceeds to inform Moses that that entire generation would die in the wilderness *because of what they had done* (Num. 14:21-23). Forgiveness does not cancel the consequences of sin.

---

9. Note in 16:23 that, immediately following the exit of the 'scapegoat', Aaron washes and changes clothes before performing the remaining sacrificial procedures in 16:24b-25. This creates a frame around the central (and unique) ritual actions of the day (cf. 16:4).

10. I provide a longer defense of this reading in '*I Will Walk Among You*', 168-72.

What might those consequences be? For serious sins like the rebellion explicitly in focus in Leviticus 16 (16:16, 21), the penalty is death (cf. Nadab and Abihu in 16:1) or being 'cut off' (e.g., Lev. 17:4; 20:2-3).[11] Such removal from the divine presence is the nation's anticipated fate, even following atonement. In fact, banishment would constitute a mitigated punishment in view of the more immediate (and severe) fate enacted upon Nadab and Abihu. However, Leviticus 16 makes provision for a goat, bearing the sin of the people (16:10) and acting as their substitute, to be banished to a 'cut-off land' (16:22, my translation; NIV 'remote place') in their stead. Therefore, the 'scapegoat' performs an essential and complementary function within the wider ritual. Together, the two goats secure atonement for sin *and* removal of sin's consequences. In this way, high-handed sins would not be held against the nation even if individuals (like Nadab and Abihu) acted defiantly.

Leviticus 16:23 marks a major transition in the ritual. Aaron takes off his linen garments, washes, and puts on his regular high priestly attire (16:23-24; cf. 8:7-9). Washing *after* a ceremony is highly unusual. At a literary level, *post*-requisite washing and dressing forms a frame with their *pre*-requisite counterparts in 16:4. The effect is to draw attention to the ritual outlined in-between (16:6-22). At a theological level, passing through water to approach the divine presence is an important motif in the Old Testament.[12] Combined with plain linen clothing (see discussion above), washing

---

11. For what being 'cut off' signifies, see discussion at 5:1-13.

12. For example, the Israelites cross the Red Sea in order to worship Yahweh at Mount Sinai. For elaboration, see L. Michael Morales, *Who Shall Ascend the Mountain of the Lord? A Biblical Theology of the Book of Leviticus* (NSBT 37; Downers Grove: IVP, 2015), 77-93.

emphasizes the ritual's most important component: entering the very presence of Yahweh to present blood.

Having washed and dressed, Aaron performs ascension offerings for Himself and for the people (16:24). The fat of the purification offerings is also burnt (16:25). The remainder of 16:26-28 provides post-ceremony instructions.

Prescriptions for perpetual observance (16:29-34a)

The final section of Leviticus 16 is demarcated by a shift of addressee. Aaron is no longer the recipient (cf. 16:2). Instead, the language is second-person *plural*. This is a command to the whole community (including foreigners, 16:29) to make what began as a response to Nadab and Abihu an annual event. The chiastic arrangement of 16:29-31 emphasizes the ongoing nature of the Day of Atonement, as well as its central purpose:

> 'This is to be a lasting ordinance' (16:29)
>> 'you must deny yourselves' (16:29)
>>> 'not do any work' (16:29)
>>>> 'before the LORD, you will be clean from all your sins' (16:30)
>>> 'a day of Sabbath rest' (16:31)
>> 'you must deny yourselves' (16:31)
> 'it is a lasting ordinance' (16:31)

Structure conveys theology. The Day of Atonement would be the means of providing the comprehensive cleansing ('from all your sins') Israel required to continue dwelling with Yahweh. For this reason, enacting the ritual annually on the tenth day of the seventh month (September/ October) becomes a lasting ordinance (see further discussion at 23:26-32). Moreover, in marked contrast to the tone of Israel's other feast days, this is a solemn affair. Self-denial is mandated for all (16:29, 31); at minimum, fasting is implied (cf. Ps. 35:13-14; Isa. 58:3). The people must *participate*, not merely observe. Physical privations also help conceptualize the seriousness of confessing sin (16:21) and remembering sin's consequences (cf. 16:1). Furthermore, all work is prohibited; there is no reason to be otherwise engaged.

The singular importance of the rite meant the Day of Atonement would outlast Aaron. Leviticus 16:32 makes clear that his son must succeed him and take on the annual task of donning the linen garments, entering the holy of holies, and making atonement for the priests, people, most holy place, tent of meeting, and altar (16:32-33). The conclusion simply records that 'it was done, as the LORD commanded Moses' (16:34b).

One of the (many) striking things in Leviticus 16 is the absence of forgiveness language (compare 4:20, 26, 31, 35; 5:10, 13, 16, 18; 6:7). This is important to note. The focus, instead, is on *purification*. The cumulative sins and impurities of the Israelites defile people and tabernacle. This is true for ritual matters, as Leviticus 11–15 has clarified. But it is also the case for moral faults, a point Leviticus 18–20 will expand upon. While sin and impurity are distinct categories, they overlap. Becoming ritually impure is often unavoidable and hence not wrong in itself. However, to ignore boundaries around impurity *is* sinful and results in people being cut off (e.g., 7:20-21). Furthermore, to ignore purification procedures is also wrong and the person who does so is held responsible (17:16). On the other hand, moral faults defile, especially grievous or 'high-handed' sins (e.g., 18:24). It is this accrued defilement that the Day of Atonement addresses. Once a year, global atonement is made (16:34). The result? 'You shall be clean before the LORD from all your sins' (16:30 ESV). Here, at the center of Leviticus, at the heart of Old Testament law, is a profound statement of the grace of God who does not treat people as their sins deserve.

The magnitude of this moment should not be missed. Many ceremonies involve a ritual repetition of the past (e.g., Passover or Communion). Likewise, the Day of Atonement intentionally recalls past events. Aaron's distinctive dressing (16:4) uses identical language to the dressing of Adam on his exit from the Garden (Gen. 3:21). Thus, Aaron approaches Yahweh representing an excluded humanity, reversing the primordial expulsion to make atonement and so prevent Adam's fate being levied upon Israel. Donald Parry draws out the significance:

> Once a year on Yom Kippur, the Day of Atonement, Adam's eastward expulsion from the Garden is reversed when the high priest travels west past the consuming fire of the sacrifice and the purifying water of the laver, through the veil woven with images of cherubim. Thus he returns to the original point of creation, where he pours out the atoning blood of the sacrifice, re-establishing the covenant relationship with God.[13]

Additionally, reference to Sabbath in 16:31 alludes to the seventh day of creation (Gen. 2:1-3; cf. Exod. 20:8-11). Enjoining Sabbath rest on the Day of Atonement evokes

13. Donald W. Parry, 'The Garden of Eden: Prototype Sanctuary,' in *Temples of the Ancient World: Ritual and Symbolism* (ed. Donald W. Parry; Provo: Deseret Books and FARMS, 1994), 135.

the seventh-day rest of creation's climax *at the very same time* as the high priest enters God's presence in the most holy place. In this way, Leviticus 16 ritually recapitulates the time and space of the original creation and, in so doing, brings aspects of that past into the present. Once again, Leviticus explains the significance of the cult in terms of new creation. This is the extent of restoration on offer.

From text to message

Leviticus 16 is theologically rich and crucial to the book. Yet due diligence must be taken to hear its message clearly. Using Hebrews/Referring to Hebrews 9–10, many interpreters are quick to draw connections between the Day of Atonement and the ministry of Jesus. Such impetus is valid (see below). Yet, one need not look far to find examples of overreading or even plain misreading. Perhaps the most common issue is making Hebrews a lens through which to understand Leviticus, without ever considering that the opposite may be the case. In fact, understanding Leviticus 16 (in detail!) is the necessary foundation for correctly reading Hebrews 9–10. The author of Hebrews simply presumes audience familiarity with Leviticus and writes accordingly. So, while making canonical connections is vital for Christian readers, connections must be based on a sensitive reading of the texts.[14]

Getting the message clear: the theme

Aaron is commanded to make comprehensive atonement for the people and tabernacle by bringing sacrificial blood

---

14. One example relates to the 'scapegoat'. Many have suggested that the goat functions as a type of Christ. However, the New Testament does not make this link. Moreover, in the early church, interpretation was divided between those who saw the 'scapegoat' as a type of Jesus and those who viewed it as a type of Satan. Caution is needed.

into the most holy place. The result is the cleansing and re-consecration made necessary by the sins and impurities of the Israelites. Enacted annually, the Day of Atonement enabled ongoing communion between Yahweh and His people.

Getting the message clear: the aim

By recalling Nadab and Abihu, Leviticus 16 warns of the death threatened by unremedied sin and impurity. Yet, Yahweh, determined not to banish His people, graciously provides a mechanism for dealing with all the sins and impurities of Israel. Aaron is invited ritually to reverse Adam's expulsion from the Garden by entering sacred space to sprinkle sacrificial blood and make atonement. A goat is appointed substitutionally to bear the exile deserved by the people. The result is complete cleansing of both people and tabernacle. Hence, careful obedience to ritual instruction allows the stage to be reset and life with God to flourish. In all of this, Leviticus 16 declares the mercy and understanding of a God who knows human frailty and fault but who nevertheless acts to overcome.

A way in

Robert Murray M'Cheyne was a famous Scottish pastor and preacher (many continue to use his read-the-Bible-in-a-year plan). Even though he died in 1843 at the age of twenty-nine, he was renowned for being a man of integrity and personal holiness. Yet, despite this, M'Cheyne made a remarkable diary entry towards the end of his life. He stated his wish to spend *more time* in confession. In fact, he longed to set aside *one whole day a month* for confessing sins to God. Why would a devoted Christian of outstanding godly character want to do that? Perhaps our surprise says less about M'Cheyne than it does about our complacency towards sin. It is easy to content oneself with the notion that confession simply involves admitting 'I'm a sinner' without ever grappling with the specificity and seriousness of our wrongdoing. Even worse, some justify glibness with an appeal to Christ's death, as if our present sinning was of no consequence to God. Leviticus 16 instructs us in a better way.

Nobody likes to be mischaracterized. Being misunderstood can produce tears or anger. We act quickly to defend our name and reputation. But is it possible that we might have mischaracterized Old Testament law? Certainly, dismissive attitudes are easy to come by. One doesn't have to ask around too much before encountering words like 'boring', 'pointless', 'tedious', and 'unnecessary'. Yet, a verdict on the law is implicitly a verdict on the lawgiver. These are God's words after all. But is our characterization justified? Leviticus 16 says no. Instead, this artistically brilliant passage paints a compelling portrait of a God who not only understands our human predicament but provides needed cleansing. Here, at the very heart of Old Testament law, we find grace and grace in abundance.

Ideas for application

- Sin is serious, has consequences, endangers the sinner, and is not easily dealt with. All this should provoke an earnest seeking of God's appointed means of atonement.

- We ought to be moved to thankfulness as we see God's unwavering determination to remove the sin and impurity that would otherwise prevent His dwelling amongst His people.

- God is a consuming fire. Nadab and Abihu experienced this directly (10:1-2; 16:1). Aaron is warned to take note (16:2, 13). The book of Hebrews extends the same warning to Christians (Heb. 10:27; 12:29). The logic is clear: if Israel had a right to be afraid, how much more should those who have experienced the fullness of God's revelation in Christ (Heb. 12:18-27)? We must not make what Christ has done for His people an excuse to sanction complacency or frivolity. There is no room for cheap grace.

- Public confession of sins was a crucial component of the Day of Atonement (16:21) and implies specificity rather than a vague sense of wrongdoing. The New Testament also makes confession of sin paramount – confession to God (1 John 1:9) *and* to fellow believers (James 5:16). Our corporate gatherings should make space for both.

- The Day of Atonement sharpens our grasp of what Jesus accomplished for His people. Accordingly, Hebrews 9–10 draws extensively on Leviticus 16 to defend faith in Christ. Jesus went through the greater, heavenly tabernacle (Heb. 9:11), entering by means of His own blood (Heb. 9:12) to effect a deeper purification than previously possible (Heb. 9:13-14). Having appeared in God's presence (Heb. 9:24), Jesus secured a once-for-all 'doing away with sin' (Heb. 9:26, 28). Therefore, as the ultimate high priest, Jesus has opened the way for *anyone* to enter the most holy place (Heb. 10:19-21), leading to confidence in approaching God (Heb. 10:22) and a dire warning to those who would turn back from such provision (Heb. 10:26-27).

- Followers of Jesus should be characterized by absolute confidence in their standing with God, based on the surpassing excellence of Christ's high priestly mediation on their behalf.

Suggestions for preaching

Sermon 1

- **Understand Leviticus 16.** Leviticus 16 begins with a flashback to Nadab and Abihu, which raises again the specter of unremedied sin and impurity. The problem from Leviticus 10:1-3 is further heightened by the intervening material in Leviticus 11–15, which hints that Aaron's sons' fate may be shared by others. This backdrop underlies the ritual outlined in 16:3-10 and expanded in 16:11-28. The purpose of the ceremony is fully to cleanse people and tabernacle from sin and impurity and to have a goat endure a living banishment in the people's stead. This is Israel's preeminent rite of restoration. Due obedience would allow the tabernacle to continue to function and permit Israel to dwell in Yahweh's presence. Unsurprisingly, annual reenactment is mandated (16:29-34).

- **Understand what Leviticus 16 is doing.** There are four primary things that Leviticus 16 as a text is doing. First, it makes assertions about ritual practice and demands obedience. These instructions come directly from God and must be heeded. Second, Leviticus 16 warns readers that unremedied sin and impurity ends in banishment from God's presence. That was Adam and Eve's fate, and it has been the fate of all people since. But, third, Leviticus 16 invites a reversal. Aaron is instructed how to safely pass by the cherubim embroidered on the curtain to enter the presence of God and make atonement. Thus, fourth, Leviticus 16 is a declaration about God's nature and character: His unapproachable holiness and His mercy in providing means for ritually and morally impure people to be cleansed. This revelation of God's character creates hope that the representative access pictured in Leviticus 16 – one person, once a year – will one day be the experience of the many.

- **Understand Leviticus 16 today.** It is not surprising that the author of Hebrews turns to Leviticus 16 to explain the significance of Jesus, for He brought to completion what God had already begun and foreshadowed. Jesus was made the permanent high priest of the heavenly tabernacle, having entered that most holy place by the sacrifice of Himself. His blood secures eternal redemption and the complete purification anticipated by Leviticus. Thus, Jesus opens a new and living way into the holy of holies so that everyone who experiences His cleansing from sin and impurity can enter with confidence and full assurance.

Suggestions for teaching

Questions to help understand the passage

1. Why does 16:1 refer to the death of Nadab and Abihu?

2. Have a look at Exodus 28 and compare the clothes Aaron is to wear on the Day of Atonement (16:4). Why are they different?

3. Draw a floorplan of the tabernacle. Read through 16:11-28 and mark where each aspect of the ritual occurs.

4. What different words does Leviticus 16 use to describe wrongdoing? How would you define each one?

5. List the unique aspects of the Day of Atonement ceremony.

6. What is the purpose of the 'scapegoat' (16:20-22)?

7. What does the Day of Atonement accomplish? What is its purpose?

8. Why does the chapter end with commands to annually reenact the ceremony (16:29-34)?

9. Why is Leviticus 16 placed here in the book?

Questions to help apply the passage

1. Imagine being present at a Day of Atonement ritual. Describe what impact it would have on you (think in physical, mental, emotional, and spiritual terms).

2. Is confession of sin a regular part of your life as an individual and as a church? Should it be?

3. What attribute of God does Leviticus 16 make you ponder?

4. In what ways does Leviticus 16 help you better understand the presentation of Jesus in Hebrews 9–10?

5. Think back over the last week. Would you say your life reflects the fact that sin endangers the sinner?

6. What does Hebrews 4:15-16 mean to you?

10.
Sacred Blood
(Leviticus 17:1-16)

Introduction

Why is blood so important? The question first arises in Leviticus 1 and reaches a crescendo by the time one reaches Leviticus 16. Blood is powerful: it can remove impurity, make atonement, consecrate priests and tabernacle, and secure divine forgiveness. But what qualifies blood for such extraordinary ends? Leviticus 17 tackles the question head on by giving a theological rationale for the use of blood, which becomes essential for understanding the mechanism and symbolism of sacrifice in the Old Testament.

Leviticus 17 is therefore closely tied to chapters 1–16, as it continues to address matters of offerings made to Yahweh, priestly mediation, and the responsibilities of worshippers. At the same time, Leviticus 17 also anticipates chapters 18–27. The 'foreigner' first mentioned in 16:29 and occupying a prominent place in Leviticus 18–27 is important here (17:8, 10, 12, 13, 15). The passage also addresses inexpiable sins (e.g., idolatry) which attract terminal punishment (e.g., being cut off). This aligns with the shift of focus as one moves into the second half of the book from primarily dealing with cultic matters to addressing moral and ethical violations which have no sacrificial remedy. I say 'primarily', because the shift is not absolute (and is sometimes overstated by commentators). Leviticus 1–16 also conveys ethical demands; ritual requirements are an ongoing feature of 18–27. Nevertheless, the relative weighting is noticeably different.

Thus, at a literary level, Leviticus 17 functions as a hinge chapter, which connects the seemingly different halves of the book.[1] The material in chapters 1–16 has a bearing on 18–27, and vice versa. At a meta level, the reconciliation with God made possible in 1–16, climaxing with entry to the most holy place, is seen to have necessary implications for how one acts towards one's neighbor in 18–27. Vertical restoration has horizontal consequences. Ethical and ritual concerns are not mutually exclusive, nor are they easily separated. Once again, Leviticus makes the point that all of life is 'before Yahweh'.

Listening to the text

Context and structure

Leviticus 17 comprises the next unit of text following chapter 16 and is marked out by the divine speech formula in 17:1 ('The LORD said to Moses'; cf. 18:1). The passage has two main concerns: (1) blood must be offered in the right place and to the right deity (17:1-9), and (2) blood must never be eaten (17:10-16).[2] Fourfold use of the phrase

---

1. For this reason, some commentators include Lev. 17 with 18–27, while others suggest it forms a unit with Lev. 16.

2. The focus on 'blood' is emphasized by a thirteenfold use of the term (only Lev. 4 has more occurrences in the Old Testament).

'any person' (17:3, 8, 10, 13, my translation; Heb. '*ish* '*ish*) divides the chapter into four paragraphs fronted by a narrative introduction. Each paragraph prohibits certain acts and demands that violators be 'cut off' (17:4, 9, 10, 14).[3]

> Narrative introduction (17:1-2)
> Slaughter of domesticated animals (17:3-7)
> The location for all offerings (17:8-9)
> Prohibition against eating blood (17:10-12)
> Regarding hunting and gathering (17:13-16)

Working through the text

Narrative introduction (17:1-2)

The narrative introduction in 17:1-2 continues the theme of Yahweh addressing *all* Israel (cf. 22:17-18). Although some commentators understand Leviticus 1–16 to be addressing priestly concerns and 17–27 those of the people more generally, such a tight divide does not work. As we have seen, Leviticus 1–16 is much more than mere instruction manual. Its rhetorical and theological sights are set higher than that. Even though the material addresses cultic matters (like sacrifice and purification) the text was nevertheless written to be heard and heeded by *everyone* (see, e.g., 1:2). Likewise, Leviticus 17–27 is not just for the people (including foreigners), but for Aaron and his sons also (17:2; cf. 21:1, etc.). Moses continues to convey to every person 'what the LORD has commanded' (17:2).

Slaughter of domesticated animals (17:3-7)

The first section concerns the right location for *slaughtering* domesticated animals: oxen, lambs, and goats (17:3; NIV,

---

3. Concerning what being 'cut off' signifies, see discussion at 5:1-13.

somewhat unhelpfully, has 'sacrifice'). Slaughter must not simply occur anywhere one might choose ('in the camp or outside of it'; 17:3). Rather, large domesticated animals were only to be killed at the entrance to the tent of meeting (17:4).[4] In this way, Leviticus 17 assumes that slaughter is a sacred act. Accordingly, the instructions insist these animals be presented as fellowship offerings, including the requisite sprinkling of blood and incineration of fat (17:5b-6; cf. 3:2-5). This type of offering had no atoning function but was a means of procuring meat and formed part of a cultic meal shared with both Yahweh and other people (see discussion at 3:1-17). While it might seem reasonable to be able to slaughter livestock anywhere, Yahweh's verdict on perpetrators is stark: 'that person shall be considered guilty of bloodshed; they have shed blood and must be cut off from their people' (17:4).

To be guilty of bloodshed is a serious matter in the Old Testament, which consistently condemns wanton shedding of blood. Violence and bloodshed were the hallmarks of Cain's lineage (Gen. 4:10, 23-24) and the reason for the flood (Gen. 6:11-13). Bloodshed and murder pollute

---

4. Astute readers will notice the conflict with Deuteronomy 12, which allowed for non-sacral slaughter of livestock 'in any of your towns' (Deut. 12:15). Important to note is the shift of setting from nomadic life in the wilderness camp to the settled life in Canaan assumed by Deuteronomy. Again, it becomes evident that Old Testament law is highly contextual. Laws may be adapted or modified to suit new situations (see 'Preaching and Teaching Old Testament Law'). In Deuteronomy 12, the overriding concern is to preserve exclusive worship of Yahweh with respect to Canaanite practices. Permitting non-sacral slaughter would remove the temptation of popping into the local Canaanite shrine to obtain some meat, instead of journeying to the 'place' Yahweh would choose to put His name.

the very land itself (Num. 35:33).[5] Somewhat strangely to Western ears, Leviticus 17 also classifies wrongful killing of animals as 'bloodshed'. There is a subtle rebuke here, perhaps, concerning our exercise of dominion over creation. Privileged position does not justify autonomous or indiscriminate action. Yahweh is concerned about more than the human inhabitants of the earth.

But why does wrongly locating slaughter attract such severe censure? Two related reasons are given. The first is that the animal has not been offered 'to the LORD' (17:4, 5 [x2], 6). Simply butchering livestock at home would rob Yahweh and priests of their respective dues (the fat presented as a pleasing aroma, 17:6; the right-hand-side breast and thigh as the priests' share, 7:31-32). It would thus constitute an implicit disavowal of Yahweh's lordship and a snubbing of His open invitation to enjoy table fellowship with Him. The second problem is made clear in 17:7. Not only were Israelites failing to bring potential offerings to the tabernacle, but they were also actively sacrificing their livestock to 'goat idols' (NIV) or 'goat demons' (ESV), an overt act of spiritual prostitution deserving of strict condemnation (cf. Exod. 22:20). Sacrifice was not merely misplaced but misdirected. The legislation is aimed at spiritual reformation.

It is important to note the explicit rationale provided: 'bloodguilt shall be reckoned to that man ... *so that* the Israelites will bring their sacrifices' (17:4-5, my translation,

---

5. I discuss the theme of land defilement more thoroughly in G. Geoffrey Harper, 'What Hope for the Land? Geospatial Defilement and Cleansing in the Old Testament,' in *Hope for the World in the Old Testament: Studies in Honour of J. Gordon McConville* (eds. Alison Lo, Jamie A. Grant, and David G. Firth, [forthcoming]).

emphasis added). Commands are not only given, they are explained. Hence, it becomes clear that readers are not merely to become obedient to divine instruction but are also to understand why such instruction is required. The end goal is not bare conformity, but growth in ethical and moral reasoning.

The location for all offerings (17:8-9)

The second section considers ascension offerings and other sacrifices. The language is all-encompassing: 'sacrifice' is an umbrella term for all kinds of offerings, whether animal or non-animal (cf. 17:3). The problem to curtail is the same as in 17:3-5. Henceforth, *every* sacrifice and offering must be brought to the entrance of the tent of meeting in order to be presented *to the* LORD. Failure to heed the instruction will again result in a person being cut off from the people (17:9). This is another reminder that Israelite religion was never meant to be purely mechanical, merely a matter of ritual performance, irrespective of inner disposition. That remains a weak caricature despite the prevalence of the view in some Christian circles. Sacrifice was relational, a personal transaction between offerer and Yahweh. The legislation in 17:8-9 aims to guard that ideal.

Also important is the inclusion of the resident alien (Heb. *ger*) in 17:8. These instructions are for 'any Israelite or foreigner' (see, similarly, 17:10, 13, 15). This is a reminder that neither sacrifice nor Torah's instruction were for Israel alone (see also discussion at 1:1-2; cf. Num. 15:13-16). The scope of God's concern for humanity and His planned restoration has always been global. Israel was merely the firstfruits of a far greater harvest to come. That global purview is increasingly foregrounded in Leviticus 17–27, with its repeated and explicit consideration of foreign nationals living amongst the Israelites.

Prohibition against eating blood (17:10-12)

The combined focus on Israelite and foreign resident continues into the third section with its universal ban on eating blood (cf. 3:17; 7:26-27; 19:26). While one might expect the prohibition to be against *drinking* blood rather than *eating* blood, the expression is shorthand for eating meat from which the blood has not been drained (cf. 17:13). Avoiding blood is not novel. The prohibition is consistent across the Old Testament. Genesis 9:3-4 is foundational and states with universal applicability, 'Everything that lives and moves about will be food for you .... But you must not eat meat that has its lifeblood still in it'. The New Testament reiterates the injunction for Gentile believers. The decision of the Jerusalem Council is summarised by James: 'It is my judgment, therefore, that we should not make it difficult for the Gentiles who are turning to God. Instead we should write to them, telling them to abstain from food polluted by idols, from sexual immorality, from the *meat of strangled animals and from blood*' (Acts 15:19-20 [emphasis added]).

The penalty for eating blood in 17:10 is severe. Yahweh becomes the explicit agent in an expanded statement of punitive action: '*I* will set my face against the person who eats blood and *I* will cut him off from among his people' (my translation, emphasis added). To act in such a deliberate, 'high-handed' manner would signal that the perpetrator had already turned their back on covenant fellowship. Complete relational separation, from God and His people, is therefore commensurate and would be enacted by God Himself. Cutting off would assuredly take place.

The reason why blood must be respected is explained in 17:11, which begins with 'For' or 'Because'. The subunit is arranged as a chiasm which draws attention to this central rationale:

> Any Israelite or foreigner who eats blood will be cut off (17:10)
>
> > The blood is the life and has been given for making atonement (17:11)
>
> No Israelite or foreigner may eat blood (17:12)

The first clause in verse 11 is straightforward: 'the life of the flesh is in the blood' (ESV). At one level this is simply an observation from experience. When the blood of any creature is drained out its life is similarly depleted. No blood, no life. It is important to note, therefore, that in Leviticus blood – especially sacrificial blood – represents *life*, not death as often assumed. Deuteronomy conveys the same understanding: 'the blood is the life' (Deut. 12:23). Thus, to eat blood would be to consume the life of the creature. In this way, the Old Testament makes a distinction between an animal's body which may be eaten and an animal's life or 'breath' (spirit?) which may not (cf. Eccles. 3:19-21). Once more, human dominion over creation has limits.

Additionally, Yahweh declares, 'I myself have given it [the blood] to you upon the altar to atone for your lives because it is the blood that makes atonement by the life' (my translation).[6] Divine agency is again paramount ('I myself

---

6. The final clause of 17:11 is tricky to translate. The ESV's rendering ('by the life') has the most to commend it and reads the clause as indicating means: i.e. the blood atones *by means of* (or, *on the basis of*) the life

have given'); this is gracious provision. Making atonement through application of blood to the altar is a repeated theme throughout Leviticus 1:1–6:7. Here, the underlying mechanism is revealed. Substitution is the key motif, conveyed by a threefold use of the Hebrew word *nephesh* ('life'): the life (*nephesh*) of the creature is in its blood and, when offered upon the altar, blood makes atonement for your lives (*nephesh*) by means of the life (*nephesh*) (17:11). Blood sacrifice pivots on the offering of one life in place of another.

It is now clearer why sacrificial animals are required to be 'without blemish' (literally 'blameless' or 'perfect') (1:3, 10; 3:1; etc.).[7] The term is more usually employed to describe people (e.g., Noah in Gen. 6:9) and is a requirement expected of God's people (e.g., Gen. 17:1; Deut. 18:13; Josh. 24:14; Ps. 15:1-2). Yet, people frequently fail to live blamelessly, fracturing relationship with God and others and inviting divine wrath. Making atonement placates divine wrath and secures reconciliation with God by substitutionally offering a without-fault life as a ransom payment in place of an at-fault offerer. That blameless life is offered by means of blood applied to the altar. As the final clause in 17:11 says, 'it is the blood that makes atonement by the life' (ESV). It is not the death of the animal which secures atonement, forgiveness, and cleansing, but its life offered up to Yahweh by means of slaughter and subsequent

---

contained within. For detailed discussion of the options, see John W. Kleinig, *Leviticus* (ConcC; Saint Louis: Concordia, 2003), 357-58, and Hartley, *Leviticus*, 273.

7. There is also a cost factor. 'Perfect' specimens were more expensive and therefore constituted a better gift (cf. Lev. 22:18-25; 2 Sam. 24:24; Mal. 1:13b-14).

application of blood. The entire sacrificial process must be enacted. As John Kleinig notes, 'Blood by itself did not atone. Nor did blood atone through the ritual slaughter of the animal and through its removal from a living animal. It atoned by being applied to the altar.'[8]

Yahweh has appointed the blood of animals to this sacred task, which permanently removes it from everyday use. At the same time, the role of blood in making atonement should not be taken as the key to the entire cult. Leviticus also has a category for *bloodless* atonement (5:11-13).

Regarding hunting and gathering (17:13-16)

The final section of the chapter provides instructions for non-sacrificial meat. While domesticated animals like sheep and goats must be offered to Yahweh at the tabernacle, that is not the case with wild animals hunted for food. Nevertheless, due diligence with respect to blood is still mandated. The blood of wild animals and birds was not used for making atonement and need not be applied to the altar (cf. 17:6). Instead, it must be drained out and covered with dirt (17:13). The rationale and punishment are the same as 17:10-12: 'You must not eat the blood of any creature, because the life of every creature is its blood; anyone who eats it must be cut off' (17:14).

If 17:13-14 deals with hunting, the remaining verses turn to 'gathering'. Once more, the instructions apply to everyone, whether 'native-born or foreigner' (17:15). In view are animals found dead or torn by wild animals. Such carcasses would not have been properly drained of blood. Nor was it possible to enact post-mortem draining.

---

8. Kleinig, *Leviticus*, 365.

However, because eating blood is not defiant disobedience in these cases, it is permitted (although not for priests, 22:8). The contact with an animal carcass makes the person impure (cf. 11:39-40), but the meat need not go to waste. This is a gracious concession, especially for the poor. To find one's goat or sheep dead in the morning would represent great loss; the thought of simply disposing of the body would be unimaginable. At least this way, the meat could be used.

Persons who became ritually impure in this way were expected to enact appropriate cleansing by washing and waiting (17:15) (note that Gentiles also became impure and needed to enact cleansing rites). Refusal to do so, however, would reveal a more sinister disposition. Leviticus 17:16 thus concludes that such a person 'shall bear his iniquity' (ESV). This verse reveals the fuzzy line that exists between the concepts of sin and impurity. Ritual impurity by itself is not sinful or wrong (see discussion at 11:2b-23). However, failing to heed instructions properly for cleansing was sinful, as it would signal a casual disregard for Yahweh's dwelling place (15:31).

From text to message

Leviticus 17 is essential for understanding the rationale of blood sacrifice, not only in Leviticus but in the rest of the canon. And yet, aspects of the text may sound surprising. For this reason, extra care is needed to ensure that we listen to and teach Leviticus 17 on its own terms and avoid the temptation to make it say what we want it to say. Of course, this chapter also needs to be read canonically, and the interpreter will have to wrestle with how the text sits in relation to the wider scriptural testimony regarding blood and sacrifice. But he or she must attend to the contours of this passage first. To do otherwise runs the risk of eisegesis – that is, reading *into* rather than *out of* the text. In the end, if a biblical passage does not fit comfortably with our preconceptions, it offers a valuable opportunity for growth.

Getting the message clear: the theme

Israel, as well as any foreigners living in its midst, must understand that an animal's blood is its life and that Yahweh has apportioned it for making atonement on the altar. Accordingly, blood must not be misplaced, misdirected, or misappropriated lest Yahweh's wrath be provoked, and the perpetrators be cut off.

Getting the message clear: the aim

Leviticus 17 reveals the singular importance of blood for securing atonement and, by doing so, forbids misuses of blood as well as promoting its right function. Slaughter and sacrifice must occur in the right place and the right manner. By outlawing potential and actual idolatrous acts, exclusive worship of Yahweh is preserved. Thus, Leviticus 17 is realistic in its recognition of the potential for incorrect behavior. Commensurate warnings are sounded. However, an invitation to grow in understanding is also offered in hope of not only changed practice, but changed thinking. The implication is that not only do the Israelites need to be taught, they can be. So, while the people have already been declared a holy nation, they must also *become* a holy nation. In these ways, Leviticus 17 testifies to the transformational nature of God's work, taking people from what they were to what He desires them to be. Positioned here in the book, this passage cautions that the comprehensive purification offered in Leviticus 16 should not produce complacency, but rather continued growth in holiness.

A way in

For mountaineers, a compass is essential. Without a compass to navigate by, it is surprising how quickly one can become lost or disorientated, even more so when in fog or snow. The consequences might simply be time wasted. But they can be far more serious. Yet, for all the benefits of compasses, they are not always useful. At the North Pole, a compass becomes entirely useless. There is no east or west. There is no more north. The only direction one can walk is south. With respect to salvation, Jesus is like the North Pole. One cannot go beyond Him. In fact, to arrive at Jesus and then attempt to walk further is inevitably to head in the opposite direction ('south'). Warning people against following such a senseless path is the reason the book of Hebrews was written. 'Blood' constitutes a vital part of the argument. Leviticus 17 helps us understand why.

Ideas for application

- God is at work to transform His redeemed people. Reconciliation makes sanctification necessary.

- The statement in 17:11, 'It is the blood that makes atonement for one's life', finds its ultimate realization in Jesus. Guilty sinners now look to a better sacrifice. For this reason, 'blood' remains a crucial concept in the New Testament and is linked to the breadth of what atonement signifies. The blood of Jesus:

  o is poured out for the forgiveness of many (Matt. 26:28)

- ○ cleanses from all sin (1 John 1:7)

- ○ cleanses consciences (Heb. 9:14)

- ○ justifies sinners (Rom. 5:9)

- ○ ransoms persons from every tribe and language (Rev. 5:9)

- ○ sanctifies people (Heb. 13:12)

- ○ gives victory over Satan (Rev. 12:11)

- ○ brings near those once alienated from God (Eph. 2:13)

- ○ gives confidence to enter holy places (Heb. 10:19)

- ○ reconciles all things to God by making peace (Col. 1:20)

- ○ secures eternal redemption (Heb. 9:12)

- Hebrews 9:11-12 assumes the logic of Leviticus 17:11 as it describes Jesus as high priest, securing atonement through the application of His own blood in the heavenly tabernacle.

- In light of the previous point, the warning to respect sacred blood in Leviticus 17 is reiterated (and ramped up) in Hebrews 10:29 in relation to Jesus: 'How much worse punishment, do you think, will be deserved by the one who has trampled underfoot the Son of God, and has profaned the blood of the covenant by which he was sanctified, and has outraged the Spirit of grace?' (ESV).

- The concept that blood equals life, intrinsic to Leviticus 17, should caution against too quickly understanding every reference to the 'blood of Jesus' as being shorthand for 'Jesus's death'. Each case needs to be evaluated on its own merits.

▪ Against the backdrop of Leviticus 17, the shocking nature of Jesus's statement in John 6:54 is more keenly felt ('Whoever eats my flesh and drinks my blood has eternal life'). Jesus's logic is drawn directly from Leviticus. Blood represents life and it is only by imbibing Jesus's blood that a person may share in His eternal life.

▪ The command to avoid blood is reiterated by the Jerusalem Council: 'abstain from what has been sacrificed to idols, and from blood, and from what has been strangled, and from sexual immorality' (Acts 15:29 ESV). The instruction appeals to the 'Israelite and foreigner' scope of Leviticus 17–18 (which tackles the same topics) as well as the Old Testament notion that these three things – idolatry (Jer. 3:1-2, 9), blood (Num. 35:33), and sexual immorality (Lev. 18:24-25) – defile the very land itself.

Suggestions for preaching

There are many ways to preach Old Testament texts that also maintain an eye on their canonical context. A linear route (Old Testament to New Testament) is not the only path to take. The sermon outline below begins with a New Testament passage before proceeding to see how exploring its Old Testament background clarifies and adds further depth.

Sermon 1

▪ **Transgressing sacred blood.** The author of Hebrews issues a strong warning to believers about falling into the hands of the living God (Heb. 10:31). The reason for vigilance is potential trampling of the Son of God by treating His blood as unholy, thereby despising the means of atonement God has provided. To understand why the warning is delivered so forcefully, we need to grapple with Leviticus 17, a text shaped to instruct readers about the importance of blood. In Leviticus, the significance of blood is assumed in chapters 1–16; Leviticus 17 explains the underlying rationale and throws light on Hebrews and the person and work of Jesus.

- **The importance of sacred blood.** The four sections of Leviticus 17 build a composite picture of the importance of sacred blood. While non-sacred blood can simply be disposed of, sacrificial blood was uniquely set apart for making atonement. The underlying mechanism is revealed: the life of the creature is in the blood and, by means of application to the altar, a substitution of one life for another is accomplished. Accordingly, sacred blood must never be misplaced, misdirected, or misused. This is a universal command, for Israelite and Gentile alike. There is one means of atonement for all people, everywhere. There is no other way to be reconciled to God. Thus, to despise that means is to reject God's offer to humanity and rightly occasions punitive separation from God and His people. This holds true for those 'outside' (the 'foreigner') and for those already 'inside' (the people rescued from Egypt and gathered around the tent).

- **The sacred blood of Christ.** With the force and substance of Leviticus 17 in mind, we are in a much better position to understand Hebrews 10. The author builds on Leviticus 17 to extend and expand its discussion of blood to Jesus. Like blood in Leviticus, Jesus's blood accomplishes atonement for Jews and Gentiles alike. But there is a difference. Jesus is the *ultimate* means of atonement: He is a better high priest, a better sacrifice, and provides better blood. An *a fortiori* (i.e., this is greater than that) comparison is marshalled to convince a wavering audience that any step away from Jesus is to reject God's full and final means of salvation. Jesus's sacred blood must be respected.

Sermon 2

For the shorter ten-part series outlined in 'Ideas for a Preaching or Teaching Series in Leviticus', I suggest that Leviticus 16 and 17 can be taken together ('Bloody Atonement'). Covering both passages in one talk brings together process (Lev. 16) and rationale (Lev. 17). Thus, while the sermon has less time for exploring the respective details of the texts, the payoff is a more holistic understanding of blood sacrifice accomplished in one hit.

Suggestions for teaching

Questions to help understand the passage

1. Why is Leviticus 17 addressed to the *entire* nation (17:1-2)?

2. What does 'guilty of bloodshed' mean in 17:4?

3. What were the personal, social, and theological ramifications of being cut off from one's people (17:4, 9, 10, 14)?

4. Why did all sacrifices need to be brought to the entrance of the tent of meeting?

5. Does the reference to 'goat demons' in 17:7 help to limit the possibilities for what *aza'zel* (NIV 'scape-goat') means in 16:8, 10 (see discussion at 16:2b-10)?

6. Read 17:11 in several different English versions (e.g. NIV, ESV, NLT, NASB). What does this verse mean? How does it connect to the broader biblical themes of sacrifice and atonement?

7. Explain why the regulations for domestic (17:3) and non-domestic (17:13) animals are different.

8. What significance does inclusion of the 'foreigner' have in Leviticus 17?

Questions to help apply the passage

1. Leviticus 17 is explicitly addressed to Israelites *and* non-Israelites. Does this affect the way you read and think about Old Testament law?

2. Regarding sacrifice and atonement, what does Leviticus 17 contribute to your understanding? What questions does it raise for you? How will you answer them?

3. Is 'cutting off' still a possibility for *Christian* people? What biblical support can you muster to validate your conclusion?

4. It is surprising that Israel was worshipping 'goat demons' (17:7) at the very same time that Yahweh was present in the tabernacle. What can you learn from this about the nature of idolatry in the lives of God's people?

5. Does the prohibition against eating blood apply today? How might Genesis 9:3-4 and Acts 15:19-20 influence your answer?

6. Are there aspects of your faith and practice that have become mechanical rather than relational?

7. Do you consider the Scriptures to be a means of growing people in moral reasoning? Can you think of examples from your own life to demonstrate?

11.
Let's Talk about Sex
(Leviticus 18 and 20)

Introduction

It is hard to imagine a more pressing issue for Christians at the beginning of the twenty-first century than sexual ethics. Believers in Jesus have their own sexual history and internal desires to deal with, as well as massive societal and legislative changes. The result is a host of personal and pastoral problems linked to identity, gender, sexual orientation, habitual sins, education of children – the list seems almost endless. Who does not feel daunted by the sheer complexity of it all?

Thankfully, God is not silent on the matter. In Leviticus 18 and 20, personal and corporate morality comes explicitly to the fore with a focus on sex and idolatry. Israel too, it seems, needed instruction and teaching with respect to these things. There is a commonality to human experience in the world. As Ecclesiastes reminds, there is nothing new under the sun. Yet, God's speaking raises its own problems. Foremost is whether (if at all) sexual prohibitions given to ancient Israel have any bearing on Christian practice today. Can these instructions simply be imposed without modification? Or, if modification is required, who chooses which commands to promote and which to set aside? How do we avoid the temptation to simply pick and choose to suit ourselves (and thereby justify our own life choices)? There is an interpretative complexity in Leviticus 18 and 20 that must be addressed.

Again, the good news is that the passage gives readers guidance. Most obvious is the crystal-clear central point driven home by a repeated refrain: 'I am Yahweh your God', together with its shortened form, 'I am Yahweh' (my translation). The phrases appear thirteen times each throughout 18–20[1] and culminate in the climactic declaration of 20:26, 'You are to be holy to me because I, the LORD, am holy, and I have set you apart from the nations to be my own.' Among all the nations, Israel was chosen to become Yahweh-like. Yahweh was the ethical ideal to which the nation was to aspire. The enduring call in Leviticus 18 and 20, therefore, is for *imitatio Dei*, to act like God.

Listening to the text

Context and structure

Following chapter 17, Leviticus 18–20 represents the next major block of material. Although each of the chapters can stand alone and is marked off by the divine speech formula ('The LORD said to Moses', 18:1; 19:1; 20:1), they are also united by a consistent focus on the holiness required by God's people. This is a word for all 'the Israelites' (18:2; 20:2), for 'the entire assembly of Israel' (19:2). The three chapters are also arranged in a concentric (ABA) pattern in which Leviticus 18 and 20

---

1. 'I am Yahweh your God' (18:2, 4, 30; 19:2, 3, 4, 10, 25, 31, 34, 36; 20:7, 24); 'I am Yahweh' (18:5, 6, 21; 19:12, 14, 16, 18, 28, 30, 32, 37; 20:8, 26).

frame chapter 19. The framing chapters deal with the same topics (sex and idolatry), albeit from different perspectives, and thus belong together: Leviticus 18 lists prohibitions and Leviticus 20 details corresponding punishments. This ABA arrangement also positions the command to love one's neighbor (19:18) at the center of the triad. The effect is to convey that fidelity to God and becoming like Him will be expressed (at least in part) by loving one's neighbor.

Leviticus 18 and 20 can be outlined as follows:

> Obey my laws and live (18:1-5)
>
> Avoid sexual immorality (18:6-23)
> > With respect to close relatives (18:6-17)
> > With respect to others (18:18-23)
>
> Avoid the defiling practices of the nations (18:24-30)
>
> Punishments for spiritual prostitution (20:1-8)
>
> Punishments for sexual immorality (20:9-21)
>
> Avoid the defiling practices of the nations and be distinct (20:22-26)
>
> Punishment for spiritual prostitution (20:27)

Working through the text

Obey my laws and live (18:1-5)

Leviticus 18 opens with a refrain that will occur a further twenty-five times in chapters 18–20: 'I am Yahweh your God' (18:2, my translation). Rationale is thereby made explicit. Why heed any of the following instructions, constrictive as they might seem? I am Yahweh. Moreover, I am Yahweh *your* God. With these words, the covenantal relationship between Israel and Yahweh is directly recalled.

Israel had bound itself to Yahweh (see Exod. 24:1-8). He was their God; they were His people. Thus, the underlying context of the chapter is relationship, but not between equals. Exodus records Israel's swapping of a tyrannical master (Pharaoh) for a benevolent one (Yahweh). But He is master, nonetheless. Benevolence must not be mistaken for softness. Yahweh's design for Israel was *transformative*, to make them into a holy nation. In Leviticus 18, transformation extends to sexual practice.

Immediately, there is a sharp countercultural challenge. Six commands – three negative ('do not do' [x2], 'do not walk'; 18:3) and three positive ('do', 'keep' [x2]; 18:4-5) – drive home the central point: Israel must not base its sexual ethic on Egyptian or Canaanite norms, but on Yahweh's decrees. There is an awareness that different cultures have different sexual values and taboos, a fact as true in the ancient world as the modern. Nevertheless, Leviticus 18 asserts that it is not a case of 'each to his or her own' or 'when in Rome'. Yahweh, as creator, calls people to heed His principles.

God does not leave His people guessing what those standards might be. Because Israel's past (Egypt) and future (Canaan) experience would likely lead them in wrong directions, Yahweh graciously speaks (18:1). Thus, Leviticus 18 cannot simply be dismissed as the self-generated standards of an ancient people who really did not understand the complexity of the world. These instructions also come as direct speech from God. And Yahweh speaks to enable life and flourishing: 'Keep my decrees and laws, for the person who obeys them will live by them' (18:5).[2]

---

2. There is a longstanding and entrenched legacy of misconstruing the force of 18:5. The verse has been read as saying something akin to 'keep my laws perfectly and you will inherit eternal life' and thereby used to

Avoid sexual immorality (18:6-23)

The central section of Leviticus 18 lists various prohibitions in relation to sexual practice. The section divides into two panels (18:6-17 and 18:18-23). The first is framed by references to 'close relatives' (18:6, 17; cf. 18:12, 13) and its prohibitions fit under the broad umbrella term of 'incest'. The Hebrew phrase used throughout, 'to uncover nakedness' (see ESV, NASB), is idiomatic for having 'sexual relations' (so NIV, NLT) or 'sexual intercourse' (HCSB). Outside of proper bounds, exposing nakedness frequently connotes a shameful or violent act (18:8, 10, 14, 16; see also, Gen. 9:21-22; Exod. 20:26; 1 Sam. 20:30; Ezek. 16:36-37). The resulting prohibitions are parsed as masculine singular. Accordingly, men must not uncover the nakedness of their

- mother (18:7)
- father's wife (i.e. stepmother) (18:8)
- maternal or paternal sister (18:9)
- granddaughter (18:10)
- half-sister (18:11)
- paternal aunt (18:12)
- maternal aunt (18:13)
- uncle's wife (18:14)
- daughter-in-law (18:15)

---

highlight the inability of the law to save. That, however, is a profound misreading of the text. In context, 'Keep my laws and live' includes heeding the means offered for restoring relationship with God following sin or defilement (especially 4:1–6:7; 12–16). Sinless perfection is nowhere in view. Rather, doing the law is not antithetical to faith but is, in fact, premised on it. This is precisely James's point in the New Testament: genuine faith manifests itself in righteous *doing* (James 2:20-24).

- sister-in-law (18:16)
- wife and her daughter (18:17)
- wife's granddaughters (18:17)

The prohibitions extend to blood relations (e.g., mother) as well as non-blood relations (e.g., one's stepmother or daughter-in-law). The common denominator is membership in the extended family unit (which, in the ancient world, often meant living in close proximity). The integrity of the household is at stake. These regulations also frankly recognize that women are often most vulnerable *at home*. Yahweh's decrees are geared to protect the powerless.

Yet, this observation raises a troubling question: why is 'daughter' not on the list? Young girls are often the primary victims of incest, so why is sex with one's daughter not prohibited? At this point, it is useful to bear in mind that Hebrew literature is subtle, euphemistic, idiomatic. Sometimes, in Hebrew legal texts, the most obvious case is omitted. It is a rhetorical device aimed at the reader or hearer that says, 'It would be shameful to have to spell *this* out; surely, you must know. Isn't it self-evident?' Omitting 'daughter' is therefore not an oversight. If anything, it communicates that sexual misconduct with one's daughter is the most pernicious form of incest.

This is another reminder that Old Testament law is better conceived as common law rather than statutory law (see 'Preaching and Teaching Old Testament Law'). Laws listed are not meant to be exhaustive. Rather they are meant to be sufficient to instruct and shape moral reasoning. Readers are meant to learn from the examples given and apply that knowledge to new situations as they arise. Just because someone can think of an example not listed (like 'daughter') or a novel variation (e.g., polyamorous marriage) does not mean that practice is permitted.

This insight also helps with the male-centric nature of Leviticus 18. The chapter is almost entirely, but not quite (see 18:23), addressed to men (the commands are parsed as masculine singular; 18:5 states, the *man* who obeys will live). Does Leviticus 18 have anything to say to women? The answer, of course, is yes. Again, approaching the text as common law helps. Ethical standards are applicable to everyone; women simply need to adjust for context. Accordingly, Israelite women must not have sexual relations with their father, their mother's husband, and so on. These precepts are universal.

The second panel (18:18-23) deals with sexual matters beyond the limits of incest. A man must not marry two sisters at the same time, setting up a destructive rivalry between them (18:18). A man must also not have sex with a woman while she is having her period (18:19). The reason given – implicitly here, but explicitly in 15:19-24 – is that contact with menstrual blood would make him ritually impure. Hence, to *deliberately* contract major impurity (lasting seven days; 15:24) would indicate a despising of Yahweh's presence (cf. 15:31). It is for this reason that doing so results in the couple being cut off (20:18) rather than simply becoming impure as in Leviticus 15:24 (which depicts *accidental* contact).

Leviticus 18:20 prohibits adultery, a sin that received widespread condemnation in the ancient world. While 18:21 seems oddly placed on a first reading, a wordplay connects it with the previous verse: 'To your neighbor's wife you will not give your seed [i.e. 'semen'] ... and from your seed [i.e. 'children'] you will not give [one] to pass [through fire] to Molech' (18:20-21, my translation).

Leviticus 18:22 is probably one of the best-known (and most debated) verses in the book. Although uncontroversial throughout most of history, recent cultural shifts have brought the condemnation of homosexual practice in this verse under the microscope. This is not the place to resolve all the difficulties, textual or pastoral.[3] A couple of things are important to note. First, in line with the wider chapter, the wording assumes a male audience. Hence, 'With a male, you [masculine singular] must not lie with as you lie with a woman' (my translation). As we have seen, however, this does not therefore sanction lesbian sexual relations. The moral reasoning on display needs to be applied to analogous contexts. Second, the focus of the passage relates to prohibited sexual *acts*, not orientation. A person who experiences same-sex attraction can live in fidelity to Yahweh as much as anyone. Third, the relative weighting of the overall passage is crucial to observe. Only one verse proscribes homosexual activity; fifteen verses prohibit heterosexual acts. It seems the biggest threat to God's people is not homosexuality, but heterosexuality. A raft of *heterosexual* transgressions would cause Israel to be vomited from the land (cf. 18:24-28). That observation ought to temper our discussions.

Leviticus 18:23 prohibits bestiality. The second half of the verse uniquely delivers a command to women: 'A woman must not present herself to an animal to have sexual

---

3. One of the most helpful books I have read on the topic is Ed Shaw, *Same-Sex Attraction and the Church: The Surprising Plausibility of the Celibate Life* (Downers Grove: IVP, 2015). For detailed analysis of the key passages and their cultural settings, Robert A. J. Gagnon, *The Bible and Homosexual Practice: Texts and Hermeneutics* (Nashville: Abingdon, 2001), has yet to be surpassed.

relations with it.' The command is delivered in the *third* person ('A woman'), rather than the second-person address ('you') found throughout. This is important and implies that while Moses is addressing a male audience, those men are to convey Yahweh's teaching to their entire households.[4] These are instructions for everyone, whether men or women.

Avoid the defiling practices of the nations (18:24-30)

The final section returns to drawing a contrast between Israel's sexual conduct and that of the Canaanite culture they are about to experience (cf. 18:3). Leviticus 18:24-28 is arranged in a repeating pattern (see *Table 11.1*).

(a) Do not defile yourselves (18:24)	(a') Do not do detestable things (18:26)
(b) This is how the nations were defiled (18:24)	(b') These things were done by the people of the land (18:27)
(c) Even the land was defiled (18:25)	(c') The land became defiled (18:27)
(d) The land vomited out its inhabitants (18:25)	(d') The land will vomit you out (18:28)
(e) You must keep my decrees and laws (18:26)	

Table 11.1

Reiteration drives home the central point: do not follow Canaanite sexual norms, for they will defile people and

---

4. For further discussion, see my essay, 'First Things First: Reading Genesis 1–3 in Its Pentateuchal Context,' in *The Gender Conversation: Evangelical Perspectives on Gender, Scripture and the Christian Life* (ed. Edwina Murphy and David I. Starling; Eugene: Wipf & Stock/ Morling Press, 2016), 45-55.

land.[5] The central pivot (e) sets the alternative basis of Israel's conduct: Yahweh's decrees and laws. The shift from 18:25 to 18:28 is also arresting. The assertion that the land vomited out the defiled and defiling Canaanites (d) is recast as Israel's assured fate if it follows the same path (d'). This potential for national catastrophe becomes the motivator for individual censure in 18:29: 'Any person who does any of these detestable practices must be cut off from his people' (HCSB). Sexual immorality has communal consequences. Sex is not just a private affair.

This final section of Leviticus 18 is essential for determining the applicability of its regulations. The whole tenor of the passage is universal, with prohibitions embodying principles that apply to all peoples in all times and places. Obviously, that is true for Israel throughout its generations, but it is also the case for foreign nationals living among the people (18:26). More than that, these laws judge Egyptian and Canaanite practices (18:3, 24, 30). Failure to keep Yahweh's sexual standards is the given reason for Canaanite expulsion from the land, even though they were unaware of those standards. Thus, these regulations cannot simply be written off as timebound, culturally specific mandates that applied only to Israel, or as laws which were only valid within the borders of the land.[6]

---

5. In Lev. 11–16, the language of defilement refers to *ritual* impurity which is usually unavoidable and unintentional and could be cleansed. In Lev. 18 and 20, the same terminology is used to refer to *moral* impurity which, in contrast, is avoidable, intentional, and has no remedial measures. Care must be taken not to collapse these two distinct categories into one another.

6. This is a strategy frequently employed by so-called revisionist writers. See, for instance, Joel Hollier, *A Place at His Table: A Biblical Exploration*

Punishments for spiritual prostitution (20:1-8)

Leviticus 20 works in conjunction with Leviticus 18 by outlining the respective punishments for those who transgress sexual and idolatrous boundaries. The first section returns to the offering of one's seed (i.e., 'children') to Molech (20:2; cf. 18:21). The punishment is death, enacted by public stoning (20:2). Human punishment is mirrored on the divine plane. Yahweh Himself will set His face against such a person and cut them off. This is because idolatry defiles the sanctuary and profanes Yahweh's name (20:3; cf. 15:31; see also discussion at 11:2b-23). The ideal is God and nation maintaining the same standard of holiness. But even if the people turn a blind eye to spiritual prostitution (20:4), Yahweh will set Himself against it and cut the culprits off (20:5-6). As Leviticus 20:8 makes clear, Yahweh will make His people holy, one way or another. Yet, the passage expects willing participation; hence, there is the call in 20:7: 'Consecrate yourselves and be holy.'

Punishments for sexual immorality (20:9-21)

The next section revisits sexual sins detailed in Leviticus 18 to stipulate punitive measures. As with spiritual prostitution (20:1-8), the consequences are severe. The most frequent punishment prescribed is the death of the guilty parties, whether they be male or female (e.g., 20:10, 11), human or animal (20:15, 16). Other consequences, diminishing as the chapter proceeds, include being cut off (20:17, 18) and remaining childless (20:20, 21). The seemingly harsh sentences follow logically from 18:24-28 (also reiterated

---

of Faith, Sexuality, and the Kingdom of God (Eugene: Cascade, 2019), 84-102.

in 20:22). National wellbeing is at stake. Sexual acts are not merely private; Leviticus again makes the point that relationship with God intrudes into every dimension of life. Moreover, immorality defiles the land, causing it to vomit out its inhabitants.[7] Against that potential future, Israel must extinguish those who endanger the collective by their individual rejection of Yahweh's standards. The assumption throughout is *willful* disobedience (victims of rape, for example, are not considered here; cf. Deut. 22:23-27).[8] Accordingly, 'their blood will be on their own head' (20:9, 11, 12, 13, 16, 27).

Avoid the defiling practices of the nations and be distinct (20:22-26)

Leviticus 20:22-26 reiterates the central thrust of 18:24-28: Israel must not follow the practices of the Canaanites which resulted in them being abhorred by Yahweh and vomited from the land. However, the underlying reason is further clarified. Yahweh has *separated* Israel from the nations (20:24; cf. Exod. 19:4-6) in a manner analogous to how the nation must *separate* between pure and impure foods (20:25; cf. 11:47). Israel must not defile itself by means of illegitimate food (20:25) or illegitimate sex (18:24). Instead, Yahweh decrees, 'You shall be holy to me, for I the Lord am holy and have separated you from the peoples, that you should be mine' (20:26 ESV). Thus,

---

7. Regarding land defilement and its potential remedy, see my longer treatment in 'What Hope for the Land?'

8. In relation to 20:13, the case has been made that what is envisioned is either homosexual rape (whether as judicial punishment or otherwise) or pederasty. However, this misses the force of the text, which assumes a *consensual* act that renders *both* partners liable to punishment.

Leviticus 20 ends where chapter 18 began: relationship with Yahweh and its implications for life.

Punishment for spiritual prostitution (20:27)

The final verse forms a frame with the opening section (20:1-8) and reiterates fidelity to Yahweh alone. Anyone who consults spirits must be put to death by communal stoning (cf. 20:2), and 'their blood will be on their own heads'.

From text to message

As one reads through Leviticus 18 and 20, it is hard not to think of narrative episodes from earlier in the Pentateuch: the seeming brother and half-sister marriage of Abraham and Sarah (Gen. 20:12; cf. 18:9),[9] the sibling rivalry between Jacob's wives (Gen. 29:31-30:24; cf. 18:18), or the incestuous relationship between Lot's daughters and their father (Gen. 19:30-38; cf. 18:7). These allusions add further weight to the Levitical injunctions: prohibited acts are real possibilities *even among God's people* and must therefore be censured. The Pentateuch's stories thus invite and make necessary the instruction in Leviticus. The legislation, in turn, presents the ideal that Israel must aspire to. In this way, story and law combine to accentuate Yahweh's plan to create a people for Himself who will increasingly reflect and embody His own holiness. Against this backdrop, Leviticus 18 and 20 become much more than lists of dos and don'ts. Once more, the keynote is restoration along creation lines: faithfulness to God expressed in sexual faithfulness towards neighbor.

---

9. I say 'seeming' because it is not altogether clear whether Sarah was in fact Abraham's half-sister or whether his statement to that effect is further fabrication wielded in the service of self-preservation.

Getting the message clear: the theme

In the context of covenantal relationship with Yahweh, Israel is called to express holiness through sexual propriety with respect to God (at a spiritual level) and others (at a physical level). Culture-transcending standards define the boundaries of permitted behaviors. Transgression renders one defiled and defiling and, because it endangers the wider community, calls for extreme censure.

Getting the message clear: the aim

Leviticus 18 and 20 list a series of prohibitions and corresponding punishments which instruct regarding Yahweh's standards of sexual and religious propriety. Divine commands are negatively framed ('Do not') and thus seek to curtail wrong behavior by acknowledging that God's people will not naturally avoid improper practices. Hearing God speak directly and personally ('*You* shall not') suggests that I, the hearer, am the greatest threat to my neighbor's wellbeing. Accordingly, threatened punishment and remembrance of Canaanite expulsion from the land function to warn and deter. Instead, there is an invitation to increasingly embody the holiness of God by heeding His instruction, rather than that of surrounding culture. Even enacting punishment becomes an expression of godlikeness as people learn to imitate Yahweh's zero-tolerance stance against wickedness. These chapters therefore serve the wider purpose of the book to call into being a transformed and obedient community who will experience life in God's presence.

A way in

Dale Kuehne's insightful book *Sex and the iWorld* suggests that a new sexual ethic is emerging in the Western world.

That ethic has three foundational and non-negotiable elements:[10]

1. A person may not criticize someone else's life choices or behavior

2. A person may not behave in a manner that coerces or causes harm to others

3. A person may not engage in a sexual relationship with someone without his or her consent

Once these maxims are upheld, any sexual act or behavior is permitted. As Christians, we do not live in a hermetically sealed environment. We live and breathe the cultural air around us. We watch the same movies and read the same books. Like the proverbial frog in a slowly warming pot of water, we may not even notice the changes around us, or *in* us. So, when matters of sexuality are debated in the public square, it is perhaps not surprising to find Christians positioned on all sides. Many are not even sure what to think anymore; it is easy to feel overwhelmed. We need help. We need instruction. We need to hear God's voice in all of this. Thankfully, He has not remained silent.

If the author of Leviticus 18 and 20 was looking for a theme tune to introduce his material, he would find it hard to go past Salt-N-Pepa's number one hit, *Let's Talk about Sex* (you can find the lyrics online). Yet, while talking about sex may be a hallmark of contemporary society, that is not necessarily true of church culture. Try singing Salt-N-Pepa's song in church and see how awkward it feels! Nevertheless, as we turn to Leviticus, God invites us to

10. Dale S. Kuehne, *Sex and the iWorld: Rethinking Relationship beyond an Age of Individualism* (Grand Rapids: Baker, 2009), 71.

do exactly that (talk, that is, not sing!). Sexuality is an inextricable part of every human's experience and carries potential for great good or great harm. We must hear what God has to say. So, let's talk about sex ...

Ideas for application

- The fundamental identity of God's people is not indexed to sexuality but relationship with God.

- Cultural norms are not a reliable guide for determining sexual standards. We need God's instruction if we are to live well in this world.

- The sexual standards expressed in Leviticus tap into something transcultural. They applied to resident foreigners, Egyptians, and Canaanites as much as Israel. The New Testament simply continues that logic and applies sexual prohibitions from Leviticus to Jew and Gentile alike (e.g., 1 Cor. 6:9-10). Likewise, in the early church, limitations regarding suitable marriage partners (not a close relative, not already married, not of the same sex, not an animal) were a direct application of Leviticus 18.

- Idolatry is akin to spiritual adultery. Our experience of sexual sin at a physical level helps us understand the impact of promiscuity at a spiritual one. This is a powerful metaphor the biblical writers use time and again (e.g., Jer. 2-3; Ezek. 23; Hosea 2; Rev. 17).

- God intrudes into the sexual lives of His people. Nothing remains private or beyond the purview of transformation for those who have been redeemed at great cost.

- Jesus teaches that sexual fidelity includes what we think as much as what we do (Matt. 5:28).

- Christians must honor God with their bodies, especially in matters related to sex (1 Cor. 6:18-20). Failure to avoid sexual immorality invites God's punishment (1 Thess. 4:3-8).

- Sexual immorality is not the unforgivable sin (whether homosexual or heterosexual). The offer of forgiveness following repentance is made to all. The measure of God's people is not who they were, but who they are becoming in Christ (cf. 1 Cor. 6:9-11).

- Sexual sin has communal consequences. Like yeast in dough, immorality can spread. For this reason, Paul commands severe measures to cut off Christians who persist in unrepentance (1 Cor. 5:1-5, 9-11; cf. Rev. 2:20-23).

- The laws of Leviticus 18 and 20 do not set the ethical benchmark for Israel (or the church). Rather, they mark the limits past which punishment is levied. The ethical standard is always to become like God Himself. 'This is how we know we are in him: Whoever claims to live in him must live as Jesus did' (1 John 2:5-6).

Suggestions for preaching

Each time I preach this part of Leviticus, I ask around to see who has heard a sermon on it before. I have yet to receive a positive response. While I am sure there are many exceptions, my straw poll is troubling, nonetheless. These are essential chapters for constructing a biblical view of sex and sexuality. The amount of space devoted in the Scriptures to talking about sex is indicative of the topic's importance. The church needs to hear Leviticus 18 and 20. Yet the church also needs to hear Leviticus 18 and

20 taught with pastoral sensitivity. The preacher is not addressing blank slates. Chances are everyone in the room (preacher included) has propagated or experienced sexual sin. An attitude of humility is apropos.

Sermon 1

- **Obey my laws and live (18:1-5).** The underlying framework of these chapters is relationship with Yahweh, a point driven home by the repeated phrase, 'I am Yahweh your God'. As their God and King, Yahweh commands His people to heed His sexual ethic, rather than that of the surrounding culture. There is a recognized contest of values, yet a promise too: the person who obeys will live.

- **Avoid sexual transgression (18:6-23).** The prohibitions of 18:6-23 are driven by the twinned concerns of loving God and loving others. Sexual immorality defiles people in God's eyes. Moreover, there is a frank recognition of the potential for individuals to harm others through wrongful sexual actions. Accordingly, various immoral practices are proscribed. Although the chapter is written addressed to a male audience, 18:23 indicates that these laws were to govern entire households. This is Yahweh's instruction for everyone. Transformed relationship with God (Lev. 1–16) must overflow into transformed relationship with others. God is saving a community.

- **Universal applicability (18:24-30).** Although it may be tempting to confine the prohibitions of Leviticus 18 to an 'Israel only' box, that is not an option the text leaves open. Yahweh's decrees appeal to creation norms and are thus applicable to all peoples. Israelites, resident foreigners, Egyptians, and Canaanites are all explicitly held to the same standard. There is no favoritism. Just as the land was defiled by the Canaanites and vomited them out, it will likewise eject Israel if they pollute it with sexual sin. Thus, those who endanger the collective through willful disobedience must be cut off.

- **Commensurate punishment (20:1-27).** Leviticus 20 expands on and clarifies the punishment due to those who sin sexually. The penalties are severe, reflecting the level of danger posed to the community. Moreover, even if human justice should fail, Yahweh declares that He himself will enact punishment. There is no room for hidden sin before the One who sees all. In this way, Leviticus 20 adds considerable rhetorical force to the prohibitions of chapter 18 by increasing the urgency of the warning and the seriousness of the deterrent.

- **What about us?** Rather than dismiss the sexual prohibitions of Leviticus 18 and 20, the New Testament affirms and reiterates them. Even the penalty of being cut off from one's people finds an analogy in excommunication from the church. This part of Leviticus calls for sober reflection. First, we ought to acknowledge our complicity; there are few who can say they have not sinned sexually, especially when our thought life is included. Our conversations about sex should be tempered with humility. Second, we must heed the warning sounded in Leviticus. The sexually immoral will not inherit the kingdom of God. Repentance may be called for. Third, we can experience God's forgiveness. It is not who we were that counts, but rather who we are becoming in Christ.

Sermon 2

A second approach to this unit would be to preach Leviticus 18 and 20 as separate sermons for which the chapter outlines above could serve as frameworks. A sermon on Leviticus 18 would be able to focus on the chapter's prohibitions and their potential application for today. The Leviticus 20 talk could do the same with respect to punishments for disobedience. Two sermons would give the preacher substantially more time to tease out the (tricky) hermeneutical issues that surround moving from Old Testament to New. There is substantial continuity, yet discontinuity too. Learning to relate the Old Testament rightly to Christian faith and practice is one of the most crucial, and difficult, aspects of theology. Preaching Leviticus 18 and 20 would be a wonderful opportunity to instruct a congregation regarding how to do that task well.

Sermon 3

Leviticus 18 and 20 would make an excellent basis for topical talks on sex and idolatry. This could even be combined with a talk on wrongful shedding of blood (based on Lev. 17). These three things – bloodshed, sexual immorality, and idolatry – are the most heinous sins from an Old Testament point of view and are consistently excoriated, especially by the prophets. In addition, they are also the only sins that pollute the land (Lev. 18:24-25; Num. 35:33; Jer. 3:1-2, 9), putting them in a unique category. It is not surprising that New Testament teaching follows suit (e.g., Acts 15:28-29). These are biblical themes worth exploring.

Suggestions for teaching

Questions to help understand the passage

1. What should 'I am Yahweh your God' (18:4, etc.) convey to readers? What does this phrase evoke in the context of the Pentateuch thus far?

2. Brainstorm or research Egyptian and Canaanite attitudes and practices with respect to sex (from the Bible or elsewhere). Why was Israel commanded to not do likewise (18:3, 24; 20:23)?

3. What does 18:5 mean?

4. How would you categorize the various prohibitions in 18:6-23? Which laws are the same today? Which are different?

5. Why is Leviticus 18 addressed to men? To what extent should this shape application?

6. What does it mean that the land became defiled (18:25, 27)?

7. How does the personification of the land vomiting out inhabitants (18:25, 28; 20:22) contribute to the force of the passage?

8. Why are sexual misdemeanors and idolatry (especially Molech worship) treated together?

9. Do the differing punishments in Leviticus 20 reveal a spectrum of seriousness with respect to sexual sin?

10. Why are people required to carry out punishments instead of it occurring through direct divine intervention (20:2, etc.)?

11. Summarize the message of Leviticus 18 and 20 in one sentence.

Questions to help apply the passage

1. Does belonging to God, or being in Christ, constitute your core identity – the foundation upon which everything else is based? How do you know?

2. What sexual ethic was conveyed in the last movie you watched or in the last book you read? Compare and contrast this with Leviticus 18 and 20. What strikes you?

3. Which of the prohibitions in 18:6-23 come across as self-evident? Which do you find troubling? What is influencing your response in each case?

4. Are the prohibitions in Leviticus 18 and 20 universally applicable or culturally limited? Defend your answer.

5. Do you think the punishments listed for immorality in Leviticus 20 are commensurate or too severe? Does the New Testament provide any guidance concerning whether Christians should enact them?

6. Leviticus 18 and 20 testify to God's transformative agenda for His people with respect to sex (incorporating both thought and action). Where are you most tempted sexually? What practical things can you do to avoid sin?

7. Do you think you, your family, and your church talk enough about sex-related matters? Why do you think this is the case? Can you think of specific (and helpful!) ways to foster better conversation?

12.
Holiness Everywhere
(Leviticus 19)

Introduction

'Love your neighbor as yourself.' If there is any verse in Leviticus that people know, this is it. Indeed, Jesus said that, alongside the command to love God, Leviticus 19:18 epitomized the very heart of the law. Unsurprisingly, therefore, many have highlighted the singular importance of Leviticus 19. Marcus Kalisch regards the chapter to be 'in some respects the most important section of Leviticus if not of the whole Pentateuch.'[1] Likewise, Samuel Balentine avers that 19:17-18 is the very 'epicenter of the book.'[2]

Importance notwithstanding, however, Leviticus 19 is not straightforward. Following the narrator's introduction, the chapter consists entirely of commands.[3]

---

1. Marcus M. Kalisch, *Leviticus, Part II: Containing Chapters XI to XXVII* (London: Longmans, Green, Reader & Dyer, 1872), 257.

2. Samuel E. Balentine, *Leviticus* (Interpretation; Louisville: John Knox, 2002), 166.

3. Those working on the Hebrew text will note (perhaps with surprise) that Leviticus has a relatively low number of imperative forms.

While the famous injunction to love others might be familiar to most Christians, the remainder of this chapter is certainly not. Commands seem randomly dispersed and touch on disparate, even strange, aspects of life. The requirement to love one's neighbor is immediately followed by a prohibition against mating different kinds of animals (19:18-19). Instruction regarding sex with a betrothed slave (19:20-22) is placed side-by-side with a prohibition on eating uncircumcised fruit (19:23-25). Even the total number of commands is disputed, with commentators counting from thirty to over fifty. All these factors make discerning the structure and flow of the chapter difficult (see below).

Yet the keynote of the passage is immediately apparent: *Be holy because I am holy* (19:2). Once again, Yahweh extols His people to emulate His character and ways. What Leviticus 19 drives home so powerfully is that Yahweh's call for holiness extends to all aspects of life. Nothing is off limits. There is no divide between sacred and secular. Accordingly, the chapter's instruction intrudes into religious, personal, relational, ethical, agricultural, social, and internal affairs without distinction. Each of these is an arena within which holiness must be expressed. The mere fact that this would not be our list of commands to instill holiness makes Leviticus 19 rich ground to till. There is much to learn here about what God deems important. Thus, while Leviticus 19 may be a challenging passage to teach, the effort is decidedly worth it.

Commands for the most part are conveyed through use of *yiqtol* and *weqatal* verbs which nevertheless carry imperatival force. Indeed, *weqatal* forms are often used in Hebrew to convey strong commands from a greater person to a lesser.

Listening to the text

Context and structure

Leviticus 19 is framed by chapters 18 and 20 in an ABA pattern. The three-chapter unit is united by a concern to foster holiness among all who live in proximity to God (although Lev. 19 does not directly address the resident foreigner as do chapters 18 and 20). Standards of holiness are formulated in *contrast* to the surrounding nations (especially 18:3, 24-30; 20:22-26) and in *imitation* of Yahweh (especially 19:2). The driving rationale is a constant reminder of who God is: 'I am Yahweh your God' and 'I am Yahweh' appear a total of twenty-six times throughout Leviticus 18-20.

A   Be holy to Yahweh, unlike the nations (prohibited sexual relations) (Lev. 18)

  B   Be holy because Yahweh is holy (Lev. 19)

A'   Be holy to Yahweh, unlike the nations (punishments for sexual violation) (Lev. 20)

As mentioned above, discerning the internal structure of Leviticus 19 is difficult. Various ways of subdividing the commands have been suggested. Jacob Milgrom concludes that the chapter 'comprises a miscellany of laws' with 'no common theme.'[4] However, bearing in mind the intricate arrangement attested elsewhere in Leviticus, the lack of order in this passage may be deliberate (I will return to the theological and hermeneutical implications of this below). Indeed, Wenham suggests that the randomness

---

4. Jacob Milgrom, *Leviticus 17–22: A New Translation with Introduction and Commentary* (AB 3A; New York: The Anchor Bible, 2000), 1596.

of material in Leviticus 19 reflects the diversity of life in a manner analogous to Proverbs.[5] The effect is to emphasize the key concern of the chapter: Yahweh expects holiness in every sphere of existence without distinction.

Although other arrangements are possible (consult the commentaries), I divide Leviticus 19 into two quite uneven sections:

> The thesis: Be holy because I am holy (19:1-2)
> The demonstration: Keep all my decrees (19:3-37)

Working through the text

The thesis: Be holy because I am holy (19:1-2)

Leviticus 19 continues the broad address of the previous chapters: 'Speak to the entire assembly of Israel' (19:2; cf. 17:2; 18:2). These are Yahweh's words to everyone. Matters of identity and formation are central. The opening command is worded in plural form: 'You shall be holy' (19:2 ESV; KJV 'Ye shall'). The explicit reason follows: 'because I, the LORD your God, am holy.' Once more, Israel is reminded of its set-apart status (cf. 20:26). However, election and calling are not an implicit acceptance of the nation as is. Rather, Israel must increasingly come to resemble its God. *Imitatio Dei* ('imitation of God') must be a way of life. The commands that make up the remainder of the chapter need to be understood in this context. They are not rules to follow so that Israel might somehow curry divine favor and earn a standing with God; instead, they are a call to holiness for a people *already* delivered by Yahweh's gracious action and *already* bound to Him ('I am Yahweh *your* God').

---

5. Wenham, *Leviticus*, 264.

Nor are they empty moralism. Yahweh's instructions are an invitation to godlikeness. The correct theological pigeonhole for Leviticus 19 is sanctification.

The demonstration: Keep my decrees (19:3-37)

The growth in holiness enjoined by Leviticus 19 impacts individual, family, and national life. The point is reinforced throughout the chapter by the language of address, which switches between 'you' singular and 'you' plural (for non-Hebrew readers, consulting the KJV is a useful way to see this). For example, 19:9-10 begins by addressing the collective: 'When you [pl.] reap the harvest'. But then the text zooms in to the individual's responsibility not to harvest everything in one's own field or vineyard so that the poor and resident foreigners might find food (the book of Ruth is the premier illustration of what this might look like practically).[6] The effect is to drive home the point that 'society' consists of individuals. Only when each individual *Israelite* reflected Yahweh's character and virtues would *Israel* be a holy nation and fulfill its calling with respect to the world (cf. Exod. 19:4-6). Thus, Leviticus 19 confronts two very real human tendencies: (1) to dodge ethical

---

6. Note that the poor and foreigners are provided access to food in 19:10 but *not as a handout*. They have a responsibility to work to gather food. The legislation thus addresses not only material poverty but has implications for emotional and psychological wellbeing. The poor are treated holistically as *persons*, not simply as a social problem to fix. Here, as elsewhere, Leviticus has much to contribute to contemporary discussions of social justice. I consider some initial soundings in '"I Will Walk in Your Midst": The Implications of Leviticus 26:3-13 for Social Wellbeing,' in *Justice, Mercy and Wellbeing: Interdisciplinary Perspectives* (ed. Peter G. Bolt and James R. Harrison; Eugene: Pickwick, 2020), 71-88.

responsibilities by deferring them to a higher power (for Israel, perhaps the priesthood or the elders; for us, maybe the church or government); and (2) to assume that because some will probably take care of this, everyone need not.

The sanctification sought is also comprehensive. As noted earlier, Leviticus 19 is broad in its scope. All of life is addressed. Commands touch on the whole spectrum of human existence from ritual matters (e.g., 19:5-8) to ethical (e.g., 19:11), from the field (e.g., 19:19) to the courtroom (19:15), from internal disposition (e.g., 19:17) to societal obligation (e.g., 19:30). The holiness Yahweh desires is all-of-life holiness. Israel must be set apart in every way. Whereas 'holy' has thus far been a ritual category used to describe the status of people (8:12), places (16:2), and objects (5:15) (see also discussion at 6:8–7:10), in Leviticus 19, 'holy' takes on an explicitly moral dimension. This does not trump the prior definition but instead adds nuance: holiness has ritual, temporal, spatial, *and* ethical dimensions.

Within the confines of this current book, there is not sufficient space to work through every command in 19:3-37 in detail. Readers are encouraged to consult the commentaries (for a list of recommended works, see the 'Further Reading' section at the end of this volume). Instead, what I want to do is explore some of the broader features of the text which aid interpretation of the specifics, as well as apply the results to some salient examples along the way.

The laws listed in Leviticus 19 are a mix of positive (e.g., 'Keep my decrees', 19:19) and negative (e.g., 'Do not deceive one another', 19:11) commands. In this way, holiness is portrayed to be as much a matter of what one actively does as what one avoids. The legislation also utilizes apodictic and casuistic forms. Apodictic commands are bare imperatives stated with universal application (e.g., 'Do not use dishonest standards when measuring length, weight or quantity', 19:35). Casuistic laws, on the other hand, present a scenario for consideration and usually begin with 'When' or 'If'. For instance, 19:23-25 imagines the future eating of fruit in Canaan ('When you enter the land'). As landowner (cf. 25:23), Yahweh is entitled to the first viable crop from newly planted trees (in the fourth year, 19:24). This harvest is given to God in thankful anticipation of the harvests to follow (19:24-25; cf. 23:9-14). Casuistic formulations enable hearers to visualize a concrete outworking of a principle as a means of enabling application to similar life situations (see also 19:5-8, 9-10, 20-23, 33-34).

Perhaps one of the more striking aspects of the laws in Leviticus 19 are their affinity with the Decalogue (i.e., the Ten Commandments). The opening verses are immediately evocative: respect for parents (19:3; cf. Exod. 20:12 and Deut. 5:16), keeping Sabbath (19:3; cf. Exod. 20:8 and Deut. 5:12), and a prohibition on making idols (19:4; cf. Exod. 20:4 and Deut. 5:8). Other verses follow suit: 'Do not steal' (19:11; cf. Exod. 20:15 and Deut. 5:19) and 'Do not swear falsely by my name and so profane the name of your God' (19:12; cf. Exod. 20:7 and Deut. 5:11). However, exactly where and how the Ten Commandments are reiterated in 19:3-37 remains debated.[7] While parallels like those just noted are clear, other suggestions become more

---

7. For a comparison of six different views, see Milgrom, *Leviticus 17–22*, 1600. Keen readers can explore the issues further in David T. Stewart, 'Leviticus 19 as Mini-Torah,' in *Current Issues in Priestly and Related Literature: The Legacy of Jacob Milgrom and Beyond* (ed. Roy E. Gane and Ada Taggar-Cohen; SBLRBS 82; Atlanta: SBL, 2015), 299-323.

tenuous. Milgrom cautions accordingly: 'an examination of some of these parallels reveals that they are grounded on exegetical quicksand.'[8] Nevertheless, Leviticus 19 clearly repeats most Decalogue commands.

It is intriguing that Leviticus 19 does not reiterate those commands precisely.[9] For a start, the scope is different. For instance, while Exodus 20:16 (and Deuteronomy 5:20) prohibits giving false testimony, Leviticus 19:11 enjoins truth-telling more universally: 'Do not lie.' The sequence is different too. In fact, in 19:3-4 the order is *reversed* (Exodus 20 lists idolatry, Sabbath, and parents ['father' then 'mother']; Leviticus 19 has parents ['mother' then 'father'], Sabbath, and idolatry). Rhetorically, the reversal is important and suggests that how one lives in relation to other people is as important as how one lives in relation to Yahweh.[10] Thus the artistic arrangement of the text drives home its central message: holiness towards God necessitates holiness towards neighbor.

Decalogue commands are also not presented as a unified block, but are interspersed with other instructions. Yet, at the same time, language from the Ten Commandments frames the entire chapter. Statements in 19:3, 36 ('I am Yahweh your God . . . I am Yahweh your God who brought you up from the land of Egypt' [my translation]) evoke Exodus 20:2, 'I am Yahweh your God who brought you out of Egypt, out of the land of slavery' (my translation).

---

8. Milgrom, *Leviticus 17–22*, 1600.

9. There are also differences between Exod. 20 and Deut. 5 (especially regarding the rationale for Sabbath observance). For details, see J. Gordon McConville, *Deuteronomy* (AOTC 5; Leicester: Apollos, 2002), 121-22.

10. Balentine, *Leviticus*, 161.

Reinforced by the repetition of 'I am Yahweh' throughout, Leviticus 19 implies *all* its material has the same claim on Israel as the Decalogue. Thus, the Ten Commandments may not be as neat a summary of the law as is sometimes suggested (or is implied by plaques hanging in some church buildings). In fact, Jesus, when asked which commands best encapsulated the whole law, quoted Deuteronomy 6:5 and Leviticus 19:18, neither of which are part of the Decalogue (Matt. 22:36-40).

The implications of these observations are enormous (see also 'Preaching and Teaching Old Testament Law'). Leviticus 19 actively resists allowing readers to compartmentalize its instructions. The point is made starker when a comparison is made with other ancient law codes which did treat religious, moral, and legal matters in *separate* collections.[11] In contrast, Leviticus 19 (and the Old Testament generally) deliberately merges all the above categories into a holistic presentation. It is a case of all in or all out; there is no middle ground. Faithful obedience is everything or it is nothing. Thus, to split Old Testament law into categories would be to subvert the intent of the text.

How then do we interpret and apply Leviticus 19 in a *Christian* context? In a word: carefully! The interpretative challenge is self-evident. While one senses an ongoing obligation to love one's neighbor based on 19:18 (indeed, Jesus commands it), does the following verse mean I must sort through my wardrobe to remove clothing made from two types of material?

---

11. Shalom M. Paul, *Studies in the Book of the Covenant in the Light of Cuneiform and Biblical Law* (VTSup 18; Leiden: Brill, 1970), 43.

Again, this is not the place to resolve every difficulty. A couple of the stranger (at least to our ears) injunctions will need to serve as examples. Returning to 19:19 ('Do not wear clothing woven of two kinds of material'), what are we to make of this? As with all interpretation, paying careful attention to text and context is crucial. First, the command forbids *wearing* mixed fabric, not making it.[12] Second, priestly attire *was* made of blended fabrics (wool and linen, Exod. 28:4-8).[13] Leviticus 19:19 is aimed at preventing other Israelites from dressing (and acting) like priests (an actual problem; see Num. 16). As my cotton-polyester blend shirt entails no risk of my performing priestly duties, it does not contravene the principle underlying 19:19, although perhaps donning a surplice and pretending to be a minister might. Likewise, while forbidding tattoos has long been a hallmark of conservative Christian culture, in context, 19:28 prohibits marking one's body (or cutting it) *for the dead*. In view are pagan practices associated with death and mourning. While Israelites could mourn for loved ones (cf. 10:6; Num. 20:29), they were to eschew the practices of surrounding nations. Tattoos without similar associations would seem to be fair game (cf. Rev. 19:16!).

---

12. I am indebted to Sklar, *Leviticus*, 248, for this section.

13. Deuteronomy makes the point more explicit. A vineyard must not be planted with two types of seed lest the entire crop become *holy* and therefore be off limits to the viticulturist (Deut. 22:9). It is wool and linen (i.e., the mix for priestly garments) that is expressly forbidden (Deut. 22:11). Mixtures belong to the realm of the holy. Roy Gane therefore concludes: 'the laws regarding mixtures seem intended to protect the distinction between the ordinary domain of laypersons and the sacred sphere of the sanctuary' (*Leviticus, Numbers*, 338).

There are real riches to be mined in Leviticus 19 for those with time to explore. Again, I will illustrate with one example: the well-known injunction to 'love your neighbor as yourself' (19:18).[14] The previous verses add definition to who constitutes one's 'neighbor': the poor (19:10), foreigners (19:10), laborers (19:13), the disabled (19:14), associates (19:15), one's brother (19:17), and fellow citizens (19:18). Thus, 'neighbor' pushes beyond peers and close relations to include the marginalized and even those of different ethnicity (also, 19:34). This climactic command is a call to love other humans without distinction.

The command to love also needs to be read as part of the two-verse unit in which it is found. The implied setting is an act of wrongdoing: a 'brother' has caused harm, serious enough to evoke hatred. Both verses follow an identical movement from prohibition, to instruction, to rationale (see *Table 12.1*).

	19:17	19:18
Prohibition:	You shall not hate your brother in your heart	Do not take vengeance, and do not keep [a grudge against] the sons of your people
Instruction:	You shall surely rebuke/reprove your neighbor	but you shall love your neighbor as yourself
Rationale:	so you will not bear sin against him (or 'because of him')	I am Yahweh

Table 12.1

---

14. Here, I am drawing on my essay, 'Joseph and His Brothers: Genesis 44–45,' in *Gospel Shaped Forgiveness: Forgiving One Another as God Has Forgiven Us* (ed. Kit Barker and G. Geoffrey Harper; ACTMS Eugene: Wipf&Stock, [forthcoming]).

The arrangement in parallel panels invites further reflection. Reading the prohibitions side-by-side indicates that fostering hatred in one's heart can overflow into acts of vengeance, even against a 'brother' (cf. Gen. 4:1-10). As 'heart' in Hebrew idiom signifies the mind rather than emotions, this suggests *planned* revenge. Instead, 19:17 dictates a better route. Rather than hating and taking vengeance, the wronged person must rebuke. This is a concrete act of loving one's neighbor (cf. Prov. 27:5). Note that love is *commanded*. One must possess a loving disposition, displayed in action, toward the very person one hates. The reason is clarified in the twinned rationales. Loving rebuke will mitigate the potential to end up bearing sin on account of the wrongdoer (presumably by taking vengeance). This response is also paralleled with the statement: 'I am Yahweh'. The point is clear: loving wrongdoers by rebuking them for sin and opening the door to repentance and restoration is exactly how Yahweh has acted towards Israel. Thus, in line with the entire chapter, individual Israelites must heed the call to emulate Yahweh in their dealings with neighbor. All of this is wonderfully suggestive for how 19:17-18 intersects with New Testament teaching and Christian application. As indicated, Leviticus 19 is a veritable treasure trove for theological reflection.

From text to message

Leviticus 19 is theologically rich and has much to contribute to Christian faith and practice. Nevertheless, it is a difficult passage to teach verse-by-verse. The first reason is simply time. A Bible study group may be able to work through the thirty-plus instructions before coffee, but a sermon is unlikely to do so, especially given a twenty-to thirty-minute timeframe. There are simply too many commands to cover adequately in one sitting. The second limiting factor is interpretative. To understand and apply Leviticus 19 well means wrestling with the bigger question of how Old Testament law applies to Christians, a complex topic at the best of times. While some of that work can be covered in a sermon or study, there are limits. It also reduces the time available to work through the text. Of course, one could preach a much longer sermon or tackle the chapter across several talks or studies. Anything short of that will inevitably involve a measure of compromise.

Getting the message clear: the theme

Leviticus 19 commands Israel increasingly to emulate and embody the holiness of the God who rescued them from Egypt. Yahweh's decrees intrude into all dimensions of individual and corporate existence and position holiness as an all-of-life response to who God is.

Getting the message clear: the aim

Running through the heart of Leviticus 19 is a call to remember. Israel must remember its deliverance from Egypt, recall the character of Yahweh, and consider the covenantal relationship established at Sinai. Then, considering these things, individuals and nation must imitate their God, becoming holy as He is holy. Accordingly, the text takes great pains to resist compartmentalization of life into religious and secular concerns, to combat reductionism when it comes to obedience and transformation. Instead, deliberate blending of Decalogue commands with a range of other ethical, ritual, social, and relational decrees communicates that the goal to which Israel must aspire is holiness as a state of being. All-encompassing sanctification is therefore mandated; that is what becoming a holy nation must entail.

A way in

For an Irishman in Australia, summertime brings mixed feelings. The long evenings of northern Europe are fondly remembered, but the consistently warm temperatures and daily sunshine go a long way to compensate. One of the key indicators that summer has arrived is that the car is full of sand. I can testify that the old saying is true: sand gets *everywhere*. Attempts to get kids to 'brush off all the sand before you get in' are an exercise in futility. Before you know it, there is sand under the rug, sand in the cutlery drawer, sand between the sheets – even grains of sand embedded in the soap. Sand gets everywhere. But if we replace 'sand' with 'holiness' we immediately get to the heart of Leviticus 19. God has a new saying He wants His people to be able to testify to: holiness gets *everywhere*.

It is impossible to be half-married. How would that work anyway? 'Sorry, only married during business hours.' 'Could you come back next week? I'll be on duty then.' Certainly, people can *act* as if they were only married for part of the time, but that is something entirely different. That would indicate a mismatch between objective identity and behavior. It would be like claiming to be a half-parent or to be half-graduated. That is simply not the way things work. There are moments that change objective reality. You are either married or you are not; you are either a parent or you are not; you have either graduated or you have not. There is no in-between. The same logic applies to knowing God. There is no half-relationship, as if you could somehow confine God to only part of the week or to just some of the things you do. It is all or nothing. In or out. If you have any doubts about that, Leviticus 19 is here to persuade you otherwise.

Ideas for application

- Like Israel of old, Christians must live up to their calling as a 'holy nation' (1 Pet. 2:9; cf. Exod. 19:6). Identity comes first, then commensurate action. Recognition of this shared vocation allows James 2:1-13, for instance, to draw heavily upon the themes of Leviticus 19:11-18 to instruct believers in holiness.

- Holiness must become extensive. Nothing falls outside of God's remit or transforming intention. This is the positive flipside to the doctrine of total depravity: sin must be undone in every dimension of individual and corporate life.

- Obedience to God's instruction is essential, but only when rightly placed. It must never become a means of earning God's favor. But, when God graciously bestows His favor upon someone, obedience is the required response.

- Loving the unlovable is what God does. Those who belong to Him must display a family resemblance. How people relate to one another is a measure of their godlikeness. Accordingly, Paul says that loving others is the fulfillment of the law (Rom. 13:8-10).

- Loving one's neighbor must be without distinction. Jesus suggests that the crucial question is not 'Who is my neighbor?', but rather, 'Who can I be a neighbor to?' (Luke 10:29-37).

- Jesus reiterates the same all-or-nothing loyalty expected in Leviticus 19: 'If anyone comes to me and does not hate father and mother, wife and children, brothers and sisters ... such a person cannot be my disciple' (Luke 14:26).

- God cannot simply be tacked onto life. Elijah condemned Israel's wavering on that front (1 Kings 18:21). Jesus, likewise, warned His followers about the impossibility of trying to serve both God and money (Matt. 6:24).

- Christians are called to rebuke others for sin – motivated by concern for the holiness of God's people – and to extend forgiveness to all who repent (Matt. 18:15-17; Luke 17:3-4).

- The prophets consistently reprimanded Israel for its lack of care for the weak and the marginalized (e.g. Isa. 1:16-17; Amos 2:6-8) and extolled the opposite virtue (e.g., Micah 6:8). Here is a metric for evaluating the biblical character of a church community: How well are the vulnerable cared for?

- God's people are His means of extending provision to others, from not gleaning the edges of one's field (Lev. 19:9-10) to providing for the needy (Acts 4:34-35; 2 Cor. 9:5-13).

Suggestions for preaching

Sermon 1

This sermon works through the entire text of Leviticus 19 to drive home the comprehensive nature of the instruction and seeks to confront the sacred-secular divide endemic to Western culture (and churches).

- **Be holy because I am holy (19:1-2).** Leviticus 19 opens with a command that encapsulates its overarching message: a call to emulate and embody Yahweh's holiness. The context is relational. Yahweh is Israel's God; Israel is Yahweh's people. There ought to be a recognizable affinity in character and action. Deliverance from Egypt is recalled in 19:34, 36. This positions the chapter's call to holiness as a call to sanctification for an already rescued people. It also encourages remembrance of Yahweh's character as displayed in the exodus. This is the God Israel is to imitate.

- **Be holy in all things (19:3-37).** The remainder of the chapter lists specific commands that relate to all manner of life situations. There is very little arrangement evident. This creates a 'lurching' effect, similar to Proverbs, in which seemingly disparate aspects of life are set side-by-side. The arrangement (or lack thereof) helps to drive home the central message of the chapter: Yahweh desires holiness in every part of life without distinction. Ritual, ethical, inner, outer, spiritual, physical, personal, and societal holiness are all equally important. Leviticus 19 subverts any attempt to prioritize commands by blending novel instructions with others taken from elsewhere in Leviticus and the wider Pentateuch, especially the Decalogue.

- **Be holy because I am holy (1 Pet. 1:16).** Peter quotes Leviticus 19:2 to apply the command to Christians, to those who have already received new birth in Christ. In this way, Peter reiterates the call of Leviticus 19 for comprehensive sanctification. Total reconciliation with God necessarily leads towards total transformation.

Therefore, Christians too must be a 'holy nation' (1 Pet. 2:9), a people set apart as a witness to the 'Gentiles' (1 Pet. 2:12 ESV). Love for neighbor is the preeminent evidence of new birth (1 Pet. 1:22-23).

Sermon 2

With a similar purpose to sermon 1, this talk attempts to convey the breadth of Leviticus 19, but does so by sampling commands that are representative of different aspects of life. This allows more time to develop a richer understanding of each injunction while also demonstrating that holiness must be an all-of-life pursuit. An outline with suggested verses follows (the main headings form a jingle that can be used as both summary and takeaway).

1. Holiness here, holiness there
   a. Holiness at home (19:3a, 29)
   b. Holiness in the vineyard (19:10)
   c. Holiness towards God (19:12)
   d. Holiness towards others (19:16b)
   e. Holiness of inner life (19:17-18)
   f. Holiness of outer life (19:27-28)
   g. Holiness and spiritual relations (19:31)
   h. Holiness and foreign relations (19:33-34)

2. Holiness, holiness everywhere
   a. Leviticus 19 is a comprehensive call to holiness (19:37)
   b. The rationale: Be holy because I, Yahweh your God, am holy (19:2)
   c. God doesn't change, but His people need to
   d. Christians are also God's 'holy nation' (1 Pet. 2:9)

Sermon 3

Another option for preaching Leviticus 19 is to focus on one specific section and develop it more fully. Leviticus 19:17-18 is well suited to this, as most people are already familiar with verse 18. I have also heard 19:9-10 preached to great effect. This kind of sermon will inevitably discuss context and so the remainder of Leviticus 19 and its place in the book can also be incorporated. The real advantage of this approach is that it better teases out the interpretative issues that bear upon reading and applying a specific Old Testament legal text. Doing so gives a congregation tools to tackle the remainder of the chapter as well as similar passages elsewhere. Of course, this approach is not mutually exclusive and can be combined with the other options outlined above.

Suggestions for teaching

Questions to help understand the passage

1. Why is this a word for the 'entire assembly' (19:2)?

2. How would you define holiness according to the book of Leviticus? Why does Yahweh command Israel to 'be holy' (19:2)?

3. Which of the Ten Commandments can you find represented in 19:3-37?

4. Why does Leviticus 19 repeat commands from elsewhere in the book (e.g., 19:5-8, 26) and from elsewhere in the Pentateuch (e.g., 19:3)?

5. Does Leviticus 19 have a discernible structure? How does your answer influence interpretation of the text?

6. Why does Leviticus 19 keep alternating between 'you' plural and singular, and between apodictic and casuistic formulations?

7. Is Leviticus 19 primarily about (a) loving God or (b) loving neighbor? How is the relationship between (a) and (b) best defined?

8. Why did Jesus say that Leviticus 19:18 represents the heart of the law (Mark 12:30-31)?

9. Give a reason for why three chapters (Lev. 18–20) filled with commands appear at this point in Leviticus.

Questions to help apply the passage

1. In Romans 8:4, Paul speaks of the righteous requirements of the law being met *in* us who have the Spirit. What do you think he means? How does this influence your understanding of Leviticus 19?

2. Which command in Leviticus 19 do you find strangest? In what ways does paying close attention to text and context help you understand it better?

3. Leviticus 19 is written to deliberately combat potential attempts by readers to create a divide between sacred and non-sacred. Are there aspects of your life which, to all intents and purposes, look like they fall outside of God's jurisdiction? What will you do about it?

4. Out of the range of issues touched on in Leviticus 19, which do you find the most challenging and why?

5. Compile a list of what Leviticus 19 says about issues of social justice. To the extent these things reveal God's viewpoint, how do you and your church community fare?

6. How do you understand interpersonal forgiveness to work? How does your understanding fit with 19:17-18, Matthew 18:15-17, and Luke 17:3-4?

13.
Acknowledging the Holy
(Leviticus 21–22)

Introduction

For many readers, Leviticus 21–22 simply occasions disbelief. Why are we thinking about priests and sacrifices again? After all, Leviticus has already devoted ten chapters (Lev. 1–10) to discussing the topics. What more possibly needs to be said?

For others, the problems go much deeper. Leviticus 21, especially, grates. Its unambiguous declaration that any priest with a 'defect' is forbidden to 'come near to offer the food of his God' (21:21) sounds strange to the modern ear and smacks of discrimination. Even more troubling is that these words come as Yahweh's speech. Dismissing the disabled is by divine decree. Consequently, these verses have negatively influenced the selection and ordination of ministers in the history of the church. Little wonder, perhaps, that the passage has been deemed oppressive and even labelled a 'text of terror'. There are more than a few who argue that this is a text to be actively resisted.

Yet in Leviticus 21–22, the theme of holiness that has been building through previous chapters reaches a crescendo.

'Holy' appears thirty-two times and is unmistakably the keyword (compared to four occurrences in Lev. 19 and six in Lev. 20). Statements regarding Yahweh's innate holiness continue (21:8; cf. 19:2; 20:26). In addition, six times readers hear that Yahweh is also the one who makes people and places holy, meaning 22:32 is the seventh, climactic occasion this phrase appears in the book (20:8; 21:8, 15, 23; 22:9, 16, 32). Becoming holy is not simply the fruit of human effort; it is a divine bestowal. But that gift must be guarded. That which is holy can be desecrated. Sacrifice can become unacceptable. Even Yahweh's holy name can be profaned – that is, publicly diminished – by His people. The penalties, including death, are severe. There is something vitally important to grasp here for the preservation of ongoing relationship between God and His people.

Listening to the text

Context and structure

The divine speech formula in 21:1 ('The LORD said to Moses') and a shift of addressee from all Israel (20:2; cf. 18:2; 19:2) to specifically Aaron's sons, the priests (21:1; cf. 21:16; 22:2), demarcate Leviticus 21–22 as a new unit. The chapters are also united by topic: preserving the holiness of priests, the sacrifices they offer, and their God.

Leviticus 22:17-33 also shares affinities with 17:1-16. Addressees are identified verbatim: 'Speak to Aaron and his sons and to all the Israelites and say to them' (17:2; 22:18). Both passages consider ascension offerings made by Israelites *and* resident foreigners (17:8; 22:18). Moreover, the chief concern of both texts is to preserve right procedure in relation to private sacrifice: the use of sacred blood in Leviticus 17 and the quality of the animal in Leviticus 22.

These connections serve to frame Leviticus 17-22 and tie the material together. Moreover, the forceful conclusion of 22:31-33, with its amalgamation of key phrases drawn from the preceding chapters, acts as a conclusion, not only to 22:26-30, but to all of chapters 17–22. John Kleinig lays out this part of Leviticus as a loose chiasm:[1]

A   Use of blood from animals for atonement (17:1-16)

   B   Defilement of the land (18:1-30)

      C   Holiness of the congregation (19:1-37)

   B' Penalties for defilement of the land (20:1-27)

   C' Holiness of the priesthood (21:1–22:16)

A' Animals acceptable for sacrifice (22:17-33)

Leviticus 21–22 contains five instances of the divine speech formula which demarcate the major sections (21:1, 16; 22:1, 17, 26). The chapters can be divided accordingly:

Priests: who they can bury and marry (21:1-15)

Blemished priests: what they may and may not do (21:16-24)

Priestly honoring of holy offerings (22:1-16)

Blemished animals: what may and may not be offered (22:17-25)

Animals acceptable for offering (22:26-33)

Working through the text

Priests: who they can bury and marry (21:1-15)

Leviticus 21:1-15 is explicitly addressed to the priests (21:1). However, as 21:24 makes clear, even a word specifically

---

1. Kleinig, *Leviticus*, 353.

directed towards a subset of the people (in this case, Aaron; cf. 21:17) nevertheless constitutes Yahweh's instruction for the entire nation. When it comes to Leviticus, there are no secrets. Mutual accountability is thereby enabled. Adherence to priestly strictures becomes a corporate concern.

The limitations outlined in this section extend to two matters: (1) death and mourning, and (2) marriage and children.[2] The topics are addressed in order, first for ordinary priests (21:1-9) and then for the high priest (21:10-15). Leviticus 21:1 states the case regarding separation from death: a priest must not 'make himself unclean for the dead among his people' (ESV). Death, especially human death, was supremely defiling (see Num. 19:11-22; for animal death, see 11:26-28, 39-40). Accordingly, a priest must not defile himself by contact with a corpse, except for persons belonging to his own household (21:2-4). Moreover, priests must not engage in pagan mourning rites (21:5; cf. 19:27-28). The rationale for both prohibitions is given in

---

2. A further restriction simply assumed by the text is that Israel's priests were to be exclusively male. While some see this as evidence of discrimination or gender bias, Milgrom's comment must be carefully considered: 'Extreme caution should be exercised in attributing prejudice, especially where it can be shown that none exists' (*Leviticus 17–22*, 1811). Foremost to bear in mind are the parallels established between Adam and the priests (especially the high priest) in Leviticus. In Genesis 2 Adam is portrayed as an archetypal priest, serving in the 'Sanctuary of Eden'. Importantly, Adam's placement and role are instituted *prior* to the creation of woman. Considering the rich tapestry of allusion to Genesis 1–3 found throughout Leviticus, this may explain why Israel's priesthood was male. Other potential reasons for the exclusion of women include the risk of menstrual defilement (and resulting consequences) as well as a concern to dissociate sexual connotations from the temple system (contra other ancient cultures).

21:6. Because priests present offerings to God they must be, and remain, holy. Proximity is the issue. That was why the inauguration ceremony of Leviticus 8 brought about a changed status: serving a holy God requires one to be holy. Intentional defilement would undermine that goal and place priest and cult in jeopardy.

Avoiding defilement likewise underlies instructions regarding marriage and children. It is 'because priests are holy to their God' that they must not marry divorcees or former prostitutes (21:7). The same logic stands behind the seemingly harsh injunction of 21:9 (cf. 10:2). Holiness must be guarded, no matter the cost. Leviticus 21:8 cements the connections. Yahweh is holy; He has made priests holy, and therefore every Israelite (the command is singular in form) must regard them as such. Priests serve Yahweh on behalf of the people. That function must not be compromised.

The following verses reiterate the above points in relation to the high priest – that is, 'the one among his brothers who has had the anointing oil poured on his head' (21:10; cf. 8:12). He too must not defile himself by corpse contact (21:11) or by marrying a divorcee or former prostitute (21:14). Yet, the strictures are more exacting. The high priest must avoid *all* contact with death, even when it is his father or mother (21:11). He must not even outwardly display signs of grief or leave the tabernacle precincts to mourn (21:10, 12). Moreover, his wife must be a virgin, ruling out a widow as potential spouse (21:13-14). This is to ensure his children are not defiled (21:15).

Evident is a spectrum of expected conduct. While commonalities exist, the requirements of holiness increase from ordinary Israelite to priest to high priest. Again, proximity is key. For those who approach closest to the divine presence, greater holiness is required (see *Figure 5.1*). The priesthood pictures an ideal, an observation that proves essential for correctly understanding the following section.

Blemished priests: what they may and may not do (21:16-24)

Leviticus 21:16-24 is addressed to Aaron alone, perhaps indicating his responsibility with respect to implementation. The legislation concerns priests who have a 'defect' (NIV) or 'blemish' (ESV). The Hebrew word (*mum*) denotes a physical flaw, not a moral deficiency. Various bodily defects are catalogued in 21:18-20. The list, consisting of twelve items (a round number), appears to be representative rather than exhaustive. Included are congenital conditions such as blindness and dwarfism as well as others that are acquired and may well be temporary, like a broken hand or foot (21:19).[3] The purpose of the legislation is to prevent any priest who has a physical defect from coming near to 'offer the food of his God' (21:17). The ban is categorical and is repeated five times in quick succession (21:17, 18, 21 [x2], 23). For priests with permanent blemishes, these words signaled a lifetime exclusion.

Unsurprisingly, 21:16-24 has caught the eye of disability theologians (as well as casual readers). Many find this passage deeply unsettling, even offensive (a point to bear in mind when teaching it). What are we to make of it? Why is this section here?

In answering those questions, my thinking has been immeasurably helped by Joshua Reeve, whose work on

---

3. 'Broken' is better than NIV's 'crippled' even though before effective setting techniques a fractured hand or foot could easily have degenerated into a permanent impairment.

21:16-24 constitutes the most persuasive reading of this difficult text. He makes several astute observations that must be borne in mind:

1. Disabled priests remained priests (in contrast to other ancient temple systems). As such, their holy status meant they could continue to eat holy and most holy food on an equal footing with their peers (21:22). Impairment did not mean diminution of status or privation for them and their families. Nor were they deemed unacceptable to God.

2. The exclusion is very specific. Blemished priests could still carry out most cultic duties (inasmuch as their disability allowed them to). They were forbidden only from approaching (or passing beyond; see ESV) the inner curtain and the bronze altar (21:23).

3. The reason for not coming near these sacred places is twofold: (1) 'because he has a blemish upon him'; and (2) so that he will not 'profane my sanctuaries because I am Yahweh who makes them [i.e., the sanctuaries] holy' (21:23, my translation). The goal of the legislation is not to promote discrimination against the disabled (cf. 19:14), but to protect the sanctity of the tabernacle.

4. This passage must be read in light of Leviticus and the wider Pentateuch.[4] In that context, the tabernacle cult is presented as a means of re-creating the cosmos in line with creation order. As we have seen, Leviticus

---

4. Reeve notes that evangelical commentators attempt too quickly to explain the passage Christologically, while disability theologians often fail to consider its wider setting within the theology of Leviticus ('Blemished Bodies', 368).

repeatedly makes this point by alluding to Genesis
1–3 (see also 'Getting Our Bearings in Leviticus').

What is ultimately at stake in 21:16-24, therefore, is the
dramatic effect of the cult within the theology of Leviticus.
Reeve concludes:

> the nonparticipation of blemished priests in rituals at
> the altar and in the holy of holies is a sign-act that points
> to God's renewal of creation. In the moment of re-union
> with God in sacrificial ritual, the officiating priest is
> required to possess as flawless a body as possible … This
> was a symbol of the created goodness of humanity in
> the edenic sanctuary, and a prophetic representation of
> God's eschatological renewal of the cosmos – a renewal
> that will include the transformation and glorification of
> human bodies.[5]

Priestly honoring of holy offerings (22:1-16)

Leviticus 22:1-16 is addressed to Aaron and his sons.
Guarding holiness is again primary: the priests must
rightly treat the 'holy things' that the Israelites 'make
holy' (i.e., dedicate) in order to avoid profaning Yahweh's
'holy name' (22:2, my translation). Although the priests
received sacrificial portions as their share (cf. 6:16; 7:7-10,
32-34), they are nevertheless instructed to 'abstain'
(ESV) or 'separate themselves' (KJV) from such when in a
ritually impure state, on pain of being cut off (22:2-3).[6]
Seven sources of potential impurity are listed in 22:4-5,
8: *tsara'at* infection (cf. 13:1-46), bodily discharges (cf.

---

5. Reeve, 'Blemished Bodies', 372-73.

6. On the meaning of 'impure', see discussion at 11:2b-23; for 'cut off', see
   discussion at 5:1-13.

15:1-15), corpse contamination (cf. Num. 19:11-22), semen (cf. 15:16-18), any crawling animal (cf. 11:29-38; 20:25), a person who might convey impurity (e.g., 15:7-8, 19-24), and meat from torn animals (cf. 17:15). Sources of major impurity must await appropriate cleansing (i.e., for *tsara'at* infection and abnormal discharges, 22:4). Minor impurity must be countered by washing and waiting until evening (22:6). When cleansed, the priest may again eat sacred offerings, 'for they are his food' (22:7).

The stakes are high. Holiness and impurity must not mix. Accordingly, Leviticus 22:9 declares that contravention of these requirements will be regarded as contempt of Yahweh and will result in death (cf. 22:3). This declaration becomes the rationale for 22:10-16. Only authorized persons, that is a priest and his immediate household, may eat holy food (22:10-13; cf. 6:18; 7:7-10, 34). The threat of death for accidental (note: not deliberate) eating by an unauthorized person could be mitigated. On realization, such a person could make restitution to the priest, including a 20 per cent levy (22:14) *and* a reparation offering to Yahweh (see 5:15-16). This hefty penalty (albeit less severe than death) meant the priests had a responsibility to ensure ordinary people avoided guilt that required payment (22:15-16). This too is part of the priestly mandate to separate holy from common and pure from impure (10:10).

Blemished animals: what may and may not be offered (22:17-25)

Leviticus 22:17-25 continues the focus on 'sacred offerings' with a discussion of acceptable and unacceptable sacrifices. The passage has immediate resonance with 21:16-24. Just as priests with a 'defect' (*mum*) are barred from serving *at the* altar, so animals with a 'defect' (*mum*) are barred from being offered *on* the altar. Again, twelve representative defects are listed (22:22-24), several of which correspond with 21:18-20. Animals with these kinds of blemish are prohibited. Instead, sacrifices must be 'without defect' (22:19, 21; cf. 1:3, 10; 3:1; etc.), although a concession is made for freewill offerings of deformed or stunted animals in some cases (22:23).

Similarity with 21:18-20 aside, the rationale for blemished animals is different. Restricted access for impaired priests is motivated by a concern for holy places (21:23). With animals, the underlying issue is they are presented as *gifts* to Yahweh (22:18), or as *food* (22:25). The value of a gift or the excellence of a meal ought to correspond with the importance of the recipient. Thus, a 'male without defect' (22:19) is the ideal (i.e., most expensive) option. Moreover, blemished animals would undermine the symbolic connection to the 'perfect' life being substituted in place of the less-than-perfect offerer (see discussion at 17:10-12). For these reasons, Yahweh declares that defective animals will not be accepted on behalf of the offerer, whether that person be Israelite or foreigner (22:20, 25).

Animals acceptable for offering (22:26-33)

The final section (without explicit addressee) provides further instruction regarding acceptable offerings. An animal must be at least eight days old when offered and must not be slaughtered on the same day as its parent (22:27-28). Thank offerings (a variant of fellowship offerings) must be conducted as commanded (see 7:12-15). Adherence to this instruction will maintain the acceptability of offerings made.

As suggested, 22:31-33 functions as a conclusion for more than just 22:26-30 (see 'Context and structure').

'Keep my commands' is plural in form, invoking the nation to heed the instruction of Leviticus 17–22. Moreover, 'keeping' is defined as 'doing' (see HCSB, ESV). Merely hearing or remembering is not sufficient; as always, *obedience* is key (cf. 26:3, 14; James 1:22-25). The clustering of terms in 21:31-33 drives home the need for such obedience. The thrice repeated phrase, 'I am Yahweh' (my translation) recalls all the instances of that expression throughout 18–22. Again, the exodus from Egypt and the subsequent binding of Israel to God is remembered (22:33; cf. 11:45; 18:3; 19:34, 36). Considering this relational context, Israel must not profane Yahweh's holy name, but must instead acknowledge Him as holy and as the one who makes people holy (22:32). Invitation and warning intermingle. The offer to share in divine holiness is real (cf. 11:44-45; 19:2; 20:7). It is also not optional: Yahweh has and is setting the people apart (cf. Exod. 19:4-6; Lev. 20:26). The priesthood embodies and visibly portrays God's transformative intentions for humanity. Conformity to that agenda is the only route to life.

From text to message

For many people, Leviticus 21–22 represents one of the book's most uncomfortable passages due to its seemingly discriminatory stance against disabled people and the potential impact on conducting Christian ministry. If that seems far-fetched, then simply read the comments made by people online or in the secondary literature. When teaching difficult texts like this, it can be very tempting to skirt the troublesome issue. However – to adopt a zoological analogy – if there is an elephant in the room, you cannot simply stick your head in the sand like the proverbial ostrich. To do so would not only be unfaithful to the text, but also to your audience. In fact, many in a given study group or congregation may not listen to much else following the Bible reading *until* you address the matter (or at least flag that you *will* address it). What becomes essential (here as elsewhere) is to help people carefully read the text in its context. This may not alleviate every problem, but it will help to ensure that we are hearing more clearly what God is saying.

Getting the message clear: the theme

Yahweh is holy and He extends holiness to people and places. Accordingly, Israel must acknowledge that which God has made holy and protect it from defilement, whether it be Yahweh's name, the priests who serve Him, the sanctuary in which they serve, or the sacrifices they present.

Getting the message clear: the aim

Leviticus 21–22 drives towards a conclusion that urges readers to keep all the Lord's commands with respect to the holy. Regarding rationale, the passage remembers deliverance from Egypt and the calling upon God's people to be set apart to the Lord. He is their holy God who is, in turn, making them holy. Accordingly, God's holiness and lordship must be acknowledged and not profaned lest the people die for treating His word with contempt or find their sacrifices deemed unacceptable. There is a warning here. Yet, there is a positive goal also. Aaron, the priests, and the people are summoned to understand God's agenda and to corporately guard against defilement that which He has made holy. By doing so, they will preserve both the portrayal and actualization of God's unfolding purpose to restore creation to Himself.

A way in

Are you any good at protecting things? I suspect you are. All of us work hard to safeguard that which we deem valuable. We protect our money. That is why you tend not to find wads of cash lying around the place; it is all safely stored in the bank (or hidden under the mattress). We protect our health. That is why we get annoyed when the person next to us sneezes without covering their nose and why every home has at least one cupboard or drawer filled with medicine, plasters, and vitamin supplements. We protect our children, our homes, our jobs. Some of us are even determined enough to protect our nation that we enlist in the military. We protect that which we deem valuable. That is the concern at the heart of Leviticus 21–22: to protect that which is valuable. Not money this time, or health, or jobs, but holiness. God is holy and He must be recognized as such. But God also extends His holiness to people and to places as part of His plan to remake and restore creation. He was doing this in ancient Israel; He is still doing it today. Holiness is valuable; it is something to guard and protect. Leviticus can teach us how.

Ideas for application

- Jesus, as a 'lamb without blemish or defect', becomes an acceptable offering that secures redemption (1 Pet. 1:19).

- In the New Testament, God's activity of making people holy is continued by Jesus. Jesus acts to present His people 'holy and without blemish' (Eph. 5:27 ESV). Holiness is both an objective status already declared (Heb. 10:10) and an ongoing process (Heb. 10:14).

- Christians are frequently called saints – that is, 'holy ones' (e.g., Rom. 1:7; 1 Cor. 1:2; Eph. 1:1). This is their new identity in Christ.

- Like Israel, Christians must acknowledge God as holy while remembering that acknowledgment needs to extend beyond mere thinking to the way one lives.

- Dedication to Jesus trumps expected family commitments and allegiances (Matt. 8:21-22 and Luke 9:59-60; Luke 14:26), although one must be careful not to disregard God's word in the process (Mark 7:11-13).

- Throughout the Gospels, those with physical impairments again serve to portray the extent of God's restorative agenda as Jesus heals the lame, the blind, the disfigured, and the crippled.

- The dynamic of Leviticus 22 is reiterated in a Christian context in 1 Thessalonians 4:7-8: 'For God has not called us for impurity, but in holiness. Therefore whoever disregards this, disregards not man but God, who gives his Holy Spirit to you' (ESV).

- As a holy priesthood, Christians must offer God acceptable sacrifices (1 Pet. 2:5). We are to present Him our very selves as holy and pleasing (Rom. 12:1). We also offer 'the fruit of lips that acknowledge his name' as well as doing good and sharing with others (Heb. 13:15-16 ESV). Indeed, providing for the physical needs of believers is deemed 'a fragrant offering, an acceptable sacrifice, pleasing to God' (Phil. 4:18).

- Christians must be very careful to guard the holiness of God's sanctuaries. These are no longer temple (or church) structures but the physical bodies of believers, bound together and indwelt by the Spirit of God (Eph. 2:22; cf. 1 Pet. 2:4-5). In a context of unchecked immorality, it is this concern that fuels Paul's pained question to the Corinthian church ('[D]o you not know that your body is a temple of the Holy Spirit within you?') and subsequent command to 'glorify God in your body' (1 Cor. 6:19-20 ESV). It also underlies the apostle's sober warning in the same letter: 'If anyone destroys God's temple, God will destroy him. For God's temple is holy, and you are that temple' (1 Cor. 3:17 ESV).

- Although there is no direct link between Old Testament priests and Christian ministers, the principle of acknowledging those set apart for service to God (21:8) continues in the New Testament (e.g., 2 Cor. 10-12; 1 Tim. 5:17; Heb. 13:17-18). Also persisting are the more exacting expectations for those assigned leadership responsibilities (e.g., 1 Tim. 3:2-13; 5:19-20; Titus 1:6-9; James 3:1).

- The command forbidding inappropriate marriage in Leviticus 21:13-14 is driven by a concern to avoid defiled offspring (21:15). Concern for the same issue stands behind Paul's declaration that 'the unbelieving husband is made holy because of his wife, and the unbelieving wife is made holy because of her husband. *Otherwise your children would be unclean*, but as it is, they are holy' (1 Cor. 7:14 ESV [emphasis added]).

Suggestions for preaching

Sermon 1

While one could feasibly divide Leviticus 21–22 into two passages (21:1-22:16; 22:17-33) and preach them separately,

taking the unit as a whole makes it easier to hear repeated
refrains (e.g., 'I am Yahweh who makes you holy') and
compare similar sections (e.g., 21:18-20 and 22:19-24). It
also allows the conclusion in 22:31-33 to govern more of
the text.

- **Guarding holy priests (21:1-15).** Through the ordination process of Leviticus 8–9, Yahweh set the priests
  apart as holy, an essential prerequisite for service in
  holy places. Because it is the LORD who makes them
  holy (21:15; 22:9), that holiness must be respected and
  maintained. More exacting standards are therefore
  placed on priests and high priest with relation to
  funerals and weddings. Priests must not deliberately
  make themselves impure and risk profaning the name
  of their God. Instead, priests must model the ideal
  worshipper.

- **Guarding holy places (21:16-24).** Priests representing the ideal become the underlying rationale for
  the prohibition against physically-impaired priests
  approaching the altar or curtain. This is not blatant
  discrimination: such priests still serve at the
  tabernacle, continue to have a holy status, and may
  eat holy food. Instead, the legislation is aimed at
  guarding the holiness of places that Yahweh makes
  holy (21:23). At stake is the portrayal and enactment
  of re-creation in the tabernacle cult in which the high
  priest, especially, is an ideal human approaching the
  divine presence. Disabled priests serve God's 'drama'
  by submitting to limited roles.

- **Guarding holy offerings (22:1-33).** Yahweh also
  makes offerings holy (22:16) and, for this reason, great

care must be taken. Offerings are God's food that He shares with the priests. Therefore, priests who are impure must desist from partaking; non-priests must not eat holy food. The penalties for violation are severe. Animals sacrificed must, like the priests who offer them, be without defect. This appropriately recognizes God's greatness and preserves the symbolism of sacrifice. Israel must heed all these commands in acknowledgment of Yahweh's own holiness and His intent to extend holiness to people and places.

- **Guarding holy Christians.** The call to acknowledge God's holiness and to guard that which He is making holy continues for Christians. In Christ, God has made Christians to be a kingdom of priests and a holy nation, set apart to serve Him (1 Pet. 2:9; Rev. 1:5). Even more remarkably, through Christ's atoning death, Christians have become a holy place in which God lives by His Spirit (Eph. 2:21-22), a holy temple that must be protected from impurity, individually and corporately (1 Cor. 5:1-2; 6:18-20). As God's priests, Christians must also offer acceptable sacrifices that are holy and pleasing to Him (Phil. 4:18; Heb. 13:15-16). In all these things, Christians increasingly embody their future destiny: serving God face-to-face in the temple of the new creation (Rev. 21:1–22:6).

Sermon 2

Social awareness of, and advocacy for, those who suffer with physical or intellectual disability has increased dramatically in the last twenty years (in the Western world at least). However, rigorous biblical thinking has not necessarily kept apace. Therefore, Leviticus 21 offers a wonderful opportunity for a church to explore what the Bible has to say on the topic of disability as a means of assessing views within and without the Christian community. This could be done as a standalone talk or added to a series on Leviticus. One helpful way to stimulate deep reflection is to compare and contrast ancient and modern views. Doing so not only fosters cultural critique (both ways) but allows the distinctive voice of Scripture to be heard and applied. One possible outline would be as follows:

1. Disability in the ancient world
2. Disability in the modern world
3. Disability in the Bible

Suggestions for teaching

Questions to help understand the passage

1. Why are God's standards for holiness higher for priests than for non-priests (21:2-15)?

2. What does 'profane the name of God' mean (21:6; 22:2, 32; cf. 18:21; 19:12; 20:3)?

3. In the context of Leviticus, what does it mean that God makes people and places holy (21:8, 15, 23; 22:9, 16, 32)?

4. Why are priests with a 'defect' prohibited from approaching the altar and curtain (21:23)?

5. Why do you think instruction addressed to Aaron (21:17) was explained to all the people (21:24)?

6. What does 'impurity' mean and why is it such a big deal in 21:1-9?

7. Why are defective animals not acceptable (22:17-25)?

8. Sacrifices are frequently referred to as 'the food of your/their/his God' (21:6, 8, 17, 21, 22; 22:25). What does this mean?

9. What is the purpose of 22:31-33? To what extent does it summarize Leviticus 17-22?

Questions to help apply the passage

1. Do the injunctions of 21:2-16 apply to Christian ministers or pastors?

2. Brainstorm what the Bible says about disability. How do you think Leviticus 21:16-24 contributes to this wider theme?

3. If a non-Christian friend asked you, having read 21:16-24, why the God of the Bible values able-bodied people more than disabled, what would you say? How could an answer lead towards explaining the gospel?

4. What does the statement, 'I am the LORD who makes you holy' (22:32) mean for Christians?

5. What does Leviticus 21–22 add to your understanding of God's call upon Christians to be a 'holy nation' and a 'kingdom of priests' (1 Pet. 2:9; Rev. 1:6)?

6. Considering that the corporate Christian 'body' is a sacred place indwelt by God's Holy Spirit, how well do you and your church community guard holiness?

14.
Holy Time
(Leviticus 23)

Introduction

In Leviticus 23, God prescribes Israel's holidays. But, at the end of the day, does it really matter what a person celebrates or when they do so? Surely these things are matters of personal choice. Leviticus 23 suggests otherwise. Here, holiness takes on a *temporal* dimension as Yahweh fills in Israel's calendar. A weekly Sabbath is mandated. Additionally, seven annual festivals are specified. All are termed Yahweh's 'appointed festivals' and are established as 'sacred' or 'holy' assemblies that Israel must observe. Accordingly, national life took on a particular shape, in much the same way that Christmas, Easter, and other public holidays bequeath a certain flow to the year in Western countries. Observing Yahweh's holy times would become another arena in which Israel displayed its set apart status among the nations.

In this way, Leviticus continues to define what holiness incorporates; it is much more than simply a moral description. While ethical standards are essential (Lev. 18–20), holiness also defines *places* like the tabernacle courtyard, and *objects* like the altar. Likewise, the ordination process of Leviticus 8 set the priesthood apart as holy. A holy status, in turn, qualified priests to offer holy sacrifices and to participate in the LORD's table as they ate holy and most holy portions of offered animals. The common denominator is Yahweh's declaration. He alone is holy. Yet Yahweh extends His holiness and, by doing so, establishes a holy realm commensurate with His nature in order that He might dwell with Israel.

It is this concern for the holy that ultimately unites Leviticus. Although a division between chapters 1–16 and 17–27 is frequently suggested, holiness terminology is almost evenly distributed between the two halves of the book.[1] A holy God has come to earth to reside among humans. Therefore, people, places, objects, and now time itself must be transformed to accommodate that glorious presence. Nothing less than a world remade will suffice. Hence, while cosmic renewal would begin with Israel, it would not end there. The prophet Habakkuk foresaw the day when 'the earth will be filled with the knowledge of the glory of the LORD as the waters cover the sea' (Hab. 2:14).

Listening to the text

Context and structure

Leviticus 23 is demarcated by an introduction to divine speech ('The LORD said to Moses', 23:1) and by repeated language which forms a frame around the unit and highlights the main topic: 'the appointed festivals of the LORD' (23:2,

---

1. The verbal form of 'holy' (*qdsh*) occurs 123 times in Leviticus, fifty-four times in 1–16 and 69 times in 17–27. The noun (*qadosh*) appears 20 times, 10 times in each half. If the 20 occurrences of *qdsh* in Lev. 27, which is not usually included in the Holiness Code, are discounted, then Lev. 1–16 contains *more* holiness language than 17–26.

44). In outlining Israel's liturgical calendar, the chapter shares affinities with Exodus 23:14-17, 34:18-26, Numbers 28–29, and Deuteronomy 16:1-17. Together, these passages build a composite picture of Israel's annual festivals.

The material in Leviticus 23 divides into seven paragraphs bounded by an introduction (23:1-2) and conclusion (23:44). The first paragraph (23:3) addresses the Sabbath, a *weekly* event. The remaining paragraphs form two panels which outline *annual* spring (23:4-22) and autumn (23:23-43) festivals. Each panel devotes more space to the final festival and concludes with the statement 'I am Yahweh' (23:22, 43, my translation).

The resulting pattern (see *Table 14.1*) is reminiscent of the layout of Genesis 1:1–2:3, which likewise consists of two series of three paragraphs (days one to three concerning *habitats* and days four to six concerning *inhabitants*) and a seventh which sits outside the scheme and details Sabbath rest (day seven). Thus, even the structure of Leviticus 23 hints at the creation themes that become important for its interpretation (see below).

Sabbath	
Passover and Unleavened Bread	Trumpets
Firstfruits	Day of Atonement
Weeks (I am Yahweh)	Booths (I am Yahweh)

Table 14.1

Leviticus 23 can be outlined as follows:

> Introduction (23:1-2)
> Weekly Sabbath (23:3)
> Spring festivals (23:4-22)
> > Passover and Unleavened Bread (23:4-8)

> Firstfruits (23:9-14)
> Weeks (23:15-22)
> > Autumn festivals (23:23-43)
> > > Trumpets (23:23-25)
> > > Day of Atonement (23:26-32)
> > > Booths (23:33-43)
> Conclusion (23:44)

Working through the text

Introduction and conclusion (23:1-2, 44)

Yahweh's command to speak to the Israelites about 'appointed festivals' in the introduction (23:2) is noted as fulfilled in 23:44, forming a frame around the passage. 'Appointed festivals' is a translation of the Hebrew word *mo'ed*, which has the basic sense of 'meeting' or 'assembly'. The term is most often used to designate the tent *of meeting* (*'ohel mo'ed*). In Leviticus 23, *mo'ed* refers to designated times for meeting or gathering – in other words, 'festivals' (NIV) or 'feasts' (ESV).[2] These occasions are proclaimed 'sacred assemblies' ('holy convocations' ESV). It is important to note the source of Israel's calendar. In all things, Yahweh remains master: 'These are *my* appointed festivals, the appointed festivals *of the* LORD' (23:2 [emphasis added]). Yahweh would define the shape of Israel's year.

Weekly Sabbath (23:3)

The first of seven paragraphs delivers a command to observe Sabbath on the seventh day of the week (cf. 19:3, 30). As a

---

2. Neither of these terms is fully adequate. The Day of Atonement (23:26-32) is neither a feast (fasting is prescribed) nor festive (solemnity and confession of sin are central). At the same time, 'seasons' (JPS) or 'times' (HCSB) is too vague. As the NIV's 'appointed festivals' is the least problematic, I adopt that term.

day of 'sacred assembly', Sabbath belongs with the festivals which follow; yet, as a weekly event, it also stands apart. This seventh day is labelled 'a Sabbath to the LORD'. It has universal applicability and must be observed 'wherever you live'. However, what the day involves is described in negative rather than positive terms: 'You are not to do any work'.

The significance of Sabbath needs to be felt. Our seven-day week owes its existence to this aspect of Israelite life. Also, in the Western world at least, we have become so accustomed to having weekends off that we forget how recent a phenomenon this is (Henry Ford was one of the first employers to introduce a five-day, 40-hour working week – in 1926). In the ancient world, by contrast, a regular day off was exceptional. Nevertheless, by prescribing rest, Sabbath occasions not only relief but anxiety: relief for those otherwise unable to cease working (e.g., slaves, as per Israel's recent experience in Egypt), but anxiety for those who could not afford to (e.g., day laborers who subsisted on daily earnings). At its core, then, Sabbath observance requires *trust*: trust in God's wisdom that He knows best how to order the lives of His people, and trust in God's provision for those who obey (see also discussion at 25:1-7).

The significance of Sabbath also needs to be assessed against the wider backdrop of the Pentateuch. Seventh-day rest evokes Genesis 2:1-3 (see, likewise, Exod. 20:10-11; 31:15-17). As noted above, the structure of Leviticus 23 reinforces a connection with creation. From the other direction, Genesis 1:14 states that the purpose of the sun, moon, and stars is to mark out 'appointed festivals' (*mo'ed*), days, and years.[3] The implications are significant. First,

---

3. If the Old Testament assumes a Jubilees calendar (a debated point), then Unleavened Bread, Trumpets, and Booths would always have

Leviticus 23 reminds readers of the idyllic order of the world as it was. Moreover, in mirroring the Genesis 1 pattern, Sabbath becomes a means of experiencing 'creation time'. In this way, 'the pattern of order established in creation is given a means of realization in the liturgical order ... By observing the liturgical order, Israel participates in the sustaining and maintaining of the divinely-constructed order of creation.'[4] Sabbath observance is more than just a day off; it is a divine means of reordering the world.

Sabbath thus carries deeper connotations that must be borne in mind. Moreover, Leviticus 23–25 extends seven-fold, Sabbath patterning to *months and years*.[5]

Spring festivals (23:4-22)

All the LORD's festivals were to be proclaimed at their appointed times (23:4). Proclamation probably indicates two things: *enactment* of the festival and public *communication* that the designated time had arrived (necessary in the days before Google Calendar).

Four 'appointed festivals' occurred in the spring. The first is a combination of Passover (beginning at twilight on the fourteenth day of the first month, i.e., March/April) and the seven-day Festival of Unleavened Bread (commencing on the fifteenth). 'Twilight' indicates that,

---

occurred on *Wednesdays*, i.e. the fourth day in Genesis 1, when the celestial bodies were created. See Wenham, *Leviticus*, 302.

4. Frank H. Gorman, *Ideology of Ritual: Space, Time and Status in the Priestly Theology* (JSOTSup 91; Sheffield: JSOT Press, 1990), 219-20.

5. Timothy M. Willis, *Leviticus* (AbOTC; Nashville: Abingdon, 2009), xxiii. Sevenfold structuring is evident in Lev. 23 in its division into *seven* paragraphs punctuated by *fourteen* occurrences of Sabbath (*shabat*) and the related word *shabaton* ('solemn rest' ESV).

as elsewhere in the Old Testament, a day was understood to begin at sunset, not dawn (23:5; cf. 23:32; hence, Genesis 1: 'there was evening and morning', not 'morning and evening' as we would put it). The remaining details for observing Passover are simply assumed (see Exod. 12; Num. 9:1-14; Deut. 16:1-8) – an early indicator that the purpose of Leviticus 23 is not primarily to convey procedural instructions.

The week-long Festival of Unleavened Bread began and ended with sacred assemblies (23:7-8). Attendance, compulsory for all Israelite men (also in the case of Weeks and Booths; see Exod. 23:17; Deut. 16:16), was facilitated by prohibiting work.[6] Like Passover, Unleavened Bread was a commemoration of Israel's departure from Egypt (cf. Exod. 12:33-34). But commemoration was more than mere remembrance. By prescribing seven days of eating unleavened bread, subsequent generations had to *participate* in exodus-like events, to act as if they had been there. Thus, these twinned festivals played a culture-forming role in their mandate that every Israelite physically experience aspects of the exodus.

The second festival, Firstfruits, is linked to when Israel would begin reaping grain in Canaan (23:10). The term itself is self-explanatory: the first sheaf of grain harvested (on this occasion, barley) must be dedicated to the LORD (i.e., as the *first fruits* of the land). On the day after the Sabbath (and accompanied by ascension, tribute, and drink offerings) the sheaf must be waved (or elevated) before

---

6. Women and children could also attend, as Jesus and Mary do in Luke 2:41-42. Wenham notes that these three festivals are termed a *hag* (Lev. 23:6, 39; Deut. 16:16), a word that carries connotations of 'pilgrimage' (*Leviticus*, 303).

the LORD (23:11-13).[7] These offerings must be presented
before any of the harvest is eaten (23:14). The language
throughout is plural, perhaps suggesting that this was a
community event, rather than something each farmer had
to enact individually. The final clause makes it clear that
Firstfruits applied not just for the first crop harvested in
Canaan, but every year henceforth.

Leviticus consistently maintains that the land of
Canaan belongs to Yahweh, not Israel. Israel are only
tenant farmers whom God permits to till His land (25:23).
As owner, it is fitting that Yahweh receives the first of
each year's crop. Nevertheless, the keynote remains one
of thanksgiving and celebration. After the long winter,
fresh bread and roasted new grain make for a veritable
feast. Once Yahweh's portion is assigned, let the party
begin! Firstfruits is also anticipatory of the remainder of
the harvest to come. Thus, the festival reminds all that
the bounty of the land is a tangible expression of God's
goodness to His people.

The timing of the Festival of Weeks (Exod. 23:16
has 'Festival of Harvest') depends on that of Firstfruits.
This allows both festivals to occur at the most germane
time for that year's harvest (always subject to the vagaries
of weather).[8] Once again, seven becomes the operative
number. *Seven* full weeks after Firstfruits ('fifty days' is an

---

7. For discussion of the terms used for each offering, see at Lev. 1–6:7
   (ad loc.).

8. In the postexilic period, the Festival of Weeks became known as Pentecost, a name derived from the Greek *pentecostos*, meaning 'fiftieth'. Based
   on 23:11 ('on the day after the Sabbath'), understood as the ceremonial
   Sabbath at the beginning of Unleavened Bread, Pentecost became fixed
   as the fiftieth day after Passover (cf. 2 Macc. 12:32; Acts 2:1).

inclusive number), on the day after the *seventh* Sabbath, an offering of new grain (this time, wheat; cf. Exod. 34:22) must be made to Yahweh (23:15-16). Pilgrimage is implied in 23:17, with a requirement for leavened loaves made from fine flour to be brought 'from wherever you live'. The significance of the occasion is marked by the full suite of offerings required (presumably donated by the community). Ten animals (with accompanying tribute and drink offerings) are presented as an ascension offering, followed by a purification offering of a goat (23:18-19). The leavened loaves, together with two lambs as a fellowship offering, are waved (or elevated) before God before being given to the priests. In this way, the priesthood (which had no tillage land; Deut. 18:1-2) could also share in the firstfruits of the wheat harvest (23:20).

The section concludes by restating the injunction of 19:9-10 not to reap to the edges of one's field, for the benefit of the poor and foreigner (23:22; 'vineyard' is omitted in the context of discussing the *grain* harvest). Repeated here, the proscription takes on added meaning. The poor and resident foreigners must be allowed their own 'harvest' so they too could bring loaves in thankfulness for Yahweh's provision. This is not just an ancient version of social welfare; it facilitates worship. 'I am the LORD your God' (23:22) is a statement that applies equally to everyone.

Autumn festivals (23:23-43)

The three autumn festivals all occurred in the *seventh* month (September/October). The first day of the month was marked by what is usually called the Festival of Trumpets. From at least the fourth century B.C., this was regarded as the *beginning* of the new year (now celebrated as Rosh Hashanah).[9] Once again, forbidding work was a means of allowing all to participate in a 'sacred assembly' at which 'a fire offering' was presented to Yahweh (23:24-25 HCSB; cf. Num. 29:1-6 which adds more detail).

The description in 23:24 is highly compressed, with a string of three noun clauses indicating the distinctive features of the festival. This was to be a day of 'complete' or 'solemn' rest (*shabaton*) and a 'sacred assembly' (my translation). The third term is more difficult. 'Remembrance' is combined with a word that indicates either loud shouting (e.g., Josh. 6:5) or trumpet blasts (e.g., Lev. 25:9). This raucous noisemaking frequently appears in military contexts (e.g., Jer. 4:19; Ezek. 21:22; Amos 1:14) where shouts (or blasts) could signal either victory or alarm. The word also appears in Numbers 10:5-6 with a more mundane sense of 'announcement signal'. The ESV perhaps best captures the sense: 'a memorial proclaimed with blast of trumpets'.[10] This was a day to invoke God's remembrance of His people (cf. Num. 10:9).

The tenth day of the seventh month was Yom Kippur, or the Day of Atonement (the name of the festival, *yom hakippurim* [literally 'the day of the atonements'] appears only here and in 25:9). I discuss the ceremony in detail above (see the discussion at Lev. 16). However, set alongside Israel's other festivals, further observations can be made.

The Day of Atonement stands notably apart. In contrast to the joyous tenor of other sacred assemblies, this

---

9. Hartley, *Leviticus*, 387.

10. Numbers 10:10 implies that every festival was accompanied by trumpet blasts.

was a solemn occasion marked by self-denial (23:27, 32), likely expressed as fasting. The ban on work was categorical (23:28, 31; cf. 16:29, 31): no one had grounds to be otherwise occupied. The rationale is given in 23:28: 'because it is the Day of Atonement, when atonement is made for you before the LORD your God'. Yom Kippur was the means of dealing with unresolved sin, impurity, and their consequences (see the discussion at 16:11-28). It was crucial for Israel's ongoing life with Yahweh. The importance of the event is matched by the gravity of the punishments threatened against those who refused to either deny themselves ('must be cut off from their people', 23:29) or who continued to work regardless ('I will destroy ... anyone who does work', 23:30). Gracious provision for sins must not be disrespected.

Israel's liturgical calendar concluded with the Festival of Booths (Sukkoth), which coincided with the olive and grape harvests and marked the end of the agricultural year (23:39; Exod. 34:22 has 'Festival of Ingathering'). The climactic nature of the occasion is marked by the preponderance of seven. The festival is a *seven*-day event that commenced on the fifteenth day of the *seventh* month (23:34); the extra day of rest prescribed in 23:36 is the *seventh* of the year;[11] and half of the chapter's use of 'seven' and 'seventh' are found in this section.[12] The festival was marked by daily offerings to Yahweh and a sacred assembly on day one and another 'closing special assembly' on day eight. This 7 + 1 pattern mirrors the 1 + 7 format of Passover and Unleavened Bread (23:4-6), framing the year.

---

11. Cf. 23:7, 8, 21, 24, 28, 35.

12. 'Seven' occurs six times (23:34, 36, 39, 40, 41, 42) and 'seventh' three times (23:34, 39, 41).

For the entire festival, all native-born Israelites were to live in booths (23:42). Rejoicing is commanded. Having gathered 'the fruit of splendid trees' (ESV) and leafy branches, the people are told to 'rejoice before the LORD your God for seven days' (23:40). But celebration and partying are not just an end in themselves. Rejoicing serves the formation of shared cultural memory. The joy and jubilation and the living in temporary shelters all evoke the exit from Egyptian slavery. Festival participation takes on a teaching function: 'This will remind each new generation of Israelites that I made their ancestors live in shelters when I rescued them from the land of Egypt' (23:43 NLT). Every generation of Israel must remember it is equally indebted and bound to the LORD. Unsurprisingly, the section concludes: 'I am Yahweh your God' (23:43).

In this way, Israel's festal calendar began and ended with 7 + 1-day events which explicitly remembered the exodus (23:6, 42-43). Noting this is crucial. There is more going on than perhaps first meets the eye. In fact, all the key aspects of God's salvific action on Israel's behalf are embedded in the annual schedule. Events recalled (and re-enacted) deliverance from Egypt (Passover) and the journey through the wilderness (Unleavened Bread, Booths). God's gracious provision of atonement and cleansing was reapplied (Day of Atonement). The fulfilled promise of a land flowing with milk and honey was celebrated (Firstfruits, Weeks). Yahweh's eschatological goal to restore the world along creation lines was not only remembered, but experienced (Sabbath). Israel's calendar thus surveyed the entire sweep of Yahweh's unfolding purposes – past, present, and future – and, in doing so, became a gospel-reminding device.

From text to message

It is essential to realize (and communicate) that Leviticus 23 is not a public service announcement to ensure that people were properly informed about their holiday entitlements. In fact, as noted, lots of necessary information is missing. The purpose of this passage lies beyond simply conveying information. The danger of not recognizing this is that one might be tempted to mine parallel passages in Numbers and Deuteronomy as an exercise in gap-filling. Thus, *we* might end up making Leviticus 23 into a public service announcement and miss the theological and rhetorical purposes that have resulted in *this* text. The focus must be on discerning what function chapter 23, as written, serves in Leviticus, and how this liturgical calendar furthers the aims of the book.

Getting the message clear: the theme

Yahweh declares a schedule of weekly and annual events that Israel must observe. The calendar is designed to encourage acknowledgement of God and His past and present activity on Israel's behalf. Communal participation becomes a means of culture formation in hope that all generations might know Yahweh as their God.

Getting the message clear: the aim

Leviticus 23 commands Israel to keep weekly Sabbaths and hold regular festivals. This is an unmistakable statement that Yahweh's lordship extends even to time. Provoking memory is central to observance. Israel must remember God's past acts of deliverance and, by re-enacting key events, participate in them. In this way, future generations would be taught. Moreover, the current blessedness of life with God is to be acknowledged, celebrated, and enjoyed.

Yet redemption is presented against a larger backdrop. Themes of Sabbath and seventh-day rest evoke the order and beauty of Genesis 1. Israel is invited to bring aspects of creation into its lived experience. In turn, recapitulation of the past (creation time, divine presence, rest, blessing, and satiety) becomes a declaration of Yahweh's intent to restore the *world* along creation lines. Israel, as firstfruits, guarantees eschatological hope for the nations.

A way in

As a child, I can remember attending harvest services at church. It was always a source of amusement to see the front of the room bedecked with pumpkins, potatoes, leeks, and carrots – and to see the pastor have to climb over them to reach the pulpit. It was also fun being able to run up and grab an apple when church was finished. However, I have not been to a harvest service in decades. Is that just the inevitable end to a tradition, a matter of little concern? Or has something vital been lost? But there is a bigger question lurking: To what degree does the rhythmic pattern of annual life bear upon faith? And, if our calendars do have an impact, is it for better or for worse? That is a question Leviticus 23 can help us think through.

The onset of COVID-19 in early 2020 sent diaries (virtual or otherwise) into a tailspin. The frustration of having to re-arrange everything from grocery shopping to international flights drove home a very clear message: your schedule is not your own. In an instant, the illusion (and pride) that we are masters over our lives evaporated. James 4 suddenly took on renewed force: 'Now listen, you who say, "Today or tomorrow we will go to this or that city, spend a year there, carry on business and make money ..."' (James 4:13). Leviticus 23 has the same effect. This passage too sounds a clear message: your schedule is not your own. God alone is Lord of time and He expects that lordship to be recognized. Seeing what that entailed for Israel can help us reflect on what it might mean for us.

Ideas for application

- We are not masters of time. God alone is. We do not even know what will happen tomorrow. Therefore, we ought to repent of pride and submit to God's mastery, saying, 'If it is the Lord's will, we will live and do this or that' (James 4:15).

- In Mark 2:28, Jesus claims Yahweh's authority over time: 'So the Son of Man is Lord even of the Sabbath.'

- Faith and obedience must be demonstrated in all aspects of life, including time. Holiness has a temporal dimension.

- The promise of entering God's Sabbath rest still stands for those who believe. Therefore, we ought to turn from unbelief and make every effort to enter (Heb. 4:1-11).

- At the last supper, Jesus celebrated Passover and invested it with new meaning. The unleavened bread and wine became emblems of a greater deliverance: 'This is my body given for you' and 'This cup is the new covenant in my blood' (Luke 22:19-20). Future re-enactment, whether regular or irregular, becomes a remembrance of Jesus (Luke 22:19) and a participation in His body and blood (1 Cor. 10:16). Celebrating the 'Lord's Passover' therefore becomes pedagogical, as it proclaims Jesus's death (1 Cor. 11:26) and culture-forming, as it unites His followers around their Lord (Luke 22:17; 1 Cor. 10:17).

- The first Easter Sunday probably coincided with the Festival of Firstfruits, the day the first sheaves of the barley harvest were dedicated. This becomes the impetus for Paul's reference to Christ's resurrection as 'firstfruits' (1 Cor. 15:20, 23).[13]

- Because we are holistic creatures, *physical* participation can have *spiritual* benefits. For example, the simple act of eating unleavened bread could remind an Israelite person of God's deliverance, encourage faith in His goodness and protection, and grant assurance of belonging to His people. The physicality of baptism and the Lord's Supper, as well as a host of other activities (singing, fasting, kneeling, etc.), should not be underestimated.

- With the global, cross-cultural expansion of the gospel, there is no longer a set annual calendar for God's people. Therefore, we should not judge, or let ourselves be judged, in relation to the observance of special festivals or days (Rom. 14:4-6; Col. 2:16). At the same time, however, we ought to ponder how effectively we have used that freedom to construct an annual calendar that reinforces gospel truths. Or might Israel's festal calendar display greater wisdom?

Suggestions for preaching

Sermon 1

- **The Lord's weekly Sabbaths (23:1-3).** In Leviticus 23, Yahweh asserts His lordship over time. Holiness takes on a temporal dimension as God sets apart regular times for holy assemblies. Israel's working

---

13. Wenham, *Leviticus*, 306.

week must include a 'Sabbath to the LORD', a day
free from work. In this way, Israel would recapitulate
time as it was in the beginning, demonstrating both
God's intent to restore the world along creation lines
and His invitation to Israel to participate in and
perpetuate His re-creative purposes.

- **The Lord's annual festivals (23:4-44).** The remainder
of the chapter expands Sabbath principles to Israel's
annual calendar. Sevenfold patterning and prescriptions
of rest continue. Festivals are correlated both to fixed
dates and the fluctuations of harvest times. Various
feast days remember Yahweh's deliverance of His
people and allow future generations to learn through
participation. Accordingly, celebration of God's goodness is a common, but not exclusive, theme. Time is
also given for sorrow and confession of sin. In this way,
Israel's festivals were designed to evoke the past, assure
in the present, and anticipate the future.

- **The Lord's freedom and wisdom.** The New Testament recognizes God's ongoing mastery over time. It is
He who determines the appointed times for all peoples
(Acts 17:26). In the Gospels, Jesus assumes this divine
prerogative: the Son of Man is Lord of the Sabbath
(Mark 2:28). Yet Jesus does not impose His own
calendar. So, while re-enacting Jesus's modified Passover is something His followers must do (Luke 22:19),
it nevertheless remains a matter of *whenever* you eat
and drink (1 Cor. 11:26). Paul recognizes the freedom
Christians have with respect to special days and
festivals (Col. 2:16). But freedom needs to be tempered
by wisdom. Israel's weekly and annual patterns were a

means of communal gospel remembrance and participation, embracing both feasting and fasting. It is worth considering whether the traditions and 'holy days' we have constructed are as rich or as gospel-centric.

Sermon 2

Another approach to teaching Leviticus 23 is to use the text to develop and explain aspects of Christology that derive some or all their force from Israel's festal calendar:

- Jesus's offers to satisfy thirst (John 7:37-38) and give light (John 8:12) occur on the 'last and greatest day of the festival [of Booths]' (John 7:37), and correspond to the special water-pouring and lamp-lighting rites conducted on that day (see *m. Sukkah* 4:1, 9-10)

- Jesus, our Passover lamb, has been sacrificed, securing deliverance from slavery to sin (1 Cor. 5:7)

- Like the Passover lamb, Jesus's bones were left unbroken (John 19:36; cf. Exod. 12:46)

- The Lord's Supper was a re-purposed Passover meal which inaugurated a new covenant (Matt. 26:17; Mark 14:24)

- Jesus's resurrection, likely occurring at Firstfruits, emphasizes Christ as the 'firstfruits' of resurrected humanity (1 Cor. 15:20-23)

- The risen Jesus pours out the Holy Spirit at Pentecost (Weeks) (Acts 2:1)

Suggestions for teaching

Questions to help understand the passage

1. Why does Yahweh prescribe 'appointed festivals' for Israel (23:2, 4)?

2. Why is the Sabbath included (23:3)?

3. What are the similarities and differences between the various festivals? Is there a logic to their order?

4. What creation words and concepts are present in Leviticus 23? How do they function in the text and contribute to its message?

5. In what ways do Numbers 28–29 and Deuteronomy 16:1-17 throw light on Leviticus 23? How does comparison to these other passages reveal the particular force of Leviticus 23?

6. Which of Israel's festival days appear in the New Testament? Are they conducted in the same or a different manner to Leviticus 23?

7. How does Leviticus 23 contribute to the purpose(s) of the book?

Questions to help apply the passage

1. What are the advantages and disadvantages of having a liturgical calendar?

2. Israel's communal festivals prescribed 'a time to weep and a time to laugh, a time to mourn and a time to dance' (Eccles. 3:4). Does your church calendar encourage the same diversity?

3. Should Christians celebrate Christmas and Easter?

4. Read James 4:13-17. In what ways do you need to think, speak, or act differently in relation to time?

5. How would you respond to a person who said, 'Christians must observe the Sabbath'?

6. On a sheet of paper, map out an annual calendar of events that would help to embody, teach, and foster

participation in gospel truths. You may incorporate or adapt existing occasions as well as invent new ones. What do you think the impact would be on you and your church community if your calendar was enacted?

15.
The Ever-Present Lord
(Leviticus 24)

Introduction

At first glance, Leviticus 24 is odd. The passage begins with ritual prescription (24:1-9) and then shifts to narrative account (24:10-23) without segue or use of the divine speech formula which so frequently demarcates discrete subunits. Moreover, neither part of the passage seems to connect with the surrounding material. In fact, Leviticus 24 interrupts the focus on holy time that is the primary concern of chapters 23 (Sabbath and annual festivals) and 25 (Sabbath years and Jubilee). The question, of course, is why? Why is this ritual-narrative composite placed here and what function does it perform within the book?

On second glance, however, lines of continuity emerge. The olive oil requested in 24:2 is produced from the harvest which is celebrated at the Festival of Booths (23:33-43; the 'seventh month', i.e., September/October, marked the gathering of olive and grape crops). 'Lasting ordinance' in 24:3 recalls the same phrase in 23:14, 21, 31, and 41. Bread laid on the golden table in 24:5-8 fills out what must happen

'Sabbath after Sabbath' (cf. 23:3) and is made according to the same 'recipe' as loaves offered at the Festival of Weeks (23:17). The 'source of light' kept burning on the pure gold lampstand (24:2) evokes the 'sources of light' in Genesis 1:14-18 which govern the appointed times, days, and years of Israel's festal calendar (see further below). Leviticus 24:1-9, at least, is firmly embedded in its context.

Leviticus 24:10-23 also reveals connections. The passage invites comparison with chapters 8–10, the only other instance of narrative in the book. Similarities are immediately evident. Both 10:1-7 and 24:10-23 record a violation with respect to Yahweh that results in the execution of the perpetrator(s). In each instance, the occasion also becomes the basis for further legislation that warns of death for future breaches (10:8-9; 24:15-22). However, the dissimilarities are just as important to observe. Nadab and Abihu, as *pureblooded* Israelites, committed a *ritual* fault within the *tabernacle precincts*. The *mixed heritage* blasphemer, on the other hand, committed a *moral* fault somewhere *in the camp*. Leviticus 24, it seems, has something to say about the presence of Yahweh which bears upon all people, everywhere, at all times.

Listening to the text

Context and structure

Leviticus 24 follows the summary statement of 23:44 and is further demarcated as a unit by the divine speech formula in the opening verse ('The LORD said to Moses'; cf. 25:1). The second use of the formulaic phrase in 24:13 continues the narrative action begun in 24:10 (captured by NIV's '*Then* the LORD said' [emphasis added]) rather than denoting a new subunit.

Leviticus 24 is framed by the time-focused material of chapters 23 and 25. This places Leviticus 24 at the center of an ABA arrangement:

> A   Sabbaths and annual festivals (23:1-44)
>
> > B   Yahweh's presence in tabernacle and camp (24:1-23)
>
> A' Sabbatical years and Jubilee (25:1-55)

A shift of genre divides Leviticus 24 into two sections: 24:1-9 (ritual instruction) and 24:10-23 (narrative). The passage can be outlined as follows:

> Lights and bread in the tabernacle (24:1-9)
> > Lights burning continually (24:1-4)
> > Loaves present continually (24:5-9)
> A case of blasphemy in the camp (24:10-23)
> > The penalty for blasphemy explained (24:10-16)
> > Instructions regarding commensurate punishment (24:17-22)
> > The penalty for blasphemy enacted (24:23)

Working through the text

Lights and bread in the tabernacle (24:1-9)

The first section of Leviticus 24 relates to activities in the tent of meeting. First, Yahweh, through Moses, commands the Israelites to bring olive oil so that 'the lamps' might burn continually (24:2). The lamps in question are those 'on the pure gold lampstand before the LORD' (24:4) – that is, the seven-branched menorah 'that stands in the Tabernacle, in front of the inner curtain that shields the Ark of the Covenant' (24:3 NLT; for the layout of the tent, see *Figure 3.1*). These lamps, like the fire of the ascension offering (6:9-13), must never go out. Accordingly, Aaron is given the task of tending the flame through the night ('from evening till morning', 24:3; Exod. 27:21 has 'Aaron and his sons').

The word translated 'light' (*ma'or*) in 24:2 is uncommon and refers to a source of light. It is most often used in connection with the tabernacle lampstand.[1] This lampstand, constructed from pure gold, was fashioned with branches, blossoms, buds, and cups shaped like almond flowers (Exod. 36:17-22). Its seven lights, flickering on shrub- or tree-like branches, evoke Yahweh's appearance in the burning bush (Exod. 3:2-4). Thus the light of the lampstand, positioned next to the curtain within the tabernacle, represents the presence of God with His people (cf. Ps. 90:8, 'the light [*ma'or*] of your presence'). Accordingly, its light must never go out.

A second directive commands the baking of loaves for presentation on the small (90 x 45 cm) golden table housed with the menorah in the holy place of the tent (24:5-6; cf. Exod. 25:23-30).[2] The imperative is parsed as masculine singular ('You shall take' ESV), but it is difficult to identify the addressee. In context, the instruction is directed to Moses (cf. 24:1). Yet the ongoing nature of the

---

1. Exodus 25:6; 27:20; 35:8, 14 (x2), 28; 39:37; Lev. 24:2; Num. 4:9, 16.

2. Within the holy place, the altar of incense stood between the lampstand (positioned on the south side of the room; Exod. 40:24) and the golden table (positioned on the north side; Exod. 40:22). (See *Figure 3.1*.) Hence, burning incense created a cloud separating the lights (representing Yahweh's presence) and the bread (representing Israel) in a manner similar to the shielding function of incense on the Day of Atonement (16:12-13).

requirement (24:8 'lasting covenant') suggests that it is not he who would be donning the apron. Considering the location of the table, a priestly baker must be intended. Twelve (flatbread) loaves are required, each made from approximately two kilograms (two-tenths of an ephah) of fine flour (24:5; cf. 23:17). Loaves are baked weekly and, on the Sabbath, must be set out in two piles of six upon the table (24:8) with accompanying incense (24:7). Removed loaves (from the previous week) become food for Aaron and his sons as another (most holy) part of their regular share of offerings made to Yahweh (cf. 6:16-18; 7:7-10, 32-36; 1 Sam. 21:3-6). This procedure is to be enacted 'Sabbath after Sabbath' (24:8).

The presentation of *twelve* loaves is suggestive regarding their purpose. Leviticus 24:8 states, 'Every Sabbath day he [presumably the one who baked the loaves (esv's 'Aaron' is not in the text)] will set it in order before Yahweh continually; it is from the Israelites, a lasting covenant' (my translation). Twelve loaves, from the twelve tribes of Israel, symbolize the nation's covenant relationship with God. The bread functions as a visible reminder that Israel always lives before Yahweh.

The language of continuity ties 24:1-9 together. The lights that represent Yahweh's presence must shine 'continually' (24:2, 3, 4), 'evening till morning' (24:3); this is a 'lasting' statute (24:3). Likewise, the bread that represents Israel must be placed before Yahweh 'continually', 'Sabbath after Sabbath'; this is a 'lasting' covenant (24:8). The lights and bread picture or symbolize the ideal: the covenant people of God continually standing in the presence of God.

The impact of this idyllic portrait is increased through use of allusion to Genesis 1–2. The branched menorah evokes not only the burning bush, but the tree of life that stood in the Garden. The phrase 'evening till morning' (24:3) is reminiscent of the repeated refrain heard throughout Genesis 1 and 'Sabbath' recalls seventh-day rest (Gen. 2:1-3). The use of *ma'or* ('light') in 24:2 evokes the fivefold use of this word to describe the function of celestial sources of light (i.e., the sun and moon) on day four of creation (Gen. 1:14-16; cf. Ps. 74:16; Ezek. 32:8). Thus, as Israel observed the appointed times, days, and years governed by the heavenly 'lights' (Gen. 1:14) and stipulated in Leviticus 23–25, the nation would reorder itself along God-ordained lines and begin to recover the divine-human intimacy which characterized the beginning of the world.

A case of blasphemy in the camp (24:10-23)

The second section of the chapter presents a narrative account of activities 'in the camp' (24:10).[3] The story begins abruptly (literally 'And the son of an Israelite woman went out'; my translation). The effect is like a live broadcast being interrupted by breaking news. The camera pans away from Moses speaking to focus on a man of mixed heritage (Israelite mother and Egyptian father) embroiled in a fight with an Israelite during which he blasphemes 'the Name with a curse' (24:11). His exact words and motive are left unstated. Questions therefore arise. In what way did he slander Yahweh's name? Was

---

3. Bryan Bibb notes that before possession of Canaan, 'the camp embodies all of the theological significance of the land in Leviticus' ('This is the Thing That the Lord Commanded You to Do' [PhD diss., Princeton, 2005], 211).

the curse directed towards the Israelite man or Yahweh or both? Was it a deliberate comment or merely something spoken in the heat of the moment? It is impossible to know.

Uncertainty also marks the required response from those who heard the utterance (possibly because the man was not fully Israelite). Hence, he is brought to Moses and placed in custody 'until the will of the LORD should be made clear' (24:11-12). When it comes, the divine verdict is stark: 'Take the blasphemer outside the camp. All those who heard him are to lay their hands on his head, and the entire assembly is to stone him' (24:14). The laying on of hands is most likely a means of the witnesses expressing, 'Yes, this is the man' (cf. Deut. 17:6-7). Punishment is to be enforced by the *community*, signifying that it sides with Yahweh against the perpetrator.

The incident also provokes a divine declaration that transcends the immediate case. 'Anyone' who similarly curses his or her God and blasphemes the Name will be held responsible and face execution (24:15-16). 'Anyone' includes both native-born and foreign residents (24:16). All alike are considered responsible moral agents. The universality of this warning, coupled with the lack of clarity surrounding the exact words spoken by the Israelite-Egyptian blasphemer, is rhetorically powerful. *Any* careless words spoken against God – and who knows what might fall into that category – could result in disastrous consequences. Ambiguity drives home the need for extreme caution (see, similarly, 10:1-2).

The following verses (24:17-22) add further legisla-tion. Chiastic arrangement draws attention to the central point in 24:20a.

> The same standard applies to foreigner and native-
> born (24:16)
>> Whoever kills a human must be put to death
>> (24:17)
>>> Whoever kills someone's animal must pay
>>> restitution (24:18)
>>>> Whoever injures another must receive the
>>>> same (24:19)
>>>>> Fracture for fracture, eye for eye, tooth
>>>>> for tooth (24:20a)
>>>> Whoever injures another must receive the
>>>> same (24:20b)
>>> Whoever kills someone's animal must pay
>>> restitution (24:21a)
>> Whoever kills a human must be put to death
>> (24:21b)
> The same standard applies to foreigner and native-
> born (24:22)

The central point ('fracture for fracture, eye for eye, tooth for tooth') is called the *lex talionis* (or law of talion) and appears elsewhere (Exod. 21:24; Deut. 19:21; cf. Matt. 5:38). The principle of measure for measure is often misconstrued as evidence that the Old Testament is cruel and vindictive. However, the opposite is the case. Talion prescribes *commensurate* punishment; the penalty must fit the crime. This is a remarkable statement of justice in the ancient world in which even minor misdemeanours could attract horrendous consequences.

But why is 24:17-22 placed here? Certainly, there is correspondence in relation to the scope of the legislation:

this, too, applies to resident foreigner and native-born alike (24:22; cf. 24:16). The penalty is also described *verbatim*: for blasphemy and for taking a person's life, the perpetrator 'shall surely be put to death' (24:16, 17 ESV). Leviticus 24:17, 21 thus accords with the wider Old Testament stance towards murder. Genesis 9:6 is foundational: 'Whoever sheds the blood of man, by man shall his blood be shed, for God made man in his own image' (ESV).[4] For this reason, those convicted of murder were not permitted to offer a monetary payment to avoid the death penalty (Num. 35:31). Punishment must be commensurate (24:20). Taking the life of another means forfeiting one's own life. This also accounts for why the Old Testament (contra other ancient law codes) does not prescribe the death penalty for property offences. Human life is worth more than things (or animals for that matter, 24:18, 21).

Positioned here, 24:17-22 establishes a distinction between execution and homicide. The death penalty that the community are instructed to carry out is not an act of murder. However, the focus on commensurate punishment in 24:17-21 also impacts how 24:14-16 is read. To curse someone is to perpetrate an act of violence; physical, emotional or spiritual harm is intended. Hence, to curse God (24:15) or blaspheme His name is a serious offence. Stoning is therefore not only commensurate, but positions blasphemy on a par with murder. The obverse is also true: wrongfully to take the life of a human made in God's image is equivalent to profaning Yahweh's name. The episode thus cuts across ancient Near Eastern norms, which deemed a

---

4. Appeal to formation in God's image means that *every* human life is equally precious. There is no priority granted for age, gender, nationality, or social status.

person's moral goodness to be less important than correct performance of worship practices.[5] There was to be no such sacred-secular divide in Israel.

The narrative concludes with a simple fulfillment statement. The blasphemer is taken outside the camp and stoned; in doing so, the 'Israelites did as the LORD commanded Moses' (24:23). Delaying the story's denouement maintains tension with respect to the fate of the blasphemer and allows the material of 24:15-22 to be inserted.

The account in 24:10-23 demonstrates that the problems hinted at and addressed by Levitical legislation are not mere strawmen. There are real, substantive problems to correct and prevent. The blasphemy incident in 24:11 also invites and makes necessary the instruction of 24:14-22. This is a microcosmic example of how Leviticus addresses problems raised by the stories of Genesis and Exodus and, by doing so, justifies the need for its regulations.

Taking all of this into account, the two seemingly disparate sections in this unit are now seen to be of a piece. The first (24:1-9) symbolically conveys that Yahweh is continually present with His people and that His people are continually present before Him. However, what is true of the ritual world *in the tabernacle* ought to be mirrored in day-to-day life *in the camp*.[6] Yahweh's presence must govern everything that Israel is and does. The case of the

---

5. See John H. Walton, *Ancient Near Eastern Thought and the Old Testament: Introducing the Conceptual World of the Hebrew Bible* (Grand Rapids: Baker, 2006), 306.

6. The tragic nature of the episode in 24:10-23 is highlighted by the use of similar terminology to describe the ideal ('outside the curtain', 24:3) and the real ('outside the camp', 24:23). See Wilfried Warning, *Literary Artistry in Leviticus* (BIS 35; Leiden: Brill, 1999), 95.

Israelite-Egyptian blasphemer,[7] happening on an otherwise unremarkable day, provides a crystal-clear illustration that it is not sufficient to pay God heed only when in certain holy places (as was the issue in 10:1-2) or on special holy occasions (like those listed in Lev. 23 and 25). Life with God is all of life with God. Leviticus 24 thus anticipates Yahweh's dual-edged declaration in 26:12, 'I will walk among you and be your God, and you will be my people'.

From text to message

This passage presents challenges. One must account for why this material is placed here in the book and how 24:1-9 relates to 24:10-23. It also requires grappling with the way different genres can be stitched together to achieve an overarching persuasive purpose. Leviticus 24 contains legislation (24:15-22) that has been inserted into a story (24:10-23) which, in turn, has been inserted into a larger block of legislation (Lev. 23-25) that sits within a narrative framework (cf. 1:1)! Assuming purposeful intent on the part of the author, the interpreter must try and work out how this arrangement serves the aims of the book. Doing so, however, allows the teacher to reveal the beauty and literary artistry that characterizes Leviticus and to demonstrate how the text's divine author continues to speak to His people through it.

---

7. Rooke argues that the identity of the blasphemer (Egyptian) furthers the narrative's polemical edge: the Israelites have been delivered from an immoral and idolatrous society (Egypt) that had no respect for Yahweh. They must never allow those influences to re-enter their own society. See Deborah W. Rooke, 'The Blasphemer (Leviticus 24): Gender, Identity and Boundary Construction,' in *Text, Time, and Temple: Literary, Historical and Ritual Studies in Leviticus* (ed. Francis Landy, Leigh M. Trevaskis, and Bryan D. Bibb; HBM 64; Sheffield: Sheffield Phoenix, 2015), 168.

Getting the message clear: the theme

Yahweh commands that light and bread be maintained continually in the holy place of the tabernacle to symbolize His ever-presence with His people. That ever-presence has negative, albeit proportionate, consequences for those in the camp who refuse to acknowledge God in the way they live and act.

Getting the message clear: the aim

By demanding the continual presence of lights (indicating Yahweh's presence) and bread (representing Israel) within the tabernacle, a rich symbolic portrait is constructed: God dwelling with His people, and His people dwelling with Him. Allusion to Genesis 1–2 emphasizes the cosmic implications of the restoration enacted. This ideal, symbolized within the tent, makes the following narrative of 24:10-23 all the more shocking: a man curses Yahweh. The juxtaposition of episodes and the portrayal of moral fault with subsequent penalty drive home the danger threatened by proximity to Yahweh's presence – *every* day in *every* part of the camp. Deliberate ambiguity concerning what was said urges extreme caution and the incident legitimizes the need for further legislation. The message is simple but stark: take heed and be very careful how you live for punishment must, and will, be commensurate.

A way in

Living cross-culturally can be fun. It can also be funny, for onlookers at least. A host of potential *faux pas* await the unsuspecting newcomer: mispronunciation, inappropriate attire, laughing at precisely the wrong moment. But other mistakes can be more serious: driving on the wrong side of the road, ending up in a dodgy part of town, or insulting one's hosts. A failure to recognize changed circumstances can be catastrophic. One's context must dictate appropriate behavior every day. For Israel, just as for Christians, reality is fundamentally altered when God comes to dwell with His people. For recent converts, there are a host of potential *faux pas* as one adjusts to a whole new way of life. Funny anecdotes abound. But other mistakes can be more serious. A failure to recognize changed circumstances can be catastrophic. That is what we find illustrated in Leviticus 24, a passage which explores the implications of God drawing near to His people.

There is a verse in a well-known children's song that goes like this:

> *Oh, be careful, little tongue, what you say,*
> *Oh, be careful, little tongue, what you say.*
> *There's a Father up above who is looking down in love,*
> *Oh, be careful, little tongue, what you say.*

The song is simple, yet profound. It urges caution regarding what God's people say – and see and hear and do. The reason is because there is a Father who is looking down in love. But fatherly love means fatherly discipline. The Scriptures are crystal clear on this front: how a person lives has consequences. As Paul says, we will all stand before the judgment seat of Christ to receive our due for what we have done in the body, whether good or bad (2 Cor. 5:10). But how should we understand Jesus's judgment of Christians? Leviticus 24 is a great place to begin.

Ideas for application

- The lives of all humans, each made in God's image, are intrinsically valuable.

- The New Testament portrays Christians as a temple in which God dwells by His Spirit (Eph. 2:21-22; 1 Pet. 2:5). This inner, continual presence of God demands greater care, not less, lest we grieve or even outrage the Spirit who lives within (Eph. 4:30; Heb. 10:29).

- Blasphemy against God is serious. Numbers 15:30 also regards defiant sins as blasphemy, revealing that the underlying issue is a heart set against God, whether expressed in words or deeds. Jesus warns that while every kind of sin can be forgiven, blasphemy against the Holy Spirit cannot (Matt. 12:31).

- God's justice is proportionate ('eye for eye'), unflinching ('he must die'), and allows no favoritism ('foreigner and the native-born'). It functions to rebuke human tendencies to overreact, prevaricate, or promote preferential treatment. Therefore, Christians who have a responsibility to enforce discipline or punitive measures (parents, judges, police officers, teachers, managers, pastors, etc.) must strive to emulate God as they do so.

- When Jesus quotes the *lex talionis* in Matthew 5:38-42, He is not criticizing Leviticus 24:20 but rather its misapplication by His contemporaries to justify personal revenge and retaliation. Such things are outlawed for God's people.

- We must be careful not to mute what the New Testament teaches about divine judgment *of Christians*, in this life and the next. A host of passages deserve sober and careful reflection:

    ○ Jesus says He rebukes and disciplines those He loves (Rev. 3:19; cf. Heb. 12:5-11)

○ In a parable, Jesus taught that 'the servant who knows the master's will and does not get ready or does not do what the master wants will be beaten with many blows' (Luke 12:47)

○ Ananias and Sapphira died instantly for lying to the Holy Spirit, causing 'great fear' to seize the church (Acts 5:1-11)

○ Widows who dedicate themselves to Christ and then marry bring judgment on themselves (1 Tim. 5:11-12)

○ The Corinthians are urged to judge and punish immoral people within the church (1 Cor. 5:1-5, 12; cf. 1 Cor. 6:5)

○ Recent converts who become conceited face the same judgment as the devil (1 Tim. 3:6)

○ Peter cautions, 'Since you call on a Father who judges each person's work impartially, live out your time as foreigners here in reverent fear' (1 Pet. 1:17)

○ Paul says he fears the Lord because Christians will stand before the judgment seat of Christ to receive their due for things done while in the body, whether good or bad (2 Cor. 5:10-11; cf. Rom. 14:10-12)

○ Some in the Corinthian church became sick and others died when 'judged by the Lord' for disregarding the body during communion (1 Cor. 11:27-32)

○ Because of the supremacy of Christ's work, the author of Hebrews warns believers against wavering: 'For we know him who said, "It is mine to avenge; I will repay," and again, "The Lord will judge his people." It is a dreadful thing to fall into the hands of the living God' (Heb. 10:30-31)

o First Peter 4:17 announces that judgment begins with God's household

o The whole church in Ephesus is threatened with extinction unless it repents (Rev. 2:5)

Suggestions for preaching

Sermon 1

Although Leviticus 24 could be preached as two separate passages (24:1-9, 10-23), taking the text as a whole allows for a better understanding of how the subsections work together to advance the book's aim to instill holiness in all of life. It also grants deeper insight into God's judgment of His own people.

- **Constant presence (24:1-9).** With Leviticus 24, the focus on weekly and annual events (Lev. 23) shifts to the daily. The priests must maintain continuously burning lights on the tabernacle's lampstand, day and night. Twelve loaves of bread, representing the people, must remain before God always, being replaced Sabbath by Sabbath. These routine actions visualize a profound theological truth: God lives continually among His covenant people and they are forever in His presence. Realities from the beginning of creation are, in Israel, being reborn.

- **Constant threat (24:10-23).** The shift to narrative in 24:10 is abrupt. So too is the change in tenor. The ideal portrayed in the tabernacle is tempered by reality in the camp. A man blasphemes and curses God, a shocking act of covenant unfaithfulness. Eruptions of sin, it seems, are an ongoing threat among God's people. However, both sin and sinner immediately encounter the threat of Yahweh's presence. Judgment is proportionate, unflinching, and enacted without favoritism. Israel is instructed to adopt the same stance towards sin, demonstrated in the communal stoning of the Israelite-Egyptian blasphemer.

- **How constant is constant?** The theme of continuity so important to Leviticus 24 is echoed by the question concerning continuity for Christians. How, if at all, does this text apply? Connections are stronger than they first appear. The reality of mutual dwelling pictured in the tabernacle finds its correlation in God's Spirit inhabiting the temple of God's new covenant people. The divine presence continues to be ever-present. So, too, does the threat of sin, a fact amply attested by the sheer quantity of New Testament prohibitions as well as our lived experience. But the threat posed by God's presence also continues. The Holy Spirit can be grieved, the Father will judge His people, and Jesus says He disciplines those He loves. It is precisely because of our status in Christ that the stakes are raised, for Christlikeness is the Christian's destiny. Thus, both the potential and the urgent warning of Leviticus 24 carry through: God has come close, so be very careful how you live, because discipline will be commensurate.

Sermon 2

The related themes of place, presence, and purity run right through the Scriptures and are essential for understanding the overarching narrative of the Bible. Topics like temple, priesthood, and sacred space move to the foreground. Leviticus 24 could be preached as part of a topical sermon which explores this biblical-theological trajectory. A possible sermon, with suggested passages, is as follows:

1. Place, presence, and purity in the beginning (Gen. 1-2)

2. Place, presence, and purity in the tabernacle (Lev. 24)

3. Place, presence, and purity in the church (1 Cor. 6:18-20)

4. Place, presence, and purity in the end (Rev. 21-22)

Suggestions for teaching

Questions to help understand the passage

1. Why is the focus on sacred times (Lev. 23 and 25) interrupted by Leviticus 24?

2. Why must the lamps in the holy place be kept burning continuously (24:1-4)?

3. What purpose does the incense in 24:7 serve?

4. Explain why twelve loaves are placed on the golden table each Sabbath (24:8).

5. Account for the family of mixed heritage in 24:10.

6. Why is the mother's name listed, but not that of the father or the son (24:11)?

7. Why is death by stoning prescribed for blasphemy (24:14, 16, 23)?

8. Why must a murderer be executed (24:17, 21)?

9. List the similarities and differences between the case of the Israelite-Egyptian blasphemer (24:10-23) and that of Nadab and Abihu (10:1-20). How do these narrative episodes function in the book?

Questions to help apply the passage

1. What do you learn about God in Leviticus 24?

2. Leviticus 24:12 describes waiting until the Lord's will could be discerned. Is that your habit when faced with a difficult situation?

3. How do you react on hearing the death penalty being prescribed (24:14, 16, 17, 21)? Why do you think you react that way?

4. Is human life honored in your culture? Why do you think that is the case? What wisdom might 24:17 contribute to your situation?

5. Is 24:19-20 a principle to teach in church or Sunday school?

6. Think of life contexts in which you are the person responsible for ensuring just and commensurate punishment or discipline. Does your mode of operation mirror God's?

7. How do you reconcile statements regarding God's judgment of His people (e.g., 1 Cor. 11:27-32) with others that say whoever believes will not be judged (e.g., John 5:24)?

16.
God's Society
(Leviticus 25)

Introduction

At the start of the new millennium, an international coalition named Jubilee 2000 emerged with one over-arching goal: debt relief for majority world countries. Its agenda was to raise awareness by highlighting the plight of the marginalized and exploited. The movement also actively campaigned to have debts cancelled and, on that front, succeeded in clearing over $100 billion in debt owed. As a direct result, countries like Uganda and Bolivia were enabled to redirect funds to education and poverty alleviation, instead of financing loan repayments.

The Jubilee 2000 movement drew its impetus and language from Leviticus 25. The 'Year of Jubilee' outlined here was to be proclaimed in Israel every forty-nine years. The occasion functioned as a national reset point and was marked by debt release, liberation, and return to ancestral land. Aims included the preservation of inheritance and limiting resource acquisition by the rich and powerful. Notes of joy and blessing predominate. Little wonder that Leviticus 25 has been frequently mined for its contribution to matters of social justice.

And yet this passage presents its own difficulties. Many scholars have drawn attention to the improbability (even impossibility) of ever enacting what is demanded here – an argument that gathers some support from the silence of other Old Testament texts which, outside of the Pentateuch, do not directly mention this year of release. Moreover, what the chapter has to say about slavery and freedom is not straightforward. Jubilee certainly demanded the release of Israelite debt-servants, but it did not extend the same benefits to foreign servants who could be retained permanently. Justice is central, but justice for whom is the question that is left hanging. Leviticus 25 also directly speaks to ownership of the land of Canaan (a matter of both ancient and modern interest) and categorically states that the land does *not* belong to Israel but remains God's possession.

As Jubilee 2000 suggests, Leviticus 25 is a text which invites contemporary appropriation. Yet, valid application is complicated. Once again, welcome to the world of Leviticus.

Listening to the text

Context and structure

Leviticus 23–25 is arranged in an ABA pattern in which chapters 23 and 25 form a frame around chapter 24. The Sabbath principle introduced with respect to weeks (23:3) and annual festivals (23:3-43) finds a correlation in Leviticus 25 with its prescription of Sabbath (25:1-7) and 'Super Sabbath' years (25:8-13). These chapters are bound together by a focus on holy time. Re-creation themes are foregrounded as the appointed festivals, days, and years demarcated by the sun and moon (Gen. 1:14) are woven into Israel's liturgical calendar.

A Sabbaths and annual festivals (23:1-44)

    B Yahweh's presence in tabernacle and camp
        (24:1-23)

A' Sabbatical years and Jubilee (25:1-55)

However, while closely connected to chapters 23–24, Leviticus 25 also shares affinities with chapter 26.[1] Both are governed by the same introduction to divine speech ('The LORD said to Moses', 25:1; cf. 27:1) and by reference to 'Mount Sinai', which frames the two-chapter block (25:1; 26:46). Once again, it becomes evident that structural markers within Leviticus often overlap.

Leviticus 25 opens with the narrator introducing divine speech (25:1-2a). The remainder of the chapter consists of two related panels which address Sabbath and Jubilee years (25:2b-24) and the redemption of property and persons with respect to Jubilee (25:25-55). Seven subsections, marked by the Hebrew word *ki* ('if/when'), outline a range of future potentials related to life in Canaan:

Sabbath and Jubilee years (25:1-24)
    'When you enter the land' (25:2b-13)
    'If you sell land' (25:14-24)

Redemption of property and persons (25:25-55)
    'If your brother becomes poor and sells property'
        (25:25-28)
    'If a man sells a house' (25:29-34)
    'If your brother becomes poor' (25:35-38)

---

1. Connections with Lev. 27 are also apparent, especially in the use of the verb 'to redeem' (Lev. 25 [x10]; Lev. 27 [x12]) and the word 'Jubilee' (Lev. 25 [x14]; Lev. 27 [x6]) which occur only here in the book.

'If your brother sells himself to you' (25:39-46)

'If a prosperous foreigner buys your brother'
(25:47-55)

Working through the text

Sabbath and Jubilee years (25:1-24)

The introduction to divine speech in 25:1 is the penultimate instance of the formula in the book and governs the material in Leviticus 25 and 26 (cf. 27:1). The addition of 'on Mount Sinai' (ESV) is unusual (also 7:38; 26:46; 27:34) and suggests an origin prior to the material spoken from the tabernacle (1:1). It also serves as a reminder of the contextual nature of the instruction. These are Yahweh's prescriptions for a people newly rescued from Egyptian slavery, a reality explicitly recalled three times (25:38, 42, 55). As we will see below, a large portion of the rationale for this chapter's legislation lies in avoiding a repeat of the Egyptian experience in Israelite society.

The chapter's first section orients its legislation towards the future: 'When you enter the land' (25:2b; cf. 23:10). The principle of Sabbath which permeates Leviticus 23–25 again looms large (see also discussion at 23:3) with the *shbt* root occurring *seven* times in 25:2-8.[2] While Sabbath in Leviticus 23 governed weeks and months, here it is extended to years. In Canaan, the normal means of agriculture and viticulture could proceed for six years (25:3). But in the seventh year, 'the land itself must observe a sabbath to the LORD' and be allowed to rest (25:2; cf. 25:4, 5). Rest is accomplished by allowing the land to lie fallow in the seventh year – that is, unplanted and unharvested (25:4-5). Yet, for those who subsist on the

---

2. Lev. 25:2 (x2), 4 (x2), 6, 8 (x2).

land, the question immediately arises: 'Great, but what are we supposed to eat?' Verses 6-7 address that concern directly: 'The Sabbath of the land shall provide food for you ... all its yield shall be for food' (ESV). The implication is that the people and their animals would find sufficient sustenance in what the land produced by itself. That *everyone* was reduced to the status of 'hunter-gatherer' for the year was a reminder of the essential equality of all humans before God (cf. Gen. 1:27).

Further echoes of creation add force to the text. Sabbath rest and the provision of abundant food *apart from cultivation* recall the conditions of Genesis 1:1–2:3. There, God allotted food produced by the land (Gen. 1:11-12) to all creatures, human and non-human, providing for their satisfaction and blessing (Gen. 1:29-30). It is trust in this God that Leviticus 25:2b-7 demands, the creator God who meets His people's needs with generous provision. *If* Israel trusted, and *if* Israel heeded this instruction, then every seven years the nation would get to experience life as it was in Eden – a foretaste of the cosmic renewal Yahweh was inaugurating (cf. discussion at 26:3-13).

The focus on weaving Sabbath into Israel's temporal landscape continues in 25:8-13 with its depiction of a 'Super Sabbath Year'. This year was calculated by counting off seven seven-year cycles. Every forty-nine years, in the seventh month, on the Day of Atonement, trumpet blasts would proclaim liberty throughout the land (25:9-10). This fiftieth year, termed the year of 'Jubilee' (25:13; from the Hebrew word *yobel*, meaning 'ram's horn'), was set apart as holy (25:12). Like the Sabbath year, planting and harvesting were banned; the people must eat what the land produced by itself (25:11-12). The moment was also marked by a return to ancestral land (25:10, 13).

The following subsection (25:14-24) considers the normal sale (better: 'lease') of land in light of Jubilee's requirement to return property to original owners. Because of this eventuality, property values must be determined based on the number of harvests that could be gathered before the next reset (25:15-16). The temptation for fiscal underhandedness is frankly acknowledged and warned against: 'Do not take advantage of each other, but fear your God. I am the LORD your God' (25:17; cf. 25:14).

Fear of God supports the subsequent appeal for obedience: 'Follow my decrees and be careful to obey my laws' (25:18). Doing so would occasion safety and sustenance (25:18-19; cf. 26:3-10). In this way, Israel's ability to enact and enjoy the blessing of Jubilee is directly correlated to their willingness to listen and obey. This is the prerequisite for the super-abundant provision they would need to see them through three years of not harvesting (25:20-22) (see Table 16.1).

	Normal harvest years	Sabbath year	Year of Jubilee	Planting begins	Harvest begins
Year and month	1–$6^{(7)}$	$6^{(7)}$–$7^{(7)}$	$7^{(7)}$–$8^{(7)}$	$8^{(7)}$	$9^{(3/4)}$
		Year 1 of eating from the land	Year 2 of eating from the land	Year 3 of eating from the land	
(NB: The seventh month marked the end of the agricultural year and the commencement of planting ahead of the winter rains.)					

Table 16.1

The rationale for non-permanent land sales is given in 25:23-24. Uniquely in the Old Testament, Yahweh declares,

'[T]he land is mine' (25:23). This positions Yahweh as landowner and the Israelites as tenant farmers – that is, agricultural laborers who farm land belonging to another. The Israelites, therefore, have no inviolable right to Canaan (they are even described as 'foreigners and strangers' who are merely permitted to live there, 25:23). The implication is that the people must conduct themselves rightly as tenants or face eviction, a dynamic exploited by the prophets and Jesus (e.g. Isa. 5:1-7; Matt. 21:33-43). It is Yahweh's 'land rules' that govern the Promised Land. One unalterable rule concerns provision for redeeming (i.e. buying back) land (25:24).

Redemption of property and persons (25:25-55)

Redemption of land and persons is the major concern of 25:25-55 (the verb *ga'al* ['to redeem'] occurs ten times and the related noun *ge'ulah* ['redemption'] appears eight times). Leviticus 25:25-28 deals with redeeming land that has been sold due to financial hardship. If a 'brother' (ESV) becomes poor and is forced to liquidate assets to stave off starvation for his family, then a near relative must buy back the land on his behalf (25:25). Alternatively, the man may redeem his own land if his situation improves (25:26). In either case, the monies owed must be calculated based on the crops harvested since the sale (25:27). If redemption remains impossible due to continued hardship, then the land is to be automatically returned at Jubilee (25:28).

The next paragraph (25:29-34) turns to the house market ('If a man sells a residence', 25:29 HCSB). If the dwelling is in a walled city, then the period for redemption lasts for one year. After that point, the sale becomes permanent (25:29-30). Two exceptions follow. Houses in country villages are considered part of the land; they could be redeemed until Jubilee (and then reverted if not redeemed) (25:31). Houses in Levitical towns could likewise be redeemed until Jubilee because these properties constituted a Levite's inheritance (25:32-34; cf. Num. 35:2-5).

The final three paragraphs address situations of increasing destitution. In the first (25:35-38), a 'brother' (ESV) becomes poor to the point of being unable to support himself. The implication is that this person has no (or no more) land to sell (cf. 25:25-28). One's responsibility towards such a person is clearly stated: *'you shall support him* as though he were a stranger and a sojourner, and he shall live with you (25:35 ESV [emphasis added]). Blessing received from the LORD is not merely for one's own enjoyment but opens the possibility of extending generosity towards those in need. This, after all, is exactly the way Yahweh has dealt with His people (25:38).

The situation in 25:39-46 is more dire. This time a person is so poor he must make himself and his family servants of a fellow Israelite (25:39, 41). In lieu of a welfare system, indentured servitude was a common, albeit desperate, measure to weather hard times. A person (along with other able family members) would work in exchange for board and lodgings.[3] Ideally, this would be a mutually beneficial arrangement. The legislation seeks to ensure that justice reigned by highlighting limitations: the person must be regarded as a hired hand, not a slave to be taken advantage of; and he and his family must be released at the next Jubilee (25:40-41). Once more, the rationale is fear of Yahweh, who acted to end Israel's slavery in Egypt (25:42-43).

---

3. At the risk of making light of a serious situation, a contemporary (clichéd) analogy might be washing dishes to pay off a restaurant debt.

The next verses, however, raise problems for modern audiences. In contrast to indentured Israelites who regained their freedom at Jubilee (if not before), foreign servants did not. Instead, they could be willed as property to one's children and retained for life (25:44-46), although the text does not demand that this happen. This is not the place to tackle all the issues that arise.[4] However, some initial points can be made. The primary focus in Leviticus 25:25-55 is the redemption of, and limitations pertaining to, poverty-stricken Israelites. It is not a treatise on slavery. The servitude in view is also different from many modern forms. Ancient slavery was not predominantly race-based, and kidnapping was a capital crime in Israel (Exod. 21:16; Deut. 24:7). Moreover, poorly treated servants could run away *without penalty* (Deut. 23:15-16), putting the onus on masters to act justly or face financial loss. Exodus 21:5-6 even imagines a servant-master scenario becoming *voluntarily* permanent because it was so beneficial. While these observations do not remove every problem, they do help. The kind of servitude described in Leviticus 25 could be lifesaving. As elsewhere, we need to read the text against the conventions of its ancient context, not our own.

The final section (25:47-55) imagines the possibility of an Israelite becoming so poor that he sells himself to a foreign resident. This is the worst possible scenario. Accordingly, the right to redemption is forcefully stated. The man may redeem himself or any blood relative may

---

4. For further reading on the topic, see Paul Copan, *Is God a Moral Monster?: Making Sense of the Old Testament God* (Grand Rapids: Baker, 2011), 124-57; Andrew Sloane, *At Home in a Strange Land: Using the Old Testament in Christian Ethics* (Peabody: Hendrickson, 2008), 99-113; Sklar, *Leviticus*, 307-10.

redeem him (25:48-49), with the redemption price indexed to time already served (25:50-52). The impetus falls on his fellow Israelites ('you must see to it') to ensure that he is not treated ruthlessly for the duration of his servitude (25:53). If not redeemed, the man and his family are to be released at Jubilee. Again, the rationale appeals to Egyptian experience: 'the Israelites belong to me as servants. They are my servants, whom I brought out of Egypt' (25:55).

Throughout Leviticus 25, the implied addressee is a landed Israelite male, the person who has servants, hired workers, and animals in their care (25:6-7). The legislation is first and foremost directed at them: 'If *your* brother becomes poor and cannot maintain himself with *you*, *you* shall support him as though he were a stranger and a sojourner, and he shall live with *you*' (25:35 ESV [emphasis added]). Second-person language ('you') makes implementation an individual's responsibility rather than that of the state. Power, position, and wealth must serve the good of others, especially those less fortunate. The repeated use of 'brother' drives home the sense of responsibility one ought to feel, as well as caution that this might be your fate someday (cf. 2 Cor. 8:13-15). Hard times are indiscriminate and may come upon anybody. Therefore, establishment of a just and caring society has long-term benefits for all.

Yahweh's thrice-remembered deliverance of Israel from Egypt provides the underlying rationale (25:38, 42, 55). In that paradigmatic event, Yahweh overcame the Israelites' experience of slavery and landlessness. Accordingly, Yahweh terms the Israelites 'my servants' (25:42, 55); to them He has given the land of Canaan (25:38). That status and provision must not be undone by recapitulating

Egyptian norms. The Israelites must never again be slaves or become permanently landless.[5]

In the end, Leviticus 25 exists in the gap between the ideal (every Israelite family secure on its own ancestral land; cf. Micah 4:4) and the real (unforeseen economic hardship that jeopardizes life and flourishing).[6] Perhaps the same could be said regarding enactment of its vision (Lev. 26:34-35 and 2 Chron. 36:21 suggest a history of non-enactment). The text portrays an ideal of justice, rather than mandating specific administrative procedures.[7] Its aim is to persuade and to function as a call to act justly and fairly and not exploit the vulnerable. For, apart from people learning to practice justice, no legislation – no matter how ingenious – has any hope of bringing about a just society. In the end, the impracticality of Jubilee is not a matter of physical impossibility but of motivation. Thus, at the very points where there is the greatest likelihood of injustice, the text advises hearers to 'fear your God' and act accordingly (25:17, 36, 43). Right acknowledgment of God should occasion love of neighbor.

---

5. Also remembered in the Pentateuch is Joseph's oversight of the sale of Egyptian livestock, land (except that of the priests), and populace to Pharaoh in a time of famine (Gen. 47:13-22). The result was the permanent enslavement of the Egyptians (Gen. 47:21) and the formalization of a system of hierarchy and oppression. The very real potential of Israel following suit is what Leviticus 25 is concerned to avoid.

6. Deuteronomy 15 recognizes the same tension. While 'there need be no poor people among you ... There will always be poor people in the land' (Deut. 15:4, 11).

7. The following comments are drawn from Walter J. Houston, *Justice for the Poor? Social Justice in the Old Testament in Concept and Practice* (Eugene: Cascade, 2020), 59-66.

From text to message

One of the challenges of preaching or teaching this passage is the cultural distance that needs to be overcome. The ancient world was markedly different to ours. The economy was primarily based on agriculture, with the bulk of the population hovering on or around the poverty line. There was no welfare system to rely on if things took a turn for the worse. Instead, the impoverished were thrust back on kinship ties or, failing that, the sale of assets, including themselves. We need to be careful not to prejudge the text based on our own societal norms. At the same time, Leviticus 25 challenges many of our cherished assumptions. Is continual growth really the mark of a successful economy? Is land ownership in any absolute sense theologically viable? Is financial security only maintained at the expense of the poor and vulnerable (who, in this global village, may remain forever out of sight)? Careful teaching of this text can be a powerful means of exposing theological and ethical blind spots.

Getting the message clear: the theme

Leviticus 25 states that the land of Canaan belongs to God, who permits His people to reside there as tenants. Israel must therefore remember God's purposes in deliverance and learn to fear Him. Obeying His commands would enable Sabbath rest, liberty, blessing, and justice for all, lessening the worst effects of a broken world until its conclusive remaking.

Getting the message clear: the aim

Leviticus 25 portrays life in Yahweh's land as marked by Sabbath rest, trusting fear, and remembrance of an end to slavery and landlessness. In positioning God as landowner, the aim of the text is to persuade readers that they have no right to take what God has claimed for Himself. Neither land nor people are to be exploited for personal gain. Instead, the passage envisions the extension of generosity and grace towards the vulnerable and impoverished in order to inculcate those virtues in readers. It is in heeding the text's demand for compliance that justice, blessing, provision, and preservation will extend to all. In this, Israel is invited to experience, in part, the goodness of the world as it was in the beginning, a world characterized by right relationships between God, individuals, society, and land. Readers must understand that transformation and restoration lie at the heart of God's agenda. His call is for His people to become co-workers in the task of re-creation.

A way in

The words of Micah 6:8 are well-known: 'And what does the LORD require of you? To act justly and to love mercy and to walk humbly with your God.' This was a needed rebuke for a generation who considered themselves religious but who invited divine judgment for perpetuating social evils. In His own day, Jesus was just as excoriating: 'Woe to you, teachers of the law and Pharisees, you hypocrites! You give a tenth of your spices – mint, dill and cumin. But you have neglected the more important matters of the law – justice, mercy and faithfulness' (Matt. 23:23). There is a whole dimension of biblical faith that is wrapped up in how we act towards others. In this, we betray whether we are truly sons and daughters of the Father, or not. Leviticus 25 may well sound a needed corrective in our day.

It was George Santayana who said, 'Those who cannot remember the past are condemned to repeat it.' The wisdom of that statement is readily evident as one reflects on the past century. Too often, the horrors suffered by one group are, in turn, inflicted by that same group upon others. There is something cyclic and universal about human nature. Leviticus 25 frankly admits that reality. It acknowledges that, while God may have rescued His people from being landless slaves in Egypt, there was every possibility that Israel would simply mirror in its own society what it had experienced under Pharaoh. Therefore, God speaks to commend a different path. Here is a word that testifies to God's intent to establish a just and generous society, beginning with Israel and extending to the world.

Ideas for application

- God's ownership of Canaan is a microcosm of His ownership of the world. The whole earth belongs to God, who will demand an accounting for what is done upon it (e.g., Gen. 6:11-13; Rev. 11:18).

- The image of tenants working for an (absentee) landlord is adopted by Jesus to encourage faithfulness among His followers with respect to their appointed tasks (Matt. 25:14-30). Christians should work towards hearing, 'Well done, good and faithful servant.'

- Just as the Israelites were considered Yahweh's servants, so Christians have become slaves of God (Rom. 6:22; 1 Cor. 7:22; Phil. 1:1). Bought at a price, we must not become slaves to another (1 Cor. 7:23).

- Acting as redeemer for impoverished kin is wonderfully illustrated by Boaz in the book of Ruth (for a counterexample, see 1 Kings 21). The narrative account of this 'prominent man of noble character'

(Ruth 2:1 HCSB) who cares for the vulnerable fleshes out the potential of what Leviticus 25 envisions.

- In Luke 4:17-21 Jesus framed His ministry in Jubilee terms (filtered through Isa. 61:1-2).

- Compassionate *action* towards the weak and needy is the hallmark of genuine faith: 'Religion that God our Father accepts as pure and faultless is this: to look after orphans and widows in their distress' (James 1:27; cf. James 2:14-17; 1 John 3:17-18).

- Poverty affects more than just the financial. The biblical response is correspondingly broad. As Corbett and Fikkert helpfully summarize, 'The goal is to restore people to a full expression of humanness, to being what God created us all to be, people who glorify God by living in right relationship with God, with self, with others, and with the rest of creation.'[8]

- The warning sounded in Leviticus 25 against taking advantage of one's 'brother' is repeatedly echoed in the New Testament. Leaders in God's kingdom must not lord it over others (Matt. 20:25-27). The Corinthians are commanded to stop taking fellow believers to court (1 Cor. 6:1-6) and to cease disadvantaging the working class (1 Cor. 11:17-22). Profiteering at the expense of the poor is condemned by James (James 5:4-5).

- The New Testament has much to say about wealth. It can vie for a believer's ultimate allegiance (Matt. 6:24) and plunge people into spiritual ruin (1 Tim. 6:9-10).

---

8. Steve Corbett and Brian Fikkert, *When Helping Hurts: How to Alleviate Poverty Without Hurting the Poor … and Yourself* (Chicago: Moody, 2012), 74.

Worry over material things can distract from kingdom work (Matt. 6:25-34). At the same time, wealth opens opportunity for generosity, whether spontaneous (e.g., 2 Cor. 8:10-12) or commanded (e.g., 1 Tim. 6:17-19). God's people must learn to use wealth and position righteously rather than be mastered by them.

- Those who put God's requirements first will have their physical needs met (25:18-22; Matt. 6:25-33).

- Believers are called to recognize the futility of their former way of life in order to avoid repeating it (e.g., Rom. 6:20-21; 1 Cor. 6:9-11; 1 Pet. 4:3).

Suggestions for preaching

As Sam Chan so helpfully points out, one of the most effective ways to preach the good news about Jesus to contemporary Western people is to affirm their desire for things like liberty, equal rights, and social justice, but then demonstrate how those good intentions fail to achieve their full potential. Only in the gospel do these things rightly longed for find their deepest fulfillment.[9] The following sermon adopts this approach to preaching Leviticus 25. As such, it could also be used in an evangelistic setting.

- **The call for social justice.** From the 1984 Band Aid campaign, to Jubilee 2000, to the Black Lives Matter rallies of 2020, social justice is big news. And rightly so. Humans have a seemingly endless capacity to inflict harm, knowingly or unknowingly, upon others. These movements rightly bring to our attention the deep

---

9. Sam Chan, *Evangelism in a Sceptical World: How to Make the Unbelievable News About Jesus More Believable* (Grand Rapids: Zondervan, 2018).

divides and inequalities that permeate our societies, as well as our possible complicity in maintaining the *status quo*. The call to do better is apt. The Bible affirms these desires for a just and generous society. Leviticus 25 is a case in point.

- **Leviticus 25 and social justice.** Leviticus 25 extends Sabbath rest to years, and pictures people living in harmony and eating uncultivated food that the land provides. It remembers the divine deliverance from Egypt that ended slavery and landlessness. In these ways, the passage recalls creation and redemption to drive home its ethical message. With Israel, God was establishing a society marked by justice, generosity, rest, and blessing. While the text's commands and warnings recognize the non-ideal state of the world, they also highlight God's intent to transform and restore. By heeding its divine commission, Israel would function as a microcosm of what will, one day, become global.

- **Jesus and social justice.** Leviticus 25 coheres with our desire for a society governed by justice and generosity. But this passage is realistic, not idealistic, when it comes to human nature. The obstacle that prevents the utopian world we desire is us. We share a flaw that runs too deep to fix. That is why movements begin, and end. We lack the commitment, perseverance, and power to truly transform the world. But instead of despair, the Bible points us to Jesus as the supreme change agent. Unlike us, Jesus's commitment is unwavering, His perseverance eternal, His power without bounds. Jesus assures us that the foretaste of a world made new seen in His life and ministry will, on the day He returns, become global reality. In the meantime, Jesus is transforming men and women, remaking them in His image, and commissioning them as His servants in the world. Little wonder that the Bible concludes with a short but poignant request: 'Come, Lord Jesus.'

Suggestions for teaching

Questions to help understand the passage

1. Why is Sabbath so important? What biblical resonances does it evoke?

2. What kinds of things would the people eat in the seventh year (25:6-7)?

3. Why does the Year of Jubilee begin on the Day of Atonement (25:9)?

4. What is so important about return to ancestral land (25:10, 13)?

5. What are the implications of Yahweh's statement in 25:23, 'the land is mine'?

6. Why are the regulations for Levites different (25:32-34)?

7. In context, why is usury banned (25:36-37)?

8. How does instruction regarding foreign servants (25:44-46) relate to the rest of the chapter?

9. Why is Egypt repeatedly mentioned (25:38, 42-43, 55)?

10. In what ways does Leviticus 25 recognize potential for sin and how does it address this?

11. Are instructions for observing Sabbath years and Jubilee possible to enact? What difficulties would need to be overcome (at individual and societal levels)?

Questions to help apply the passage

1. Imagine you are part of an Israelite farming family. How would hearing Leviticus 25 make you feel?

2. What is God calling His people to be in this passage?

3. Leviticus 25 outlines means of financial assistance for the impoverished. But it also addresses other aspects of poverty (intrapersonal, societal, psychological, institutional, etc.). What can you observe along these lines in Leviticus 25 and how does this inform your understanding of what God was doing in Israel?

4. Is 'slave of Christ' (1 Cor. 7:22) part of your self-identity? How should Paul's phrase impact the way you live?

5. Jesus says a person cannot serve both God and money (Matt. 6:24). How do you know which is your master?

6. What are your responsibilities towards impoverished 'brothers' in your own church community and in the global church?

17.
Obedience Brings Blessing
(Leviticus 26)

Introduction

Does obedience really matter? Surely God will bless His people regardless. That is the topic Leviticus 26 addresses. Yet the passage stands apart from the other material in the book. Instead of ritual or legal instruction, Leviticus 26 voices a call for conformity that derives its force from listing promised rewards and corresponding threats. The chapter becomes 'sermonic' in tone.[1] In first-person language ('I'), Yahweh declares what He will personally bring about in the face of either obedience or disobedience.

The positive and negative outcomes listed are presented as mirror opposites, often in near-verbatim terms. Thus, the whole passage tuns on reversal. For example, if Israel obeys, Yahweh will 'not abhor' them (26:11); but if the nation decides to 'abhor' divine instructions (26:15), Yahweh says, 'I will abhor you' (26:30). Leviticus 26 thus raises the question of human agency and responsibility when it comes to covenantal demands. It seems that divine intent

---

1. Hartley, *Leviticus*, 462.

to bless is not a foregone conclusion that will simply unfold irrespective of moral and ritual propriety. Israel must learn to carefully obey. There is a real choice to be made.

Within Leviticus, this passage functions as a closing exhortation. Divine sanctions address a potential question in the mind of listeners with respect to everything the book has presented: 'What if I do? What if I don't?' The chapter's role as conclusion becomes clear with its mention of the statutes, judgments, and laws that Yahweh gave Israel on Mount Sinai (26:46). The term 'judgments' (*mishpatim*) occurs most frequently in Leviticus 18–26. 'Statutes' (*ḥuqqim*), however, only appears in this form in 10:11 (and in Deuteronomy). Likewise, 'laws' (*torot*) is distinct to Leviticus 1–16. Thus, the chapter's closing verse has been deliberately worded to encapsulate not only Leviticus 25–26, or even 17–26, but the entire book.

Here, then, is a final call to faithfulness. There is much at stake, for the contemporary reader as much as the ancient. As C. S. Lewis realized,

> I may repeat 'Do as you would be done by' till I am black in the face, but I cannot really carry it out till I love my neighbour as myself: and I cannot learn to love my neighbour as myself till I learn to love God: and I cannot learn to love God except by learning to obey him.[2]

Listening to the text

Context and structure

Leviticus 25 and 26 are closely tied together. Both are governed by the same introduction to divine speech ('The

---

2. C. S. Lewis, *Mere Christianity* (50th anniversary ed.; London: Harper-Collins, 2002), 87.

LORD said to Moses', 25:1; cf. 27:1); the chapters are framed by the phrase 'on Mount Sinai' (25:1; 26:46 ESV); deliverance from Egypt is a consistent refrain (25:38, 42, 55; 26:13, 45); and these are the only chapters in Leviticus that mention Sabbath years (25:1-7; 26:34-35, 43).

The twofold mention of Mount Sinai is important. First, it functions as another reminder of the historical setting. But, second, it reveals chronological displacement: the instruction in Leviticus 1–24, spoken to Israel *from the tabernacle* (cf. 1:1-2; 4:1; etc.), comes later than that of Leviticus 25–26 (delivered *on* Mount Sinai). Yet arranging the contents of Leviticus this way allows the book to end with the idyllic potential encapsulated by Sabbath, Jubilee, and the creation-evoking blessing of chapter 26 (see below). Heeding Leviticus 1–24 is therefore presented as the means of achieving this end, adding weight to the call for obedience in chapter 26.

Leviticus 26 can be divided into five main sections:

> Summary of the Decalogue (26:1-2)
> Promised rewards for obedience (26:3-13)
> Threatened punishments for disobedience (26:14-39)
> Future restoration (26:40-45)
> Summary conclusion (26:46)

Working through the text
Summary of the Decalogue (26:1-2)

Leviticus 26 opens with a restatement of several Decalogue demands. The exact number is debated, however, and partly depends on how one divides the Commandments (everyone agrees that there are ten, but Protestant, Roman Catholic, Orthodox, and Jewish traditions split them differently).

Nevertheless, resonance with Exodus 20 and Deuteronomy 5 is obvious: 'Do not make idols or set up an image' (26:1; cf. Exod. 20:4; Deut. 5:8), 'do not ... bow down' (26:1; cf. Exod. 20:5; Deut. 5:9), and 'Observe my Sabbaths' (26:2; cf. Exod. 20:8; Deut. 5:12). The phrase, 'I am the LORD your God' also appears in both contexts (26:1; cf. Exod. 20:2; Deut. 5:6). Furthermore, reference to the Israelites being brought out of Egypt in 25:55 recalls Exodus 20:2 and Deuteronomy 5:6. The effect achieved by summarizing key covenantal requirements in Leviticus 25:55–26:2 is to make readers consider *all* that Yahweh has commanded, in a manner akin to 26:46 (see above). This is the necessary context for understanding what the following section means by 'decrees' and 'commands' (26:3).

Promised rewards for obedience (26:3-13)

Leviticus 26:3-13 is presented in conditional language. The opening *protasis* in 26:3 ('*If* you walk in my statutes and you keep my commands and do them') outlines the essential conditions that govern the *apodosis* in 26:4-13, '*then* I will give' (my translation, emphasis added).[3] This casts the promised realities in 26:4-13 as contingent upon Israel's obedience. There is a divine intention to bless, but experiencing that blessing is conditioned by the human covenantal partner(s).

Nevertheless, *if* Israel listens to Yahweh's decrees and *does* them, blessing will ensue. Yahweh Himself (note the use of first-person language throughout) promises to bestow His favor. Promised rewards are tangible and

---

3. A complete conditional sentence contains a *protasis* which explains the condition (usually marked with 'if') and an *apodosis* which explains the result (usually marked with 'then').

concrete. Israel's harvests will be bountiful (26:4-5), leading to satisfaction and full stomachs (26:5).[4] The nation will enjoy peace from enemies (26:6, 7-8) and from the ravages of 'wild beasts' (26:6). Safety will become Israel's norm (26:5). Moreover, the people will be fruitful and increase in number (26:9). But even this increased population will not exhaust the supply of food (26:10). Yahweh will not only make His dwelling among His people (26:11; cf. Exod. 25:8) but even, climactically, asserts, 'I will walk among you and be your God, and you will be my people' (26:12). Importantly, Leviticus 26:13 indicates that these rewards are offered to an *already delivered* people. In fact, enabling this (potential) state of affairs is the very reason Israel was rescued from Egyptian bondage.

The language of Leviticus 26:3-13 deliberately evokes Genesis 1–3.[5] The people will 'be fruitful' and will 'become numerous' (26:9, my translation; cf. Gen. 1:22, 28). The land will 'give of its produce' and the 'trees will give of their fruit' (26:4, my translation; cf. Gen. 1:29). So, even though Leviticus allows for and even prescribes eating meat, the picture presented in 26:4-12 is of a *vegetarian* diet, as in Genesis 1. Moreover, the divine pronouncement that 'you will eat bread to satisfaction' (26:5, my translation) mitigates Yahweh's former decree that only 'by the sweat of your face will you eat bread' (Gen. 3:19, my translation). Incredibly, God states He will 'walk about' in the midst

---

4. The bounty pictured in 26:4-5, 10 connects with the annual festivals charted in Leviticus 23, many of which coincide with key moments in the agricultural year. Likewise, provision contingent upon careful obedience is promised with respect to the Year of Jubilee (25:18-22).

5. Interested readers can see my extended discussion of this in '*I Will Walk Among You*', 187-221.

of the people (26:12) just as Genesis 3:8 describes Him
'walking about' in the Garden. This marks the ultimate
blessing listed in 26:3-13. It also signals the climax to the
theme of increasing intimacy between Yahweh and His
people evident throughout Leviticus: from total exclusion
(Exod. 40:34-35), to speaking from the tabernacle
(1:1-2), to initial admittance (9:23), to once-yearly access
(16:12-15). The implication of 26:12 is that Yahweh will
no longer be confined to the sanctuary but will be present
everywhere in the land.[6] In this way, Leviticus 26 uses
creation language to anticipate eschatological realities even
as it invites realization in Israel's lived experience.

Threatened punishments for disobedience (26:14-39)

The idyllic picture of 26:3-13 is quickly shattered in
the following section, which progressively reverses and
undermines the potential for blessing. Thus, once more,
Leviticus remains soberly realistic; the specter of sin and
disobedience is never far from view. Leviticus 26:14-39 is
also substantially longer than 26:3-13, perhaps suggestive
that this set of realities will be the more likely outcome
for Israel. As such, Leviticus 26 adopts a similar pattern
to Deuteronomy 28 and even the extra-biblical Laws of
Hammurabi, which likewise emphasize threat over blessing
(Hammurabi has sixteen lines of blessings followed by 280
lines of curses).

As with the previous section, 26:13-39 is phrased in conditional language, albeit expressed negatively: 'But *if* you will
not listen to me and carry out all these commands ... *then* I

---

6. Jacob Milgrom, *Leviticus 23–27: A New Translation with Introduction
    and Commentary* (AB 3B; New York: The Anchor Bible, 2001), 2301.

will do this to you' (26:14, 16 [emphasis added]). As noted above, reversal is the key motif. Promise becomes threat. The possibilities outlined in 26:4-12 are progressively set against their mirror opposites. Rain in season (26:4) will become iron skies (26:19). Instead of bounty and plentiful harvests, the nation will be subject to deprivation and scarcity marked by the fruitlessness of trees (26:20) and scarcity of bread (26:26). Wild animals will multiply, depriving people of their children and depopulating the land (26:22). Enemies will come to steal food and peace alike (26:16-17).

Throughout, the focus on divine agency persists. Just as Yahweh promised to bring about blessing, so He will personally enact judgment: '*I* will do this to you: *I* will bring on you sudden terror... *I* will set my face against you... *I* will punish you... *I* will break down your stubborn pride.... *I* will multiply your afflictions' (26:16-21 [emphasis added]). What transpired would not be due to random chance. It could not simply be written off as bad luck. This is divinely-instigated punishment.

Nevertheless, punishment serves a disciplinary role. To see this, it is important to note the escalating nature of the threats. There are five subsections in 26:14-39, each introduced by the Hebrew word '*im* ('if') (26:14-17, 18-20, 21-22, 23-26, 27-39). However, in each case the phrasing is longer, highlighting the ongoing stubbornness of a nation that requires escalated threats:

- 'But if you will not listen to me ... then I will do this to you' (26:14, 16)

- 'If after all this you will not listen to me, I will punish you for your sins seven times over' (26:18)

- 'If you remain hostile toward me and refuse to listen to me, I will multiply your afflictions seven times over, as your sins deserve' (26:21)

- 'If in spite of these things you do not accept my correction but continue to be hostile toward me, I myself will be hostile toward you and will afflict you for your sins seven times over' (26:23-24)

- If in spite of this you still do not listen to me but continue to be hostile toward me, then in my anger I will be hostile toward you, and I myself will punish you for your sins seven times over' (26:27-28)

The language of sevenfold punishment indicates the thoroughness or completeness of judgment. Yet, as 26:23 makes clear, the goal is correction. The hope is that the nation will come to its senses before it is too late (cf. Amos 4:6-13).

The final threat (26:27-39) elaborates what 'too late' will look like: total dissolution of people, place, and the beneficent presence of God. Instead, Yahweh will abhor Israel and no longer respond to sacrifices offered (26:30-31). The language is graphic, describing the horrific effects of siege warfare (26:29). National annihilation is portrayed with ravaged land (26:32) and a populace either killed (26:29-31) or scattered among the nations (26:33), where the people will perish and be devoured (26:38). Even the vivid personification of the land enjoying its Sabbath rest (26:34-35) drives home the point: vomiting out the source of its defilement (i.e., the Israelites; cf. 18:28; 20:22) will make the land happy. This is banishment on a national scale. Instead of Edenic blessing, there is Adamic exile.

Yet, as in 26:3-13, the language is contingent. This need not necessarily be Israel's fate. The warning, dire as it is, remains an act of grace. Strong language and piled-up threats are aimed to dissuade.

Future restoration (26:40-45)

Grace also pervades the chapter's final section. Conditional language is again evident as Israel is positioned as having already suffered the exile threatened in 26:27-39. Silence regarding sacrificial remedy is expected; there was no sacrifice for 'high-handed' sins like rebellion (see discussion at 1:1–6:7; 16). Nevertheless, Yahweh announces (contingent) hope: '*if* they confess their iniquity and the iniquity of their fathers ... *then* I will remember my covenant with Jacob, and I will remember my covenant with Isaac and my covenant with Abraham, and I will remember the land' (26:40, 42 ESV [emphasis added]). Genuine, corporate repentance would bring restoration.[7] Even in the face of unfaithfulness, Yahweh would prove faithful (cf. 2 Tim. 2:13). He would not break the covenant but would remember His purpose in calling Israel out of Egypt: to be their God (26:45). Even though 26:40-45 does not describe return from exile, mention of Egypt subtly introduces the potential for a second exodus. The following statement, 'I am Yahweh' (26:45, my translation), reiterates the point. This is the forty-ninth and final time the phrase appears in the book[8] and it stands as a reminder that the nature and character of the God revealed in the exodus remains unchanged. Just as Yahweh heard the cries of the Israelites in the past, and remembered the covenant

---

7. For an excellent analysis of repentance in the Bible, see Mark J. Boda, '*Return to Me*': *A Biblical Theology of Repentance* (NSBT 35; Downers Grove: IVP, 2015).

8. Gane, *Leviticus, Numbers*, 455.

made with their forefathers (Exod. 2:23-24), so He will
again respond to their pleas for deliverance.

The tenfold use of the verb 'to walk' throughout Leviticus
26 highlights the central message. Walking frames the
blessing section: 'If you walk in my statutes ... I will walk
among you' (26:3, 12, my translation). Indeed, making
Israel 'walk erect' was the goal of the exodus (26:13 ESV).
However, in 26:14-39, warnings are repeated that, if the
Israelites walk contrary to God (26:21, 23, 27), then God
will likewise walk contrary to them (26:24, 28). However,
confession of having walked contrary to God in 26:40, and
of making Him walk contrary to His people (26:41), is
held out as the path to restoration. Thus, learning to walk
rightly with God is crucial; this is, after all, the hallmark of
the faithful (e.g., Enoch [Gen. 5:22], Abraham [Gen. 17:1;
24:40], and Isaac [Gen. 48:15]).

Summary conclusion (26:46)

The wording of 26:46 has already been discussed above
(see 'Introduction'). Concluding with a list of sanctions
is a common feature of ancient covenant documents. Yet
it is normally a royal personage who declares what the
gods (third person) will do if the terms of the covenant
are violated.[9] In Leviticus 26, however, Yahweh is the King
who declares in the *first person* what He Himself will do.
This first-person language used throughout the chapter

---

9. For example, *Treaty between Mursilis and Duppi-Tessub of Amurru*
   begins, 'These are the words of ... the great king, the king of the
   Hatti land,' and ends, following a long list of named deities, with
   the invocation, 'should Duppi-Tessub not honor these words of the
   treaty and the oath, may these gods of the oath destroy Duppi-Tessub'
   (*ANET* 203-205).

underlines the deeply personal connection that exists between Yahweh and His people. Rebellion is not simply a matter of breaking rules; it fractures a relationship.

As such, Leviticus 26 comes as a divine plea for relational fidelity. Yahweh's intent is to bless, but human responsibility is a real factor. Either way, whether in blessing or judgment, Yahweh will remain faithful to His word. The difference will be the lived experience of the people.

Throughout, use of allusion to Genesis 1–3 intensifies the *affective* dimension of the plea. Tacit evocation of the first humans – of their original blessedness and its subsequent loss – adds poignancy and emotive force to the chapter's appeal for covenant faithfulness. In this way, powerful associations from the past are re-presented as future images of longing and hope.[10] Potential return to Edenic life becomes the carrot *par excellence* – and Adam-like banishment the stick. In this way, the literary sophistication of the text becomes more than mere artistic flourish; it becomes another means for Leviticus 26 to achieve the ends for which it was written.

From text to message

The message of Leviticus 26 is clear and needs to be heard as much by the contemporary church as by Israel of old: obedience matters. At the same time, care is needed. The principle that underlies this passage remains true: God rewards obedience and disciplines His people when they disobey. However, the specifics of Leviticus 26 cannot simply be adopted wholesale by assuming a one-to-one correspondence. It is not that straightforward. The exact

---

10. Michael Fishbane, *Biblical Interpretation in Ancient Israel* (Oxford: Clarendon, 1988), 371.

form of the positive and negative incentives laid out in Leviticus 26 was determined by the agreement between Yahweh and Israel known as the Mosaic covenant. Those specific terms do not directly apply to the church as the people of God today. Hence, drought in Australia or food shortages in the Sudan do not necessarily indicate divine judgment as they did for ancient Israel. Therefore, teaching this passage requires interpretative wisdom. Both extremes are off limits: wholesale adoption or wholesale rejection. God's continuing word to His people lies somewhere between those horizons.

Getting the message clear: the theme

God offers Israel new creation blessings and threatens their removal contingent upon whether the nation heeds and does all He had commanded. Divine sanctions thus sound a clear call for careful obedience and warn against disobedience. Yet, God also graciously opens a way for corporate confession and restoration should rebellion bring the nation to ruin.

Getting the message clear: the aim

Leviticus 26 reminds readers of God's commands, both those of the Decalogue as well as the entire content of Leviticus. Furthermore, recalling Egyptian deliverance prompts remembrance of Israel's purpose to walk with God and be His people. Expected obedience is further incentivized by outlining the potential rewards that Yahweh promises to enact on behalf of a compliant nation. Allusion to Genesis 1–3 stimulates the imagination and creates a desire for the Edenic blessings portrayed. Yet threatened punishment for disobedience warns that future blessing is not guaranteed but remains conditional. Adam-like banishment from the place where God walks is also a possibility. The contingent nature of both blessing and punishment highlights the reality of human responsibility and drives home the urgency of the choice to be made.

A way in

The words of John Sammis's song *Trust and Obey* are well known:

> *While we do His good will, He abides with us still,*
> *And with all who will trust and obey.*

> *For the favor He shows, for the joy He bestows,*
> *Are for them who will trust and obey.*

But are those words true? Do Christians need to obey God's commands to experience His blessing? This would seem to be a foundational matter to be certain about. For some, the answer is assured: of course not. God's blessing is not dependent on obedience. Yet for others, the answer is equally clear: obedience is required. So, which is it? Do Christians need to obey God's commands to experience His blessing, or not? Thankfully, Leviticus 26 speaks to that very issue. By listening carefully to what God said to Israel, we can gain insight into the ongoing role of obedience in the lives of God's people.

When disaster strikes, it does not take long for someone to label the event as 'divine judgment' upon some real or imagined sin. From the 2004 tsunami in the Indian Ocean, to Hurricane Katrina, to the coronavirus pandemic of 2020, God's punitive design is perceived (and then blogged or tweeted about). Passages like Leviticus 26 are appealed to for support. Their unashamed focus on the geopolitical, meteorological, and biological disasters threatened by God for disobedience seems to offer a ready explanation for current calamities. But is that a legitimate reading of Leviticus 26? Can this passage be used to diagnose twenty-first century disasters? To answer those questions, we need to take a careful look at Leviticus 26 to hear what God was and is saying through this text.

Ideas for application

- God demands that His rescued and delivered people learn to obey His every command. Jesus declares that obedience is a sign of whether a person loves Him (John 14:14, 21, 23) and is the way to remain in His love (John 15:10). Therefore, those who obey will be regarded as Jesus's friends (John 15:14). The indwelling Holy Spirit is the means by which such obedience becomes possible (John 14:26; cf. Ezek. 36:26-27).

- The dynamic of reward for obedience is intrinsic to Jesus's teaching (e.g., Matt. 5:12; 6:4, 6; 10:41-42; 16:27; 25:14-23; Luke 6:35; John 13:17). So too is the loss or forfeiture of reward (e.g., Matt. 6:1, 5, 16; 25:1-13, 24-30). The remainder of the New Testament simply follows suit (e.g., 1 Cor. 3:12-14; Eph. 6:8; Col. 3:23-24; Rev. 2–3; 22:12). Like Leviticus 26, this is not salvation by works, but the obedience expected from those already saved.

- Revelation 22 similarly uses the promise of creation remade (22:1-3) and intimate fellowship with God (22:3-5) to incentivize obedience in the present

(22:12-15). The book also adopts the pattern of sevenfold judgment aimed to evoke repentance (Rev. 6–11; 15–16).

- The book of James is indispensable for understanding the place of obedience in the life of believers. It maintains that the person who *does* what the word says will be blessed in what he or she does (James 1:22-25). Thus, belief by itself is insufficient: 'What good is it, my brothers and sisters, if someone claims to have faith but has no deeds? Can such faith save them?' (James 2:14). Rather, 'a person is considered righteous by what they do and not by faith alone' (James 2:24). Therefore, 'faith without deeds is dead' (James 2:26).

- Paul asserts that the gospel brings blessing (1 Cor. 9:23). Such blessing relates to both spiritual (e.g., Gal. 3:14; Eph. 1:3; 1 Pet. 1:3-5) and physical benefits (e.g., Luke 18:29-30; Rom. 15:27; 1 Cor. 15:20-23; 2 Cor. 9:8; Phil. 4:19).

- Sin and rebellion are personal affronts to a personal God. They are not simply a matter of breaking the rules. Christians are therefore urged not to *grieve* the Holy Spirit who lives within them (Eph. 4:30).

- In the New Testament God continues to enact discipline and punishment for His people *in this life* (e.g., Acts 5:1-11; 1 Cor. 11:29-32; Heb. 12:5-13; Rev. 2:4-5). Disobedience can have temporal consequences. C. S. Lewis highlights the necessity of divine discipline: 'The human spirit will not even begin to try to surrender self-will as long as all seems to be well with it ... We can rest contentedly in our sins ... But pain insists on being attended to.'[11]

- In Leviticus 26, obedience, disobedience, and confession are *corporate* realities. This sounds a challenge to Western, individualistic conceptions and invites consideration of how such practices might be enacted at a whole-church level.

- Borrowing words and phrases from Leviticus 26, Daniel enacts the confession and repentant disposition required by 26:40 on behalf of the nation (Dan. 9:4-19). Importantly, this comes in the 'the first year of Darius' (Dan. 9:1), the king who allowed the exiles to return home (2 Chron. 36:23).

- The promise of God walking with His people (26:12) finds fulfillment in the church as sacred temple (2 Cor. 6:16; cf. Rev. 2:1).

Suggestions for preaching

Sermon 1

A temptation in many evangelical circles can be to mute the central message of Leviticus 26, or to relegate the idea that obedience brings blessing to the world of the Old Testament. The preacher therefore has some work to do to convince a congregation that the dynamic on display in Leviticus 26 persists in Jesus's teaching and the rest of the New Testament. At the same time, care must be taken to ensure that people do not hear a sermon that says 'salvation is based on your own efforts'. That is not what Leviticus

---

11. C. S. Lewis, *The Problem of Pain* (London: HarperCollins, 2002), 90-91.

26 is asserting: this is a word to those who, by grace, are *already* God's people.

- **A reminder of God's commands (25:55b–26:2, 46).** The passage begins and ends with language that evokes God's commands to His people. Deliverance from Egypt, a prohibition against idolatry, and instruction to observe Sabbath remind readers of the Decalogue. The chapter's concluding verse uses terms that connect with the whole of Leviticus. Together, this is a clear reminder of all that God expects from a people who have sworn allegiance to Him.

- **Obedience brings blessing (26:3-13).** The conditional language of 26:3-13 indicates that projected blessing is contingent upon Israel hearing and doing all that God has said. The earthly blessings listed – abundant food, safety, multiplying descendants, and absence of wild animals – take on a deeper resonance by reusing language from Genesis 1–3. Restoration of creation blessings and proximity with God are promised – all designed to make obedience attractive. Indeed, God rescued Israel from Egypt precisely so that they could experience this blessedness/blessing.

- **Disobedience brings discipline (26:14-39).** The conditional language of 26:14-39 demonstrates that reward can be forfeited. Israel had an innate tendency to disobey divine commands. Thus, a series of escalated disasters are threatened to dissuade Israel from abandoning the God who rescued them. Disobedience would bring divine displeasure and discipline, experienced as successive acts of uncreation and climaxing in exile from the land where Yahweh walks. The longer treatment and picturing of an already-exiled people suggests that this will likely be the nation's fate.

- **Confession brings restoration (26:40-45).** Leviticus 26 remains hopeful, however. Divine discipline, even severe discipline, need not be the end. Opportunity for confession and repentance is offered. God assures readers that He will hear and respond to the humble with kindness and remember His covenant commitments. Sin will not have the final word. God is steadfast in His intent to form a people of His very own, who will walk in faithfulness with Him.

Sermon 2

Culture invariably shapes one's understanding of the Bible. While it is impossible to step outside of this reality, one can nevertheless become more aware of the assumptions that are unconsciously brought to the text. For example, the influence of Western individualism means that many Christians conceive of sin, punishment, and repentance only in personal categories: it is *my* sin, *my* punishment, *my* repentance. However, with its resolute focus on the *corporate* dimension of sin, punishment, and repentance, Leviticus 26 provides an excellent opportunity to explore these issues topically as they relate to groups. There is much here for a church community to learn. A sermon outline could be as follows:

1. Corporate sin, punishment, and repentance in Leviticus 26

2. Corporate sin, punishment, and repentance in the New Testament

3. Corporate sin, punishment, and repentance in our church

Suggestions for teaching

Questions to help understand the passage

1. Why does Leviticus 25:55–26:2 recall the order and content of Decalogue commands from Exodus 20 and Deuteronomy 5?

2. Why does Leviticus 26 use conditional language ('If … then')?

3. In 26:3-13, what allusions to Genesis 1–3 do you notice? Why are these here?

4. Why is the section that lists threats (26:14-39) longer than that which lists blessings (26:3-13)?

5. Is there an order or progression to the threats listed in 26:14-39?

6. Some of the language in Leviticus 26 seems to imagine that exile has already happened (e.g., 26:34-35, 40-41). Why is this the case?

7. What is the significance of Abraham, Isaac, and Jacob being mentioned in 26:42?

8. Compare Leviticus 26 with Deuteronomy 28. What is similar? What is different?

9. Why is material given by God 'on Mount Sinai' (26:46; cf. 25:1) placed here in Leviticus?

10. What role does Leviticus 26 play in the book?

Questions to help apply the passage

1. What do you think is the main point of Leviticus 26?

2. Could Leviticus 26 be labelled a 'prosperity gospel' text? Why or why not?

3. What do you learn about God in this passage?

4. If a friend pointed out 26:27-33 and asked, 'How can you believe in a God who would do that?', what would you say?

5. Does God bless *Christians* based on their obedience and does He punish them for disobedience? What biblical evidence can you find to support your answer in each case?

6. Leviticus 26:40 describes *corporate* and *generational* confession of sin ('their sins and the sins of their ancestors'). Does this type of confession have any place in church communities?

7. Write out a short paragraph that explains the place of obedience in the life of the believer.

18.
Extraordinary Thankfulness
(Leviticus 27)

Introduction

For many readers, Leviticus ends with a resounding anticlimax. After the impassioned appeal of chapter 26, the book seems to fizzle out in a loosely tacked-on appendix which lists commands about vows and dedicated items. Even in scholarly literature, Leviticus 27 fares poorly. It is frequently left out of structural analyses and is not always considered when discussing the book's message. Yet this chapter nevertheless forms part of the received text of Leviticus and needs to be approached as such. The key questions therefore concern why this material has been placed here and how it serves the overall aims of the book.

Leviticus 27 serves several important literary functions. The chapter's focus on items voluntarily dedicated to Yahweh revisits themes and ideas found in Leviticus 1, forming a frame around the book. This enables Leviticus to begin and end with portraits of inner thankfulness and devotion finding external expression. Yet, in contrast to the ascension offerings of Leviticus 1, items dedicated in Leviticus 27 are not necessarily part of the sacrificial system. The complementary pictures of cultic and non-cultic giving combine to portray worship as an 'all of life' activity.

Leviticus 27 also contains important keywords which evoke Leviticus 25: 'Jubilee' and 'redeem'. The effect is to invite readers to consider the chapters together. In this way, the generosity towards one's 'brother' expected in Leviticus 25 finds a correlation in generosity towards one's God in Leviticus 27. The emergent picture is of an ideal Israelite, obedient and therefore blessed with abundant provision (cf. 26:1-13), who expresses tangible love to both God and neighbor. This positive portrait, bracketing Leviticus 26, serves to offset the bleak description of punitive exile in 26:27-45 and allows the book to end on a more hopeful, perhaps even prophetic note. Rebellion and punishment remain Israel's *pen*ultimate destiny. The nation will, one day, become the worshipping community imagined by Leviticus.

Listening to the text

Context and structure

Leviticus 27 is marked out as a unit by the book's final introduction to divine speech ('The LORD said to Moses'; 27:1). The wording of the concluding statement in 27:34 echoes that of 26:46. Moreover, references to instruction given 'on Mount Sinai' (which is also the last phrase in the Hebrew text of Leviticus) in 25:1, 26:46, and 27:34 serve to join these chapters together as a block. Sklar even suggests a chiastic arrangement for Leviticus 25–27:[1]

---

1. Sklar, *Leviticus*, 326 (adapted).

 A Laws about redemption (Lev. 25)

  B Blessings for covenant obedience and curses for
   disobedience (Lev. 26)

 A' Laws about redemption (Lev. 27)

The chapter divides into three main sections with major transitions in 27:2 and 27:14 marked by the Hebrew word *ki* ('if/when'). The first section (27:2b-13) concerns animate objects – persons or animals – pledged to Yahweh in fulfillment of a 'vow' (Heb. *ndr/neder*). The second (27:14-25) provides instruction for 'dedicating' or 'consecrating' (Heb. *qdsh*) inanimate items to God (houses and property). Both vows and consecration are voluntary acts on the part of the worshipper. The third main section (27:26-33) details exclusions. Some things already belong to God and therefore cannot be given to Him again: firstborn animals, devoted persons or items, and tithes. The chapter can be outlined as follows:

Introduction (27:1-2a)

Voluntary vows to Yahweh (27:2b-13)
 Persons (27:2b-8)
 Animals (27:9-13)

Voluntary consecration to Yahweh (27:14-25)
 Houses (27:14-15)
 Ancestral land (27:16-21)
 Acquired land (27:22-25)

Things already belonging to Yahweh (27:26-33)
 Firstborn animals (27:26-27)
 Dedicated things (27:28-29)
 Tithes (27:30-33)

Conclusion (27:34)

Working through the text

Voluntary vows to Yahweh (27:2b-13)

The chapter opens with Yahweh addressing the making of vows. The verb used in 27:2 (*pl'*) has the basic meaning of something being 'different' or 'conspicuous', often in a positive sense – i.e. 'to be wonderful' or even 'miraculous'. Hence, many versions have 'special vow' (NIV, ESV, HCSB; Milgrom has 'extraordinary vow').[2] Items promised to God in this manner are above and beyond anything mandated.

The making of vows is commonplace throughout the Old Testament. Often, a person committed him- or herself to fulfill a particular action *if* God delivered them from a situation of current crisis or need. For example, Jacob says, 'If God will be with me and will watch over me ... then the LORD will be my God and this stone that I have set up as a pillar will be God's house, and of all that you give me I will give you a tenth' (Gen. 28:20-22). Or Hannah promises that if God grants her a son, 'then I will give him to the LORD for all the days of his life, and no razor will ever be used on his head' (1 Sam. 1:11). Making vows in this way is viewed positively as a hallmark of genuine faith. The language permeates the Psalms (e.g., Ps. 22:25; 56:12; 61:5-8; 76:11; 132:1-5). It is also one of the key indicators given in Jonah 1 that the sailors have truly come to know Yahweh (Jonah 1:16). Vows were not a means of twisting God's arm or currying favor; rather, they underscored the seriousness of petition (comparable to fasting). Of course, as Deuteronomy 23:21-23 cautions, vows made to God

2. Milgrom, *Leviticus 23–27*, 1941.

should also be fulfilled. It is better, in fact, not to vow at all than to renege upon one's commitment (Eccles. 5:5).

The items promised or vowed to God in 27:2b-8 are persons. However, instead of depositing an actual man, woman, or child at the tabernacle (Hannah's presentation of Samuel is exceptional), a monetary payment is allowed instead, perhaps as a gracious concession for words spoken in desperate circumstances. Accordingly, relative values are set in 27:3-7 indexed to gender and age (see *Table 18.1*). These values or assessments indicate labor value, not intrinsic worth, and have affinities with slave market prices listed elsewhere (e.g., Gen. 37:28; 2 Kings 15:20; cf. Num. 18:16).

Age	Male assessment (shekels)	Female assessment (shekels)
1 month–5 years old	5	3
5–20 years old	20	10
20–60 years old	50	30
60+ years old	15	10

Table 18.1

The monetary amounts are not insignificant. Assuming the sanctuary shekel equates to eleven to twelve grams, vowing a thirty-year-old male would set a person back 600 grams of silver – a substantial figure equivalent to about four years' wages (cf. Judg. 17:10).[3] However, Leviticus once again displays its social awareness by making provision for the poor (cf. 1:14; 5:11; etc.). For such a person, 600 grams of silver would be unattainable.

---

3. See Wenham, *Leviticus*, 338.

Thus, 27:8 allows the priests to set a valuation in accord
with what a person could reasonably afford. Poverty
must not limit a person's ability to fulfill promises made
to God. Yahweh is the God of all His people, without
discrimination.

Vows could also be made in relation to animals
(27:9-13). If the animal was suitable for offering to the
LORD (i.e., from either flock or herd), then it became 'holy'
(27:9). In other words, it became Yahweh's (for discussion
of 'holiness', see at 6:8–7:10). For this reason, the animal
could not simply be swapped if the vow-maker happened
to change his or her mind (27:10). Indeed, attempting
to swap animals simply made *both* holy and therefore
off limits (27:10). Thus, Leviticus recognizes 'a human
tendency to promise God much when we need him, but
to thank him little when he meets our needs.'[4] Animals in
this category were likely presented to Yahweh as either an
ascension offering (see 22:18) or fellowship offering (see
22:21). Either way, such 'gifts' needed to be worthy of a
king – that is, costly and without blemish (see 22:19-22; cf.
Mal. 1:14). In fact, blemished animals were unacceptable
for the purpose of fulfilling vows (22:23).

For vows involving any other type of animal (e.g., a
donkey or camel), the priests had to determine its value
(27:11-12). Then, if not required by the priests themselves,
such animals could be sold off for the set amount (cf. 27:27).
Furthermore, because 'impure' animals did not become holy,
and thus irrevocably off limits, the option to redeem them
remained open. Accordingly, animals could be bought back
for their established value plus a 20 per cent levy (27:13).

---

4. Sklar, *Leviticus*, 328.

Voluntary consecration to Yahweh (27:14-25)

The change of topic in 27:14-25 is marked by the particle *ki* ('if/when'; 27:14) and a shift in terminology from *ndr* ('to vow') to *qdsh* ('to consecrate'). Whereas vows are conditional promises to be fulfilled only when certain conditions are met, consecrating is enacted immediately.[5] The result is similar in both cases: items become holy to the LORD (27:9, 14, 21, 23). While the reasons for consecration are left unstated, items were likely turned over to the sanctuary, either in fulfillment of a vow or as a generous offering to express devotion.[6] Once again, the significant cost implies an attitude of immense gratitude towards God.

In contrast to persons and animals (27:1-13), consecration in 27:14-21 relates to inanimate objects. The first two options listed – houses (27:14-15) and ancestral land (27:16-21) – belong to the person consecrating them. Several features are shared:

- The act of consecration in each case is voluntary ('If anyone', 27:14, 16; also 27:22)

- Valuation is conducted by the priests (acting as Yahweh's 'agents') (27:14, 18; also 27:23)

- Consecrated property could be redeemed by the original owner (27:15, 19)

- Redemption requires payment of a 20 per cent levy on top of the set value (27:15, 19)[7]

---

5. Gane, *Leviticus, Numbers*, 465.

6. Hartley, *Leviticus*, 482.

7. Wenham (*Leviticus*, 337) suggests that the 20 per cent levy for redeeming one's property may have functioned to dissuade casual or rash vows.

The value of land is determined by harvest potential
(27:16; also 27:23). Accordingly, proximity to the Year
of Jubilee influences the valuation (27:17-18; also 27:23;
cf. 25:14-16).[8] Land that remains unredeemed by Jubilee,
however, does not revert to the family (as per 25:23-24,
28). Instead, as property consecrated to Yahweh, it
becomes permanently holy and is henceforth considered
as belonging to the priests (27:20-21). In this manner, the
man's 'possession' (*'achuzzah*, 27:16) becomes the priests'
'possession' (*'achuzzah*; 27:21). This stipulation may have
served to encourage the redemption, and hence retention,
of family lands rather than allowing them to become
perpetually forfeit.

For non-ancestral land acquired through purchase
(27:22-25), consecration also involves valuation by the priests
in relation to Jubilee (27:23). Here, however, 'the man shall
give the valuation on that day as a holy gift to the LORD'
(27:23 ESV). In the Year of Jubilee, the land reverts to the
original family owners.

Things already belonging to Yahweh (27:26-33)

The last main section lists three exceptions regarding
what may be vowed or consecrated to Yahweh. The common denominator is that these things – firstborn animals
(27:26-27), dedicated things (27:28-29), and tithes (27:30-33)
– already belong to God, indicated by the repeated refrain

---

8. Milgrom (*Leviticus 23–27*, 2383) notes that the standard price for
barley in Mesopotamia was one shekel per homer. Thus, 'fifty shekels'
(27:16) would appear to be the value for land dedicated in the Year
of Jubilee (i.e. land that is fifty years away from the next Jubilee). If
this is correct, then depreciation in 27:18 would be at the rate of one
shekel per year.

'it is Yahweh's' (27:26, 28, 30, my translation). Leviticus 27:26 conveys the logic: 'No one, however, may dedicate the firstborn of an animal, since the firstborn already belongs to the LORD' (cf. Exod. 13:2; 34:19; Num. 8:17; Deut. 15:19). Instead, such animals were to be brought to the tabernacle (once a year according to Deut. 15:20) and offered as fellowship offerings (unless defective in some way; cf. Deut. 27:21). Firstborn animals not suitable for the altar (i.e. not from flock or herd) could be redeemed upon payment of a 20 per cent levy (27:27).

Leviticus 27:28-29 considers 'devoted things'. The Hebrew word (*herem*) denotes something or someone irrevocably given to God in a process often consummated by complete destruction (although see Num. 18:14).[9] Accordingly, no person, animal, or property that God had deemed to be devoted in this way could be redeemed, sold, or ransomed (27:28-29). Instead, devoted things were considered 'most holy' (27:28) and therefore permanently removed from everyday use.

Tithes, likewise, belonged to God. One tenth of all produce from the land (27:30) or from flock and herd (27:32) was 'holy to the LORD'. Moreover, tithed animals were not selected at the giver's discretion. Rather, random choice seems to prevail (27:32). In fact, 'No one may pick out the good from the bad or make any substitution' (27:33). In addition, while tithed animals could not be substituted or redeemed, produce from the land could (subject to a 20

---

9. The extermination of the Canaanites and their religious system is described as an act of *herem*, an irrevocable handing over to Yahweh (Deut. 7:2, 26; Josh. 6:21). It is this that makes Achan's fault so heinous: he kept for himself some of the 'devoted things' (*herem*) that belonged exclusively to God (Josh. 7:1).

per cent levy on top of its value) (27:31). Thus, there are
marked differences between Levitical 'tithe' language and
that found in some Christian usage.

Those differences only become more pronounced if the
lens is expanded beyond Leviticus 27:30-33. Ten per cent
of one's annual produce was given to the LORD (as per
Lev. 27:30, 32) becoming, in turn, 'wages' for the Levites
and priests (Num. 18:21-28). However, Deuteronomy
14:22-26 also commands the saving up of a tithe to be
spent on an extravagant party held once a year at the
tabernacle. This tithe, converted to silver for ease of
transport, could be spent however one wished: 'Use the
silver to buy whatever you like: cattle, sheep, wine or other
fermented drink, or anything you wish. Then you and
your household shall eat there in the presence of the LORD
your God and rejoice' (Deut. 14:26). In addition, every
third year, a tithe of the land was to be stored in the towns
and villages as a means of allowing foreigners, widows,
and the fatherless to eat and be satisfied (Deut. 14:28-29;
26:12-13). If these various tithes are understood as being
cumulative, then the average Israelite household could
expect to set aside around 23.3 per cent of its annual
income for predetermined purposes.[10]

Conclusion (27:34)

The words of 27:34 conclude not only the chapter, but the
book: 'These are the commands the LORD gave Moses at
Mount Sinai for the Israelites.'

---

10. There is some debate about how best to accommodate the legislation.
The three tithes could represent (1) conflicting views of tithes; (2) modi-
fications to tithing over time; or (3) complementary and overlapping
tithes.

As noted above, vows in the Old Testament are often connected to petition and represent promises made to give God something if He would only intervene. The need to regulate the fulfillment of vows and the consecration of costly items in Leviticus 27 suggests that God has aided, and will continue to aid, those in severe plight. This makes the underlying tone of Leviticus 27 one of thankfulness and joy. Psalm 66 expresses the sentiment well:

> I will come to your temple with burnt offerings
>> and fulfill my vows to you –
> vows my lips promised and my mouth spoke
>> when I was in trouble.
> I will sacrifice fat animals to you and an offering of rams;
>> I will offer bulls and goats.
> Come and hear, all you who fear God;
>> let me tell you what he has done for me. (Ps. 66:13-16)

In this way, Leviticus concludes with a compelling picture of a thankful community, coming to the one who continues to rescue and deliver, drawn ever deeper into worship and appreciation of their God. For a book so saturated with notes of divine grace, this is a most fitting end.

From text to message

Of all the passages in Leviticus, this is perhaps one of the most difficult to teach and preach. The idea of making and fulfilling vows, consecrating one's house, or irrevocably devoting persons to God is utterly foreign. The distance between Leviticus 27 and Christian spirituality can feel like a yawning chasm. Yet, points of connection exist which are suggestive regarding underlying patterns of faith. Even today, in moments of crisis, people will sometimes exclaim, 'Help me God! And if you do, then I promise I will …' Ought not such vows to be fulfilled? Or take public expressions of thankfulness and joy following experience of God's deliverance. Are such things not also suitable in Christian gatherings? Leviticus 27, despite its initial strangeness, testifies to a living relationship between God and His people, in which the cries of the needy and desperate, when met with divine mercy and aid, turn into joy-filled expressions of thankfulness. Leviticus 27 runs along gospel tracks.

Getting the message clear: the theme

Leviticus 27 regulates the fulfillment of vows and the voluntary consecration of property as tangible expressions of thankfulness towards Yahweh. Israel's God, living among His people, continues to rescue and deliver. Costly gifts, freely devoted, are designated appropriate acts of worship.

Getting the message clear: the aim

In Leviticus 27, Yahweh gives instruction regarding vows and the voluntary consecration of items. Values are set and the priests are authorized to perform case-by-case evaluation for non-standard items. Particular care is taken to distinguish between revocable and irrevocable items. Some things, once given, could be redeemed; others, however, could not and remained permanently Yahweh's. The legislation also ensures that fulfilling vows is open to all, irrespective of means, indicating that the underlying concern is not monetary value but heart attitude. In this, the passage validates vow-making and consecration as acceptable forms of worship and invites this kind of thanksgiving. The assumption that these things will indeed happen portrays a living relationship in which crisis-provoked vows are met with divine deliverance which, in turn, results in thankful vow-fulfillment.

A way in

Beginnings and endings are important. That is why we remember famous opening lines from novels or the climactic finales of great movies and musical scores. First *and* last impressions linger and often prefigure or recapitulate essential elements for readers and hearers. The same holds true for Leviticus. The book opens and closes with portraits of a community of people approaching their God to perform spontaneous acts of thankful worship and devotion. In this way, Leviticus addresses the dilemma posed at the end of Exodus, where all are excluded from the holy and glorious presence of the LORD. Leviticus 27 reaffirms that sin, impurity, and their deleterious effects will not have the final word. Yahweh will walk among His people and be their God.

On the 27th of May, 1943, former Olympian, Louis Zamperini, together with the rest of his bomber crew, crashed in the South Pacific. Zamperini was to spend the next forty-seven days adrift in a life raft before his eventual 'rescue' and incarceration as a POW. Writing about his experience years later, Zamperini said, 'After thirty-three days Mac died. We buried him at sea. Phil and I hung on. By then I had begun to do what everyone in a real or metaphorical foxhole does: I desperately asked God to intervene, saying, "I promise to seek you and serve you if you just let me live."'[11] However, after the war, Zamperini

---

11. Louis Zamperini and David Rensin, *Don't Give Up, and Don't Give In: Life Lessons from an Extraordinary Man* (London: Piatkus, 2014), xxii-xxiii.

turned to alcohol to deal with the trauma he had suffered. The turning point came in 1949 at a Billy Graham crusade where Zamperini was reminded of the promises he had made to God while floating in the Pacific. He turned to Christ and, as promised, devoted his life to serving God. Yet, long before Zamperini's ordeal, making vows and promises to God was part of the rhythm of Israelite worship. Leviticus 27 helps us understand how and why that was the case.

Ideas for application

- The proper response to experiencing God's deliverance is *public* thanksgiving in the community of God's people.

- The monetary value of items vowed and consecrated in Leviticus 27 is substantial. Yet, this illustrates a key biblical theme: giving ought to be costly. David illustrates the principle well when he exclaims, 'I will not sacrifice to the Lord my God burnt offerings that cost me nothing' (2 Sam. 24:24). Experiencing God's love and mercy should rightly result in extravagant generosity towards Him that is not constrained by what others deem financially responsible. Indeed, as Jesus said to His host when anointed with costly perfume by a sinful woman, 'whoever has been forgiven little loves little' (Luke 7:47).

- It is not the total amount that one dedicates or gives to God which counts, but the heart attitude that provokes the giving. Jesus illustrated the point by highlighting the extraordinary nature of a poor widow's tiny donation at the temple (Matt. 12:41-44).

- In Mark 7:11-13, Jesus took issue with those who piously labeled money or possessions as something 'devoted to God' simply to avoid clear fiscal responsibilities – in this case, caring for one's parents.

- We ought to give careful forethought to what we commit ourselves to do. Proverbs 20:25 cautions against glib pledges: 'It is a trap to dedicate something rashly and only later to consider one's vows.' Instead, desire, or even stated commitment, to give ought to be followed through in action. This is Paul's point when he urged the Corinthians to 'finish the work, so that your eager willingness to do it may be matched by your completion of it, according to your means. For if the willingness is there, the gift is acceptable according to what one has, not according to what one does not have' (2 Cor. 8:11-12).

- Luke portrays the piety and obedience of Joseph and Mary when he recounts how they took Jesus, their firstborn son, to Jerusalem to present Him to the Lord (Luke 2:22-23).

- The dedication of houses and lands to the Lord (Acts 4:34) and the making of vows (Acts 18:18; 21:23) continued in the early church. In line with Leviticus 27, these acts are presented as voluntary, rather than commanded, but are nevertheless used by Luke to demonstrate the deep connectedness between the church and Israel in God's unfolding purposes for His people. In fact, the seriousness of devoting property to the Lord in Leviticus 27 grants greater clarity concerning the terrible fate of Ananias and Saphira in Acts 5.

Suggestions for preaching

In this sermon, I tackle Leviticus 27 as a unit in its own right before drawing out some of the wider theological and literary implications. This approach allows the sermon to both explore the passage and to remind hearers of themes heard earlier in Leviticus. The sermon thus does double duty as an exposition of Leviticus 27 and as series finale.

- **Vows and consecration according to Leviticus 27.** Making vows to God and dedicating costly items to Him is intrinsic to Old Testament faith. The concept is found in law, narrative, and poetry. Petition and thankfulness are the driving concerns. Leviticus 27 regulates the practice by setting assessment values and by commissioning the priests as Yahweh's 'agents' to decide on non-standard items. The passage also clarifies which items could be bought back (redeemed) and which could not. Items already belonging to Yahweh are listed as exceptions: these cannot be re-given. Thus, while setting its expectations high, the passage nevertheless recognizes the potential for underhandedness, even when it comes to fulfilling vows made to God. However, the effect of conveying this legislation as Yahweh's direct words to the people legitimizes the practices of vowing and consecrating, as well as inviting these expressions of thankfulness.

- **The gospel according to Leviticus 27.** Although seemingly foreign at first glance, Leviticus 27 presents another portrait of the gospel truths so intimately woven throughout Leviticus. In view are those who, finding themselves in dire need and recognizing their own inability, cry out to God in desperation.

Petition is bolstered with extraordinary vows. And God hears the cries of His people. Deliverance is granted. Against that backdrop, Leviticus 27 invites a fitting response of thankfulness and joy expressed through public acts of vow-fulfillment and dedication. Extraordinary gifts – children, houses, and ancestral land – to match extraordinary salvation. So Leviticus ends as it began, by presenting a community living in relationship with God, marked by spontaneous acts of adoration. The community excluded at the end of Exodus has been brought near. Leviticus 27 leaves readers with a snapshot of future potential: ongoing blessing in the land where Yahweh walks.

Suggestions for teaching

Questions to help understand the passage

1. Use a concordance or digital search tool to look up occurrences of 'vow' in the Old Testament. For what reasons did people make vows to God?

2. What is the rationale for the monetary values listed in 27:3-7?

3. Explain how the Year of Jubilee affects land valuations in 27:16-25.

4. Why are the exceptions in 27:26-33 listed here?

5. What does it mean for something to become 'holy to the Lord' (27:14, 21, 23, 28, 30, 32)?

6. What is the role of the priest in Leviticus 27? Why do you think this is the case?

7. List the similarities and differences between Leviticus 1 and 27.

8. Why do you think the book of Leviticus ends with this passage?

Questions to help apply the passage

1. Is it appropriate for Christians to make vows when petitioning God for help?

2. Read Deuteronomy 23:21-23, Ecclesiastes 5:4-7, and Matthew 5:33-37. What do your words and promises say about you?

3. Can you think of worship activities that are off limits to persons of limited means? What response(s) might 27:8 suggest?

4. What can Christians learn from Israel's pattern of tithing which underwrote priestly stipends, extravagant communal partying, and aid for the destitute?

5. Is public thanksgiving part of what your church community does? What lessons could be learned from Leviticus 27?

FURTHER READING

The number of commentaries on Leviticus has increased significantly in recent times. This is good news for preachers and Bible study leaders alike as it means there are plenty of resources available. Here, I briefly chart those I have found most helpful.

When teaching Leviticus, there are three commentaries I inevitably reach for. The first is Gordon Wenham's *The Book of Leviticus* in the New International Commentary on the Old Testament series (Eerdmans, 1979). Wenham is such a sensible exegete that his commentary remains invaluable even though four decades old. He provides a thorough treatment of the text which is also sensitive to matters of Christian theology. Jay Sklar's *Leviticus*, in the Tyndale Old Testament Commentary series (IVP, 2013), is also excellent. His introductory discussion alone makes this a 'must-have' for one's bookshelf. My third go-to is the NIV Application Commentary, *Leviticus, Numbers* (Zondervan, 2004), by Roy Gane. Gane's analysis includes exploration of the Ancient Near Eastern context in which the books of the Old Testament were written, helping to clarify how Leviticus would have been understood by original readers.

Although published too late for me to interact with in this volume, Jerry Shepherd's commentary in the Story of God Bible Commentary series (Zondervan, 2021) is superb. Shepherd takes seriously the task of hearing Leviticus as Christian Scripture and his 'Live the Story' sections alone make this a necessary investment.

Beyond the volumes listed above, there are several other works worth noting. Michael Morales has written an immensely valuable theology of Leviticus, packed with exegetical insights and useful diagrams – *Who Shall Ascend the Mountain of the Lord? A Biblical Theology of the Book of Leviticus* (NSBT 37; Downers Grove: IVP, 2015). For preachers and teachers engaging with the Hebrew text, John Hartley's Word Biblical Commentary, *Leviticus* (Word Books, 1992), provides useful assistance. Michael Gorman's short commentary, *Leviticus: Divine Presence and Community* (Eerdmans, 1997), sheds light on the ritual dimension of Leviticus and contains many valuable theological insights. Finally, for those who wish to leave no stone unturned, Jacob Milgrom's massive 2,700-page magnum opus (Anchor Bible, 1991–2001) remains the definitive work. For any preacher or teacher looking for exhaustive treatment, this is the place to go.

ABOUT THE PROCLAMATION TRUST

The fundamental conviction underlying the work of The Proclamation Trust is that when the Bible is faithfully taught, God's voice is clearly heard. We are ambitious for the spread of the gospel – and of expository preaching and teaching in particular – in the UK and beyond.

There are three strands to our ministry:

First, we run the Cornhill Training Course in London, a flexible, multi-year, part-time course for anyone who wants to handle and communicate God's Word more faithfully and effectively.

Second, we run a range of conferences to equip, enthuse and energise senior pastors, assistant pastors, students, ministry wives, women in ministry and church members in the work God has called them to. We also run the Evangelical Ministry Assembly each summer in London, which is a gathering of over a thousand church leaders from across the UK and from around the world.

Third, we produce an array of resources, of which this book in your hand is one, to assist people in preaching, teaching and understanding the Bible.

For more information, please go to www.proctrust.org.uk

Christian Focus Publications

Our mission statement —

STAYING FAITHFUL
In dependence upon God we seek to impact the world through literature faithful to His infallible Word, the Bible. Our aim is to ensure that the Lord Jesus Christ is presented as the only hope to obtain forgiveness of sin, live a useful life and look forward to heaven with Him.

Our books are published in four imprints:

CHRISTIAN
FOCUS

Popular works including biographies, commentaries, basic doctrine and Christian living.

CHRISTIAN
HERITAGE

Books representing some of the best material from the rich heritage of the church.

MENTOR

Books written at a level suitable for Bible College and seminary students, pastors, and other serious readers. The imprint includes commentaries, doctrinal studies, examination of current issues and church history.

CF4•K

Children's books for quality Bible teaching and for all age groups: Sunday school curriculum, puzzle and activity books; personal and family devotional titles, biographies and inspirational stories – because you are never too young to know Jesus!

Christian Focus Publications Ltd,
Geanies House, Fearn, Ross-shire,
IV20 1TW, Scotland, United Kingdom.

www.christianfocus.com
blog.christianfocus.com